The
Ecology
of Hope

COMMUNITIES
COLLABORATE
FOR
SUSTAINABILITY

Ted Bernard and Jora Young

FOREWORD BY WES JACKSON

NEW SOCIETY PUBLISHERS

Canadian Cataloguing in Publication data:

A record for this publication is available from the National Library of Canada.

Cover design by Val Speidel, from photographs by Marian Bantjes and Louie Ettling.

The maps in this book were created by Kylie Hunt, Fred Calef and Joseph Wisby.

Printed in the U.S.A. on partially recycled paper using soy-based inks by Capital City Press, Montpelier, Vermont.

Inquiries regarding requests to reprint all or part of *The Ecology of Hope* should be addressed to New Society Publishers at the address below.

Paperback ISBN: 0-86571-355-3
Hardback ISBN: 0-86571-354-5

To order directly from the publisher, please add $3.00 to the price of the first copy, and $1.00 for each additional copy (plus GST in Canada). Send check or money order to:

New Society Publishers,
P.O. Box 189, Gabriola Island, B.C. V0R 1X0, Canada

New Society Publishers aims to publish books for fundamental social change through nonviolent action. We focus especially on sustainable living, progressive leadership, and educational and parenting resources. Our on-line catalog is available for browsing at:
http://www.swifty.com/nsp/

NEW SOCIETY PUBLISHERS
Gabriola Island, BC and East Haven, CT

 745-C

We shall not cease from exploration
And the end of all our exploring
Will be to arrive where we started
And know the place for the first time.
Through the unknown, remembered gate
When the last of earth left to discover
Is that which was the beginning;
At the source of the longest river
The voice of the hidden waterfall
And the children in the apple tree

— T.S. Eliot, *The Four Quartets*

CONTENTS

ACKNOWLEDGMENTS

This project has been thoroughly and joyfully collaborative from start to finish, so that the order of our names on the cover implies no differential contribution. At the onset, we gratefully acknowledge each other's friendship.

Many people helped us on our journey. They shared their stories, their homes, their time, and their dreams. They were a constant source of inspiration. We will ever be grateful for everything they gave us. Thanks to all who appear in the pages of this book. Special appreciation goes to Renard Phillips, Geri Spring, Lawrence Waukau, Wendy Warner, John Cook, Leah Wills, John Sheehan, Valerie Nellor, Peter Boehmer, Tom Harris, John Hall, Steve Packard, Laurel Ross, Carol Kuhre, Mary Ann Borch, Sanford Lowry, Freeman House, Barb Allison and Irene Edwards.

Our employers, Ohio University and the Nature Conservancy, provided material and financial support as well as time and space away from the bustle of offices and classrooms.

Finally, to the Young and Bernard/Lofgren families (especially Mark Young and Donna Lofgren) go heartfelt thanks for your unwavering support and encouragement.

Ted Bernard and Jora Young
August 1996

It's the W(holes), not the Donuts, that Count
————————————— Foreword —————————————

Wes Jackson

"Parochialism and provincialism are opposites. The provincial has no mind of his own; he does not trust what his eyes see until he has heard what the metropolis ...has to say on any subject.... The parochial mentality, on the other hand, is never in any doubt about the social and artistic validity of his parish. All great civilizations are based on parochialism...."
— Patrick Kavanagh, Collected Pruse (sic), (1967)

Study the above paragraph because you are about to read some "stories" in which the parochial mind rules over the provincial, which is to say the agrarian mind comes out ahead of the industrial mind.

I told the notable historian, Don Worster, the upshot of Kavanagh's paragraph. His immediate reply was, "Of course, province implies empire. Provincials are always looking to the locus of power." On the contrary, this book is in close agreement with the mind that never has "any doubt about the social and artistic validity" of the local. Since the parochial is an agrarian at heart, he or she is not impressed that the World Wide Web will make it possible for city people to occupy the rural areas and their small country towns. For those who love the Web will mostly come as provincials and stay that way, never becoming parochials.

Why make a fuss about such a distinction? Two reasons: (1) If we don't get sustainability first in agriculture, forestry and fisheries, then it won't

1

happen at all. The minerals industry can't achieve it, nor will any other area of industry, even with recycling; (2) Sustainability will be managed by those with the necessary cultural capacity — the parochials — and not by those who employ a technological 'tour de force.' Why? Because food, logs and fish come out of ecosystems running on contemporary sunlight; and when they are managed by humans in a responsible manner, the reality of the ecological mosaic becomes clear as a study of the sunlight collecting plants and their interaction with the rest of the world — our most important subject. That seems so elementary to the parochial, but the idea is not widespread.

Sitting in a hotel room one evening in Berlin in the mid-1930s, Aldo Leopold jotted down some notes to himself under the heading, "Wilderness." The third paragraph below is the really relevant one for this volume, but I include his first two also, for they show Leopold's line of reasoning leading up to the third.

"The two great cultural advances of the past century were the Darwinian theory and the development of geology. The one explained how, and the other where, we live. Compared with such ideas, the whole gamut of mechanical and chemical invention pales into a mere matter of current ways and means.

"Just as important as the origin of plants, animals and soil is the question of how they operate as a community. Darwin lacked time to unravel any more than the beginnings of an answer. That task has fallen to the new science of ecology, which is daily uncovering a web of interdependencies so intricate as to amaze — were he here — even Darwin himself who, of all men, should have the least cause to tremble before the veil.

"One of the anomalies of modern ecology is that it is the creation of two groups, each of which seems barely aware of the existence of the other. The one studies the human community, almost as if it were a separate entity, and calls its findings sociology, economics, and history. The other studies the plant and animal community and comfortably relegates the hodgepodge of politics to the 'liberal arts.' The inevitable fusion of these two lines of thought will, perhaps, constitute the outstanding advance of the present century."

These stories, for my money, are the necessary part of a journey which will lead toward "fusion of these two lines of thought."

And so we have a beginning point. We have seen the consequences of operating as though nature is to be subdued or ignored. Researchers beginning with Darwin who merely wanted to understand how the world works have given us a mature discipline in ecology which now stands ready to inform agriculture, forestry and fisheries. Some well-understood principles now provide a foundation, a body of knowledge based on our understanding of how natural ecosystems work. We can now look to systems which feature material recycling and run on sunlight. This is why agriculture, forestry and fishing, coming out of nature, have the greatest potential to achieve sustainabiltiy. The mineral economy (indeed the whole industrial economy) has no analog to look to. Material recycling with all its virtues requires reliance on "smart resource management." The living world has the advantage, for it can feature "nature's wisdom." Our work at The Land Institute in Natural Systems Agriculture, by the way, is based on the way nature's prairie works.

But back to Leopold's "two lines of thought" and the need to explore the commonalities between a human community and a plant and animal community. That exploration will require decades, or perhaps scores of years, maybe even centuries. We are interested in the revitalization of rural communities at the The Land Institute and we looked for common ideals in such cultural centers as Berkeley and Boulder, Santa Fe and Amherst, Lawrence, Kansas and Cambridge, Massachusetts. But whatever we liked in such places could not be replicated in what some despairingly call the little "holes," little towns in out-of-the-way places. If these are the holes, Boulder and Amherst are the donuts. Here one finds good coffee, micro-brewery beer, good bread, Mexican food, theater — the accoutrements of civilization. The hole of these donuts is usually a university or some other popular attraction. Farmer's markets, and Community-Supported Agriculture can flourish here. But they are still the home of the provincial, or more positively, the post-industrial, scaled down, urban life.

And what about Max, ND (population 301), a few miles south of Minot? Or Matfield Green, Kansas, (population 50), 80 miles southwest of Lawrence? And the thousands of places like them? Max and Matfield have more in common with one another that either have with any of the donuts. No theater, no Mexican restaurants, no CSA. Even if they had these advantages, they likely could not hold the young, not without educating them about the possibilities for the parochial. Here is what we are up against: these "holes" need to repopulated if the ecological world view is to more thoroughly penetrate those biotic systems which support us, thus creating wholes. Repopulation alone won't do. It is also community revitalization we need, but it has to center around the ecological world view. We dare not repopulate or develop community with the same ensemble of assumptions carried by most of our forebears, and most of us today. These assumptions include the notions of infinite resources and, more recently, infinite substitutability, as well as the attitude that, as Angus Wright put it, "nature is to be subdued or ignored." We've carried on that way long enough as we have featured the industrial or provincial mind. In other words, the "holes" need to become "whole."

Where are the good examples? I liked much of what I saw in Tuscany and Umbria a few years ago. In a cultural sense, none of the little towns of Tuscany are like Florence, but they are good enough and the weight of opinion in those towns must be parochial in nature. Of course, no one place or region can be like an ink stamp of a Norman Rockwell, or a Marlow wood cut, to be slammed down on Max or Matfield. Nor can we look to the Amish, for example, and precisely imitate them. Even so, enough good examples exist and we need not be weighed down with the obvious obstacles and give up in despair. The Ecology of Hope carries some of these stories, these good examples. And nothing beats the good example, for it represents a particular which the abstraction needs, but too often lacks.

While it is worthwhile to ask what among the donuts is sustainable, it is worthwhile only if we always come back, finally, to the non-donut. For it is here that rural revitalization and conservation in general are essential for ecological and cultural reasons. We need to formulate models of renewable economies based on ecological constraints and sustained yields. From these models we hope then to determine a sustainable carrying capacity and settlement pattern of the land, given culturally defined basic needs. But that is not enough. We need, also, to identify the more "ghost-like" barriers to the adoption of a renewable economy, be they economic, social, political or "human nature." We will need to expand on the moral and spiritual dimensions that are part and parcel of that which can be quantified in energy and material terms.

It is now time for: (1) suggestions as to how one would bring out the best of what the good examples have to offer; (2) exploration as to what our version of resources might be like; (3) exploration of what a community-based research agenda might look like; and (4) the creation of a network of people who offer ideas for curriculum in our schools.

We will need a network of people to solve the problems. We will need hundreds of little enterprises, but we dare not look at enterprise without exploring what stands behind the enterprise in terms of renewable versus non-renewable resources.

The stories in this book describe small and modest efforts — exactly the requirement for getting something done. This volume should help us address how to eliminate the "hole" and achieve the "whole." We have a long journey ahead of us. It is a journey to restore both culture and ecosystems. It is only one trip, so it has to deal with both forms of restoration at once. There is no "how to do it" manual. We have to lay down the path as we go. The dangers are subtle. The voices of destruction are soft and inviting but, make no mistake, deadly. They are the oldest forces of conquest which lie in ambush, not legions. They will willingly pervert, subvert and destroy natures' communities and human communities in one lick because the reward for destroying such communion is now, and ever shall be, power: the enemy of the parochial.

The Land Institute, Salina, Kansas

September 1996

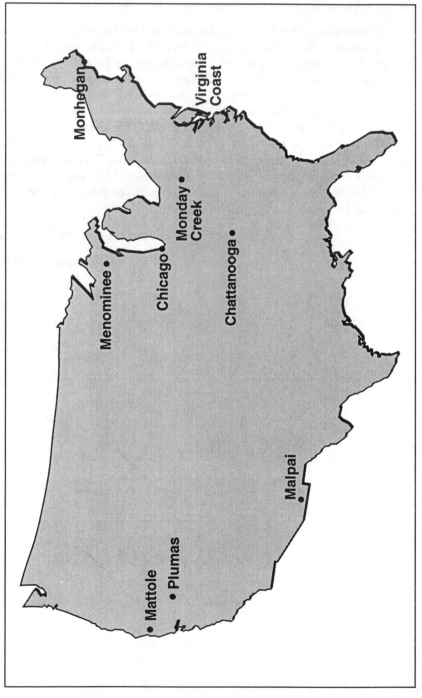

Searching For New Stories
———— Introduction ————

It's all a question of story. We are in trouble just now because we do not have a good story. We are in between stories. The old story is no longer effective.
— Thomas Berry[1]

The book you have just opened is a book of stories. The stories are about rivers and mountains, oceans and cities. There are fishers and farmers, brilliant leaders and shy woodspeople in these stories. Some parts of the stories took place long ago, many others are still being written. All are about one thing: real people trying to live more sustainably in their home places.

Like the Brothers Grimm, we have travelled across the country in search of the best stories we could find. We asked everyone we could: "Do you know of anywhere where people live sustainably with the natural resources of their region? Do you know of anyone who is developing a more sustainable approach to the future for their community?" We followed every possible lead. Our journey took us from Maine to California and back again. We travelled by airplane, automobile, horse, boat, train and modem.

Like the Brothers Grimm, we felt driven to capture these stories because we believe that "good stories have the power to save us."[2] Stories can instruct and inform us and fill us with a sense of what's possible. A good story can touch us with the magic of hope. Through the trials of the characters and epic struggles of their families, we can gain the wisdom of generations and the insights of sages.

Most of all we have collected these stories because we believe that Thomas Berry is correct. The old story no longer works. Humankind is struggling to break from a Dark Age of exploitation and abuse of our environment into a new age Berry calls "the Ecological Age." We stumble with new language for this new age. Recently coined words and phrases such as "ecosystem management," "sustainable development," "green technology" and "ecosystem health" are appearing in everything from Good Housekeeping to Scientific American to the Wall Street Journal. Their meanings are still unclear, as everyone from the United Nations Secretary General to the local park manager gropes about for points of reference.

We are all seeking direction in this age of transition. We see that we have been profoundly lost. We have been living in a time that allowed us to send our most fertile soils off to the sea, change our grasslands to deserts, convert our priceless minerals to mountains of trash, and cut down our forests until our very atmosphere is threatened. We see that even after spending so much of the earth's bounty, the world's people still suffer enormous want and despair. We know that this path cannot be the right way. There must be a better one. And good stories can help us uncover it, to discover "what the world is trying to be."[3]

The stories we share are of people who, we believe, are finding the path. These people and places are diverse, but they have much in common. To begin, they are no longer looking to government to solve their differences. They understand that they need to take matters into their own hands and fashion home-grown solutions. They are creating forums that allow for meaningful collaboration and exchange of real information. They are experimenting with new decision-making processes that seek solutions based on common ground, not compromises. They are starting to realize that they live together in a shared space, with limited supplies and no place else to go.

From their different angles and in their own language, their stories point to a new ethic — an ethic of "sustainability." Ethics are fundamental statements of right and wrong that allow individuals to function effectively within a family or community. Psychologist Mary Pipher claims that "ethics, rather than laws, determine most of our behaviors" and, in fact, form the "unwritten rules of civility [that] organize civic life."[4] Aldo Leopold further clarified the definition of ethic as a "mode of guidance" that may be used to provide direction when one is faced with a situation that is new or complex or where the results of one's actions may not be understood for a long time.[5]

The ethic of sustainability asserts that it is the responsibility of the present generation to live in such a way that the needs of future generations can still be served. This ethic recognizes that natural resources such as water, air, soil, plants and animals are the basic capital upon which all life, human and otherwise, depends. And that it is wise to learn to live off the interest generated by this capital rather than deplete the basic stores.

We believe that the ethic of sustainability is the critical foundation upon which the new age will be built. This ethic, we feel, will lead to vastly different realms. When the ethic of sustainability is truly understood, the old notion that resources can be managed in a fixed and static manner for "maximum sustained yield" will become as comical as the belief that the Earth is flat. The ethic of sustainability will make the division between preservation and utilization of the natural elements of the planet seem, at best, hopelessly naive and simplistic. It will prompt instead a constant yearning for integration of human activities into a more complete and wholly understood lifescape, a unit of organization that includes all living things and the native processes that ensure the promise of natural evolutionary change. Seeing their interdependence, communities will start to fashion resource management solutions that are faithful to the geography and ecology of their place and are responsible to the future.

It is impossible to talk about this ethic without acknowledging the prophet and land philosopher, Aldo Leopold. Leopold laid out the basic principles of an ethical relationship between humans and the earth 50 years ago. Leopold's statement of a "land ethic" is a simple one that is almost buried in his famous essay by the same name. It consists of two plain sentences. "A thing is right when it tends to preserve the integrity, stability, and beauty of the biotic community. It is wrong when it tends otherwise."[6] If, however, only these two sentences had survived, he would have provided an extraordinarily useful test of rightness upon which to build sustainable resource management.

Integrity, stability, and beauty: these are the elements of Leopold's ethical test for rightness. Integrity denotes maintaining and restoring wholeness and diversity. Stability incorporates Leopold's concept of land health, which he defined as the "capacity of the land for self-renewal."[7] Beauty demands, above all, that we approach the land with reverence and awe for the wonder of life. Recognizing the biota as things of beauty cannot help but lead to feelings of respect and, perhaps, even love. And as Leopold noted, "it is inconceivable to me that an ethical relation to land can exist without love, respect, and admiration for land."[8]

Wendell Berry envisioned that there are "scattered and sufficient examples of competent and loving human stewardship of the earth,"[9] places where the land ethic might be influencing civic life. The stories we gathered may prove Berry right — Leopold's land ethic does seem to be guiding resource management decisions in a sufficient number of places to convince us that a new era is upon us.

In Part 1, we describe some historical events we believe provide context for the stories we have collected. We present these in Part 2 of this book; they are ordered roughly east to west. Feel free to read them in any order that suits you.

It took a view of Earth from space for us to finally realize that the Earth is an island whirling in the vast sea of the galaxy. With no bridge to another land, no lifeboat off, some of the residents of "Turtle Island" are starting to understand our real dilemma. Our first story takes place on Monhegan Island, where we found a tiny island community that realized this truth three generations ago. Loving their island and their relationship to the sea, these islanders made some unique choices to limit their personal freedoms for the right to live prosperously on this beautiful rock ledge. As a result, today they enjoy a year-round stable community, 100 per cent employment, the highest per capita income in the county, a renewable lobster fishery, and an idyllic neighborhood most of us can only dream of visiting.

The Industrial Age was an age of deferred debt. Small numbers of people built huge personal fortunes and left enormous cultural and ecological liabilities for those who followed. Rusting hulks of abandoned factories, soils and waters simmering in chemical soups, cities with their hearts rotting out and a disillusioned "underclass" that has been poor for generations: these are the unpaid notes left by the excesses of the Industrial Age. By the 1970s Chattanooga, Tennessee, was one such place where the debts of the Industrial Age were coming due big time. Chattanooga was described as "the second most polluted city in America." The air and water was black with the debris of the past and the spirits of its citizens darkened by their prospects for the future.

David Orr claims that in the age of ecological sustainability the main task will be "finding alternatives to the practices that got us in trouble in the first place." He foretells that in the search for ecological sustainability it will be "necessary to rethink agriculture, shelter, energy use, urban design, transportation, economics, community patterns, resource use, forestry, the importance of wilderness, and our central values."[10] In Chattanooga, the reader will see how one city is exploding into prosperity by doing just that. By using the ethic of sustainability, Chattanooga is working its way out of the debtors prison left by past practices of the Industrial Age. They are designing a future for all citizens using the principles of sustainability as their road map and the Tennessee River as their compass.

Our next story takes place along the eastern shore of Virginia, an ocean-washed spit of land that hangs between Chesapeake Bay and the Atlantic Ocean. Here exists one of the longest stretches of undeveloped shoreline left on the U.S. Atlantic coast. Watermen and farmers have made a living more or less in balance with this wildness for over three centuries. The class structure designed and determined by the legacy of slavery meant that some would be reasonably well-placed. Others would always be "dirt poor." By the last quarter of the 20th century, however, everyone was in crisis.

In searching for a way out of this crisis, the community discovered that they have something rare and priceless. They have a cultural identity deeply tied to the land. They have the loud calls of migrating ducks in season. They have beautiful beaches and open vistas. They have bountiful waters and rich soils. In short, they have what their neighbors in Virginia Beach traded for bright lights and boardwalks and the original families of Hilton Head exchanged for fancy discount malls and second home development. The citizens of Virginia's Eastern Shore have decided to use the unique attributes of their community to guide their way to an enhanced quality of life without "losing their roots." Working together, side by side, all elements of the community have sketched out a treasure map that they hope will lead to a new future for themselves and their children. One where they will all prosper precisely because they have something that everyone else has compromised — cultural and natural integrity and beauty. They decided, unlike some communities faced with similar challenges, to take a long view. Not because they saw themselves as "visionaries," but rather "as helpers for the generations to come."

Robert Frost laments in his poem "Witness Tree" that "the land was ours before we were the land's." In Menominee, Wisconsin, we discovered what humans belonging to a place really means to the practice of forestry. We went to the Menominee Indian reservation to see what many foresters and ecologists consider to be one of the most well-managed working landscapes in the country. We found that this highly recognized forest management program evolved out of 5,000 years of living as a forest people. Since contact with the Europeans, the Menominee's profound sense of connection to the forest has inspired extraordinary courage and vigilance. These qualities, combined with a surprising openness to new information, yield a picture of a sustainable forest management program that has much to teach 21st century resource managers.

The great western range lands, the site of our next story, are indeed "A Changing Mile."[11] Historic abuses, altered weather patterns, evolving social mores, shifting government priorities, and the resettling of America are all prompting enormous challenges for the rural communities of the West. Along the vast open ranges that cross the border between Mexico and New Mexico and Arizona, we found a community responding to these changes like true pioneers.

The frontier these ranchers, conservationists, and government workers occupy is what Daniel Kemmis calls "the territory of collaboration."[12] Together they show what it means to embrace change as an inevitable part of life without losing one's roots or compromising core values. In their efforts to protect their threatened open space lifestyle, cattle ranchers are listening to lifelong environmentalists. Environmentalists, in turn, are beginning to realize that the government cannot own and manage everything that will be needed if western wildlands and the antelope that roam them are to survive. Here in the Sky Islands of the U.S. and Mexico border, if its existing stewards can find a way to thrive together, this priceless threatened landscapes may also survive intact.

Deep in the foggy coastal mountain range of northern California the last of the Mattole River king salmon are fighting for their lives. In the memory of some still living, the salmon once ran so thick that they could be thrown into the backs of wagons with pitch forks. Now the salmon run is just a few hundred in a good year. This is the story of shaggy transplants to this remote region who, loving the salmon and the memories of those who had once seen them in these great numbers, decided to try to save the Mattole River king salmon from extinction. Donning heavy waders, they followed the spawning salmon to discover that everywhere along its journey were ominous threats. The Mattole Salmon Group then entered the entire watershed of the Mattole River. They mapped its twists and turns. They found its remaining treasures and its horrible scars. They saw how the forests, soils, valleys, towns, streams, river and salmon stitched together. In an effort to understand and chronicle the rapid and profound changes of the river, they plastered their walls with images of the watershed the way grandparents line their hallways with pictures of the children and grandchildren.

In entering the watershed they encountered their neighbors in new ways. They found that together they shared a common nostalgia for the salmon and for the river named "Clear Water" by those who had come before. They realized that both are poised on the brink of extinction. To save the salmon and their river, the people of the Mattole River watershed decided to come together to search for a way back to that valley of Clear Water.

We found our next story in Plumas County, California. You get to Plumas County by travelling through catacombs of twisting, turning roads, up one mountain range and into another. Once there, you are in one of the most productive forests in North America. Not many people live in this high, rugged place and those who do realize that their living relies on the forests, mountain meadows and fast rivers. The great Feather River flows out of this county in strands of fast water that get braided together into the California aqueduct and sent to fields and taps as far away as southern California. This is the story of these forests, the river, and a community facing a sickness that threatened all three. This is the story of how they put aside blame and guilt and fashioned instead a visionary plan for their recovery. Their plan, and the process that led to it, is challenging some mighty institutions and inspiring new ideas about the economics of natural resource restoration and management.

In Chapter 10, we tell of two very different places. One is the sprawling, affluent suburbs of Chicago, where concrete, glass and steel are growing on what was once corn and before that, prairie. The other, the quiet and, for generations poor, forgotten hills of Appalachian Ohio. Many of the slopes of this region have been lying naked for more than 60 years, as they were long ago stripped bare of their protective skin for the black coal that lay underneath. People in these two places may seem different but they share a common need — a need to reattach themselves to the living fabric of their homeland. When the hills of southern Ohio were abandoned, bleeding and left for dead, the people never really recovered. When a city turns to an incoherent morass of highways, strip malls, and housing developments named after the creeks they destroy, that which is vital abandons it. In suburban Chicago and along the Monday Creek, the people are using the act of restoration to discover home and to reawaken life long dormant in both the land and in themselves.

ఌ

Admittedly these early pathfinders on the way to sustainability are tentative and many of their successes are not time-tested. Nonetheless, we share their experiences because in the darkness where we all stand, they, at least, hold some light. In the final two chapters we offer our interpretation of what these stories might be telling us. In Chapter 11, using the images shared by those we met along the way, we envision the ultimate destination — a community integrated into and respectful of the living resources that sustain it. In Chapter 12, we attempt to retrace the pathways of the communities we visited to determine if there are common markers that have allowed them to make progress. These markers may allow others a surer journey in their own search for sustainability.

We offer their stories, not because we are cockeyed optimists. We are not blind to the ominous signs of personal, community and global decay that are everywhere showcased by the media and pundits of all disciplines. Like the reader we have seen all the predictions and statistics. We do this because we believe that if there is a way out of this global crisis of ecological and human decline, it will not be found through despair or blame setting. It will be found through positive transformation, personal responsibility, and action at all levels. We do this because we see that the existing stories about our earth are "making us all sick. We need new stories. We need stories that connect us to each other, stories to heal the polarization that can overwhelm us all and stories to calm those who are frightened and who hate."[13]

Too often, when we face insurmountable obstacles such as global warming, overpopulation or species extinctions, we are discouraged from ever finding a way through. By allowing ourselves to become discouraged, we lose our courage. Our only hope is to find the courage to climb. Our only hope to build a new future is, to paraphrase William Dietrich, to re-image the planet to be the very best world it can be for all its inhabitants. And ourselves to be the very best we can be on it.[14]

Leopold's land ethic, or its equivalent, can be a Magna Carta for the land, freeing humanity to seek communities where the dream of sustainability can bond people to the land and to each other in a new way. We make no claim that this will come easily. It will require different perceptions of nature and of humankind, more guidance from nature, less anthropocentrism. It will demand management objectives, programs and practices that place health of the resources first. And the faith to know that this will ultimately lead to greater human health. It will require good science and better knowledge of the rates and kinds of change in nature. It will compel a radically new way of valuing land and protecting and sustaining it. It will demand political reconstruction and a new kind of economics. It will require us to "stop making things that sell and [start] making things that help."[15] It will oblige all decision-makers to become ecologically literate and to cultivate and nurture the courage to act against all odds for the good of our children and all children. And, perhaps most importantly, it will require us to come together in our home places in a spirit of co-operation, not competition, in a search for quality of life, not quantity of goods, with an attitude of humility, not domination.

As you follow our journey, you won't find a place where sustainability is perfectly practised. What you will find, in the best of lights, is the nascent beginnings of sustainability. In all likelihood, sustainability, in its fullest sense, exists nowhere. And perhaps may never exist. For sustainability is like pure love and equality: grand goals that should always lead human endeavor but a destination at which we will never arrive. This should not derail us. For this journey, like the journey toward human equality, had to start somewhere. Thomas Jefferson had no idea that the Declaration of Independence would eventually and inexorably lead to the termination of slavery or to the right of women to vote. Once the fundamental truth that "all men are created equal" was uttered, however, there was no way to stop the avalanche of change that would thereafter rumble down the mountain. The land ethic and the concept of sustainability, now having been articulated, have this same power. The transition will be a long and difficult one. The alternative to embracing this change, however, is even more dangerous and anything but easy.

The people and places found in this book may help to bring about this difficult transition. After you read their stories, feel free to reword them, rethink them, come up with new endings, anything you need to do to give them a hopeful meaning for you. But most of all, we encourage you to write your own stories. The world needs as many stories of hope and vision as we can find. For if we can sew enough of them quickly "quilted together, these stories will shelter us all."[16]

HISTORY RETOLD

ᛏᴏ

——— Part One ———

The Meaning of Copernicus
———— Chapter One ————

Looking at the night skies in a new way, Nicholas Copernicus touched off a revolution. His book, published in 1543, asserted that the Earth was not the center of the universe. Earth became just one of a number of objects revolving about the sun, which is the center of the planetary system. In denying our world its centrality and redefining the place of humans in the universe, Copernicus challenged conventional thinking about heaven and earth. And he threatened powerful institutions and people.

For at least a century, it was dangerous to espouse his model. In 1593, Giordano Bruno, a zealous apostle of Copernicus who had travelled widely in Europe spreading the word, was convicted by church authorities of heresy. Imprisoned for seven years and staunchly refusing to recant, in 1600 Bruno was burned at the stake. In spite of such draconian efforts by the church to persuade otherwise, by the 18th century the Copernican view of the universe became the accepted model. No one could successfully argue against a sun-centered planetary system any more than they could deny the Earth its place as one of the six known planets. Copernicus had conceived an elegant set of proposals that irrefutably answered questions, clearly explained the form and function of a sun-centered system, and provided an enticing framework for further study. The new paradigm revolutionized astronomy.

Even more important, it seemed also to unlock human imagination and creativity. As a framework for seeing the familiar in a new way, it ushered in astounding discoveries not only of Earth's rightful place in the universe, but also of the universe itself. In the arts, medicine, geography, mathematics and religion, a strikingly parallel renaissance blossomed. Copernicus, in his own way, contributed to the unique flowering of Western civilization that also produced da Gama, Michelangelo, Galileo and da Vinci.

This new vision of the cosmos came at a time in the evolution of Western civilization when the old ways of defining reality and the existing institutions did not fit with the challenges of the times or meet the needs of the people. Prevailing theory "did not compute." Ptolemy's theory of a stationary Earth that the sun and planets revolved around did not explain the many observed celestial motions. The epicycles described by Ptolemy were impossible to predict. The calendar based on this celestial theory was inconsistent. Observations of explorers like Columbus and Polo only increased the questions and needs. Europe had to have a more useful understanding of the heavens.

On the intellectual front, centuries of cloistered scholarship, hierarchical organization, and censorship made the Roman Church a barrier to new ideas. Because the new Protestant churches were teaching that truth could only be found in a literal interpretation of the Bible, scientific inquiry shifted to secular institutions.

Europe's scholars, educated in the emerging private and municipal universities, were liberated from the church's centuries of prejudice against the "pagan" classical thinkers. They were rediscovering the writings of the Greek and Arabic astronomers and mathematicians. It was in one of these secular universities that Copernicus was educated and undoubtedly began to construct his new theory.

While employed as an administrator for the Catholic Church in 1512, Copernicus began to construct his new theory and test it with crude measurements. By the 1530s he was discussing his findings with students and colleagues. He advanced the hypothesis that the known planets were revolving around the sun and that the Earth, far from stationary and from the center of it all, was rotating on its own axis, revolving in a fixed pattern within the planetary system. In short, he concluded that the familiar night skies were not at all as they had seemed for centuries.

To make such claims, Copernicus realized, was a defiant act, and as he was employed by the Catholic Church, he was reluctant to disseminate his proposals widely. Copernicus cautioned his students against speaking out and did not publish his theories until late in his life.[1] Legend has it he was handed a copy of his book, De Revolutionibus, just a few hours before his death. He died without knowing his theories would become the most significant spark in a revolution of profound importance. Like other revolutionary sparks, it was significant less for its own incendiary power than for the flames it fanned. In time, the conflagration devoured Ptolemaic thinking forever.

In the initial firestorm, Protestant theologians blasted Copernican thinking. Quoting passages from Old and New Testament scriptures, Protestants condemned the inconceivable notion of a universe not Earth-centered. They believed the human journey on Earth was but training for an eternal afterlife. How could it take place anywhere but in the center? To think otherwise would risk eternal damnation. Of Copernicus, Martin Luther exclaimed: "That fool will reverse the entire astronomy; according to the Scripture, Joshua bade the sun and not the Earth to stand still."[2]

The Copernican Revolution threatened Christianity on many counts. It forced the church to reconsider not only humanity's relationship to the divine and to afterlife, but also its own limited place in the universe. Humans could no longer presume themselves to be at the center of the universe. Heaven could no longer be imagined as a glorious celestial dome arching above a stationary Earth. Where was God in the new scheme of things? If the universe is infinite, where is God's throne? "How is man to find God or God man?"[3]

Copernicus and his followers thus challenged the very cosmology of Christianity. The Catholic Church ultimately banned De Revolutionibus, Copernicus and his followers were branded heretics and atheists, they were excommunicated, and his followers were burned at the stake. Galileo, the Copernican who most effectively confirmed and enlarged upon the system, was twice condemned by the Inquisition and forever banished from the Catholic Church. Despite inquisitions, bannings and burnings, the revolution could not be contained. It exposed too many illogical explanations; it responded too successfully to questions and doubts; it unlocked too many secrets; it opened too many vistas. It was just too useful to an expanding class of global navigators. It became the new universe of Galileo and Newton and Einstein, a universe at the core of our own vision of the night skies, a universe in which the Earth is surely not the center. Nor is man.

This upheaval in Western thought — the Copernican Revolution — is a powerful metaphor. Like most major transformations in the way humans think about the world, the Copernican Revolution shattered beliefs at the core. Though its foundations were laid centuries before, like most revolutions, it required a gifted and unconventional person to recast those foundations in new ways, to see familiar objects with new eyes, and to translate everything into language others could understand and take forward.

A small voice across a vast wilderness, Copernicus was at first heard by just a few. Those few had to hold on to the nascent vision while everyone else — the big institutions, the clergy, the "powers that be" — tried to obliterate it. Nevertheless, this new way of seeing familiar objects and of connecting them to the unfamiliar was compelling. Individual by individual, the new way spread. It set minds free, threw open doors for research and discovery, laid groundwork for great new structures of scientific inquiry, sparked a renaissance of action. The world would never be the same.

Philosopher Thomas Kuhn, to whom we are much indebted for his interpretation of the Copernican Revolution, tells us that this is the way all science marches forward.[4] An old framework, which holds center stage for a long time, begins to crumble. Inexplicable facts and conflicting observations strain its credulity and create problems. Research scientists are in crisis. There are too many puzzles. Science comes to a turning point. A new paradigm emerges to shed light on the accumulated stack of puzzles. The new paradigm is incompatible with the old; their differences are irreconcilable. Since the new effectively explains contradictions inherent in the old, it gains ascendancy and becomes the framework by which everybody understands reality. It becomes, in Marilyn Ferguson's words, a "sudden liberation from old limits."[5]

In the search for sustainable ways to manage the earth's natural resources, Kuhn's explanation of change and the metaphor of Copernicus has much to teach us. First, resource management — the policies and practices governing natural resource allocation, development and use — has come to a decisive place in history. The existing framework for making choices is not solving present problems. It does not effectively explain observed phenomena nor does it give good direction for future decisions. The present framework assumes that the earth's resources exist largely for human use. It assumes that the earth is infinitely resilient and malleable and that humans have ultimate dominion and sovereignty over all other life-forms and processes.

Thomas Berry explains how this happened:

> We were the sane, the rational, the dreamless people, the chosen people of destiny. We had found the opening to a more just society, a more reasoning intellectual life. Above all we had the power to

re-engineer the planet with our energy systems, our dams and irrigations projects, our great cities. We could clear the forests, drain the marshes, construct our railways and highways, all to the detriment of the other living forms of earth, to the elimination of needed habitat, to the obstruction of migration paths, to the cutting off of access to waterways. We could subdue the wilderness, domesticate the planet. We were finally free from the tyranny of nature. Nature was now our servant.[6]

This history seems to give us permission to manipulate any and all of earth's systems for the "commodities" valued at any given time. If humans want to live and raise corn in the floodplains of great rivers, those rivers should be diked and rerouted. If humans want ten times more cellulose fibre from a forest than that forest can produce with its native configuration of species, then we should remove all other species and grow only one type of "genetically improved" pine tree where once a whole forest grew. If humans graze livestock on grasslands until all the grasses have been consumed and soils waste away, then future generations will have to accept the consequences of expanding deserts.

When this belief system is questioned, there are no small number of institutions and individuals ready to quote scripture and hold fast to religious or legal rights and precedents. But the questions cannot be put down. Thinking people cannot accept that there is nothing to worry about:

- when as many as 20 per cent of the earth's species is threatened with extinction within the next century[7]

- when almost half of the commercial shellfish beds in the U.S. could not be harvested in 1993 because of pollution[8] and most of the earth's fisheries are on the decline[9]

- when the earth's deserts are expanding while its rich forests, freshwater aquifers, and coral reefs are declining

- when "impoverished" land is the fastest growing category of land use in the world

- when in spite of all this, even the basic needs of the people living on the earth today are not being met and human population is growing exponentially.

Rational people can come to no other conclusion. The present framework does not work. Earth's landscape is littered with failed projects, environmental debacles, unanswered questions, impossible problems, and vast contradictions. Crises abound.

Thousands of people from all walks of life are calling for change. Resource management professionals are risking their careers by questioning their organizations' methods,[10] observers and citizens are turning into activists calling for change,[11] theologians and philosophers and educators are begging us to reconsider our place in the scheme of things. Michael Frome implores us to challenge the system;[12] Matthew Fox asks that we "see the planet...as Original Blessing."[13]

As the living fabric of the earth becomes ever more frayed, many search for a new paradigm, a paradigm of sustainability. Though we often refer to sustainability as a "new paradigm," it is only partly so. Just as the insights of Greek philosophers and Arabic astronomers were lost in the Dark Ages and rediscovered by Copernicus, so also have traditions of sustainability been obliterated by the obsession of industrial societies with science and technology and control. This obsession underlies resource management and conditions us to view ancient ways as primitive and simplistic. As the new paradigm of sustainability emerges, there is renewed interest in understanding the methods and uncovering the wisdom of traditional resource managers. For in ancient civilizations are examples of human resource use that did not profoundly interrupt cycles of natural renewal.

The Copernican Revolution speaks to our generation in a second, even more profound, way. Copernicus forced humans to reconceive the position both of their planet and of themselves. Copernicus convinced the world of the radical idea that Earth is not the stationary center around which all else revolves. A similarly radical idea must take hold in modern resource management. Just as Earth is not the center of the universe, so also must we recognize that for humans to find their way they must first realize where they are. They are not at the center of the living cosmology of the Earth, they are not central and superior to all other parts of the planet. "We need to realize," writes Father Thomas Berry, "that the ultimate custody of the earth belongs to the earth."[14]

The American Conservation Movement:
Coming of Age at the Century Mark
———————— Chapter Two ————————

Conservation may be interpreted as an effort to extend abundance and opportunity. So in a sense the conservation and environmental movements became the new American frontier.

— Roderick Frazier Nash[1]

The American conservation movement, historian Roderick Nash tells us, is like the frontier itself. It's a century-long struggle of walking the difficult line between unbridled individual freedom and regulated social responsibility, between private and public lands, between utilitarian and aesthetic conceptions of nature, and between short-term profit and long-term prosperity.[2] In our brief recounting of this frontier, we seek answers to a limited set of questions. What in this "frontier experience" informs resource management in the late 20th century? What have we learned? What must we still learn? Where is the frontier now? What are the countervailing forces? Given this history, is hope justified?

Up to the 1980s there were two broad waves in conservation, both emerging from awareness of a deteriorating environment, both relying primarily on government. The first wave, beginning about 1890, focused on specific places in the landscape and whirled around a deceptively simple dichotomy about choice between preserving or using resources in these places — a dilemma that American society has never successfully resolved, perhaps because the choice is based on an inadequate understanding of both people and resources.

24

A second wave, with roots in the public health movement of the late 19th century, has rippled across the land since about 1950. It is about protecting the commons.[3] As pollution began to threaten health, safety, and the very quality of life, legislators responded swiftly. Like the first wave, the people expected the government to move into the breach. Environmental regulation, court suits, and enforcement scuffles became daily news and the work and professional identity of resource managers greatly expanded.

Beginning in the 1980s, the first ripples of a third wave — a wave based on an ecological worldview — began to wash quietly into neighborhoods and watersheds. The ecological worldview is not entirely new, for it taps deeply the writings of philosophers and ecologists of more than a generation ago and is informed by conceptions of nature long held by native peoples. We call this the ecological way.[4] Even as the work of the previous two waves still occupies the vast majority of resource professionals, this third wave is building strength. Based on a more sophisticated understanding of nature's flux and of the relationship between humans and nature as well as knowledge of collaborative, community-based action, the ecological way requires managers to think of the earth not as separate elements to be protected or used. It assumes the locus of responsibility and action is the individual and community, not a depersonalized, distant government. If it holds, it may lead us toward a more sustainable future. Then, perhaps the American conservation movement will have come of age.

THE FIRST WAVE

The Choice

This is a plea for the preservation of some tag-ends of wilderness, as museum pieces, for the edification of those who may one day wish to see, feel, or study the origins of their cultural inheritance.

— Aldo Leopold[5]

Envisioned in its entirety this river, like every river in the world, has many potential assets. It could yield hydroelectric power for the comfort of the people in their homes, could promote prosperity on their farms and foster the development of industry. But the same river by the very same dams, if they were wisely designed, could be made to provide a channel for navigation. The river could also be made to provide fun for fishermen and fish for food, pleasure from boating and swimming, a water supply for homes and factories.

— David Lilienthal[6]

The choice North Americans made over the past two centuries is now revealed in "tag-ends" of wild landscape that somehow eluded industry, cities and suburbs — whether the far-off Arctic National Wildlife Refuge or a small patch of uncut forest just over the horizon. One such place in Ohio will show what we mean.

If you drive across eastern Ohio's rolling lands of coal and corn, you'll be ill-prepared for the contrast you find in this little tag-end tract. You park in a weedy lot at the edge of an unremarkable second-growth wood, walk a few minutes toward a ravine. Remembering corn and coal, you begin to wonder. How could the forest in this ravine have survived intact? As you descend, the floor opens. Light translucent, sweet spring vapor near the ground, birdsong high above, you look upon ancient oaks, beeches, maples and tulip poplars. Their trunks more massive than any living trees in Ohio; their tops 150 feet above the ground. Something beyond words wells up.

You've entered Dysart Woods, a tiny patch of old-growth forest. Just 50 acres, it is one of the largest tracts in Ohio to escape homesteader's axe and plow, Hanna Coal Company's bulldozer and dragline. In Dysart it is possible to imagine the forest the natives knew, the forest that awed pioneers. Of this, Conrad Richter wrote: "Away back here across the Ohio, it had no fields. You tramped day long and when you looked ahead, the woods were dark as an hour or a day ago."[7] Dysart is remnant of a vast Ohio forest that in 1800 covered 25 million acres. It stands in a fragmented and simplified landscape. A landscape where for 200 years Ohioans have farmed and logged and mined, built towns and railroads, carved out interstates. A landscape commodious for people and for cows and cowbirds.

In Ohio, the choice seemed clear. A rich and rolling agricultural paradise, Ohio would be opened to settlement; its soils, waters, woods and minerals would make people prosper. In Dysart Woods, by some strange accident of history, a farmer and his descendants preserved 0.0002 per cent of Ohio's original forest. Staggered by this fact, Californian Freeman House wrote, "I felt as if I were seeing a once-great library reduced to one book with half its pages ripped out."[8]

The choice played out across the country. "Culturally speaking, we came here to subdue the continent...we have a Manifest Destiny itch to cut it down, drill it, shoot it, pave it, or just mess with it, for a profit or for the pure hell of it," wrote Audubon editor Michael Robbins.[9] Manifest Destiny drove us to defile and devour the land. But some Americans grieved. Romantics and transcendentalists called us to a higher vision, while bison and passenger pigeon were driven to the brink of extinction, forests burned and mountains were blown apart. Some, perhaps, remembered Thoreau's dictum, "In wildness is the preservation of the world."

By the turn of the century, when, like Dysart Woods, all but the last chunks of wild country were gone, a few scrambled to protect what was left. Theodore Roosevelt, the youthful naturalist who, at the hand of an assassin, suddenly found himself in center stage, read the times accurately. Loving both nature and center stage, he pledged to reverse decades of wanton resource destruction, a situation he called "the weightiest problem now before the nation."[10] Conservation became the centerpiece of his new progressive movement, which "aimed at redressing the social, economic, and political imbalances caused by industrialization, urbanization, and the concentration of economic power within the hitherto unrestrained corporations."[11]

While Roosevelt protected some of our most treasured historic and scenic spots (such as the Grand Canyon, the Olympic Mountains, and Mount Lassan), helped save the bison, and laid foundations for a system of wildlife refuges, his forestry chief, Gifford Pinchot, built an empire. Using the Forest Reservation Act of 1891, Pinchot convinced Roosevelt to withdraw more than 130 million acres from the public domain. This turned out to be significant, for the act was repealed by Congress in 1907. In six years Roosevelt set aside two-thirds of our current National Forests.

With a huge forest to manage, members of Roosevelt's "tennis cabinet" — Pinchot, Overton Price, W.J. McGee — and a few others literally wrote the book on conservation. The Forest Service came to epitomize dedicated, hard-working, incorruptible resource protectors and managers. "Every member of the Service realized that it was engaged in a great and necessary undertaking in which the whole future of their country was at stake," wrote Pinchot. "Every man and woman believed in it and its work. And out of this pride grew a strong common interest, which made the Service a thoroughly inspiring place to work."[12]

To Pinchot conservation was the very basis for American prosperity. Conservation meant resource development, the prevention of waste, benefits accruing to the many and not merely profit to the few, economic and political progress. "The earth and its resources belong of right to its people," wrote Pinchot. "Without natural resources life itself is impossible.... Without abundant resources, prosperity is out of reach. Therefore the conservation of natural resources is the fundamental material problem. It is the open door to economic and political progress."[13] Although Pinchot literally saved the forests from the wanton decimation of the 19th century, his emphasis on extraction of timber would be a legacy the Forest Service would live to rue. "Forestry is tree farming," Pinchot believed, and that was that.[14] Even to professional foresters, it became clear that "there was something deficient in Pinchot's view."[15]

But Pinchot implicitly set a standard for other emerging federal resource agencies. He appointed competent resource professionals to promote "wise use" of the nation's resources for multiple purposes. With science rapidly infusing their work, confidence bordering on arrogance, and a human-centered purpose, foresters and other resource professionals believed what Pinchot preached. They believed they could manipulate the environment to foster economic development; they believed they could uplift society and eliminate waste all at the same time. These were the illusions of an immensely optimistic age.

Meanwhile, working on a much grander scale than Dysart Woods, preservationists clamored to save what was left of the nation's wildlands. By the time they got to work in the last quarter of the 19th century, less than 20 per cent of the continent's pristine land remained intact. John Muir, the quintessential preservationist at the turn of the century, crusaded to save Yosemite and the Sierras. Others, including Roosevelt, saw to it that some of the most treasured natural areas were preserved: Yellowstone, Grand Canyon, Rocky Mountain, Glacier. David Brower, a mid-20th century version of Muir, called Muir's notion of people's parks "a new kind of foresight,"[16] and Time magazine described Muir as "the real father of conservation."[17]

Whether one assigns paternity to utilitarians like Pinchot or preservationists like Muir in retrospect seems inconsequential, for the two traditions are really part of the same wave that perceived humans and nature as separate, which, of necessity, required the government to intervene to protect for use or simply for posterity. As for Muir, ironically, one of his motives for saving wilderness was human fulfilment. He wrote in 1901, "Thousands of nerve-shaken, over-civilized people are beginning to find out that going to the mountains is going home; that wildness is a necessity."[18] As for Pinchot, despite his utilitarian bias, his National Forests unwittingly saved much of the "roadless" land base for the country's wilderness system.

The lines between utilization and preservation were further blurred by politics, ever responsive to the marketplace. Even the most unequivocally preservationist laws — the National Park Act of 1916 and the National Wilderness Preservation System Act of 1964 — were justified by recreation and human pleasure. The National Park Act mandated parks "for the use, observation, health, and pleasure of the people."[19] The Wilderness Act required that "wilderness...possess outstanding opportunities for solitude or a primitive and unconfined type of recreation."

Reflective of both the human-centeredness and government paternalism of the era, national parks were managed mostly for people. "Hotels were built, roads extended, trails improved, toilets provided and lakes stocked with fish — all in the name of providing the recreating public with what the 1916 act called 'enjoyment.'"[20] Neither is "wilderness" what it seems. William Cronon rightly characterizes it as a human construct:

> Far from being the one place on earth that stands apart from humanity, it is quite profoundly a human creation.... It is not a pristine sanctuary where the last remnant of an endangered but still transcendent nature can be encountered without the contaminating taint of civilization. Instead it is a product of that civilization.[21]

In many senses the choice was not really between aesthetics and utility. It boiled down to government taking responsibility for preserving a mythical state of nature for people's pleasure and recreation or utilizing nature for something else. Either way, it was a highly anthropocentric choice in which people and nature were separate categories.

ɘɔ

Theodore Roosevelt left the national scene in 1912. Conservation continued but with a decidedly utilitarian flavor. In the 1920s a heterogeneous collection of federal administrations began nationwide forest fire protection, conceived and constructed the Boulder Canyon (later Hoover) Dam and other hydroelectric projects, established a network of migratory bird sanctuaries, and added to the national park system.[22] These efforts laid the groundwork for New Deal conservation of the 1930s and 1940s, the second surge of progressive conservation.

For President Franklin Roosevelt, the Great Depression spurred his four successive administrations to engage in soil conservation, forest conservation, wildlife management, park improvement, and river basin development.[23] The Tennessee Valley Authority, David Lilienthal's river of many potential assets, and massive projects on the Colorado River symbolized the twin visions of utilization and control, visions harkening back to Pinchot, visions still driving North American water resource management.

In agriculture, industrial forestry, transportation, flood control, energy, even in recreation, the picture has been quite the same: extraction, control, and management. Recent threats to the biological integrity of National Wildlife Refuges throughout the United States[24] and Canada's assault on the Pacific rainforest at Clayoquot Sound are only the most recent examples of the choice.[25] The utilitarian tradition hangs tough.

THE SECOND WAVE

Ruin is the destination toward which all men rush, each pursuing his own best interest in a society that believes in the freedom of the commons. Freedom in a commons brings ruin to all.

— Garrett Hardin[26]

Environmental laws, de minimus, give the appearance of protection and sometimes the language of protection, but not necessarily the reality of it.

— H. Patricia Hynes[27]

The Commons

The ugly corruption of polluted rivers, smog alerts, fish kills, toxic dumps, and the image of a spring without birdsong were all ominous post-Second World War signs that the commons — air, water, species of plants and animals, and habitat — were in rapid decline. Freedom to abuse the commons, wrote Hardin, would bring ruin to all. Ordinary people were suddenly aware of these threats. Beginning with Rachel Carson's warnings of the biocidal impacts of agricultural chemicals in *Silent Spring*, published in 1962, people were bombarded with information that seemed to show the environment in free-fall. Their rivers were on fire and they could see and taste the foul air in their cities. They demanded that the government do something.[28] The problem was not about one place or one culprit. This was everyone's common place and the perpetrators were our sewage plants and our power plants, not just one man's factory.

By the 1960s, protecting the commons and improving environmental quality had gained national stature and political clout. President Richard Nixon, one of the most reluctant of environmental leaders, did understand the concept of political clout. On his watch, an unprecedented panoply of laws and regulations and a vast pool of tax dollars flowed to a new resource management mission, perhaps best encapsulated in Section 101 of the

National Environmental Policy Act, a cornerstone of second-wave environmental policy that said it was the federal government's responsibility to:

- fulfil the responsibilities of each generation as trustee of the environment for succeeding generations
- assure for all Americans safe, healthful, productive, and aesthetically and culturally pleasing surroundings
- attain the widest range of uses of the environment without degradation, risk to health or safety, or other undesirable and unintended consequences
- preserve important historic, cultural, and natural aspects of our national heritage...
- achieve balance between population and resource use
- enhance the quality of renewable resources and approach the maximum attainable recycling of depletable resources.[29]

Passed by a Congress that could not have foreseen its far-reaching implications, NEPA amounted to a bill of environmental rights and responsibilities. But how would these wide-ranging goals be achieved? NEPA's sponsors hoped that despoliation of the commons could be treated as a technical matter in which "value-free" science could be used to make environmental decisions.[30] The Environmental Protection Agency was created to help pull this off.

During the administrations of presidents Nixon, Ford and Carter, Congresses of the 1970s pressed forward with commons legislation: clean air acts, clean water acts, statutes to control and clean up toxic and hazardous wastes, to regulate pesticides, to protect drinking water, to reclaim lands damaged by surface mining, to protect wetlands, to save endangered species, and to safeguard human health. In this "golden age" of environmental regulation, most second-wave laws assumed without question that centralized resource management was the only way to get the job done.

Soon government's regulatory powers were unprecedented; they seemed to reach into every aspect of life. Among the regulators, EPA was king of the mountain. It not only inherited and was newly assigned enormous enforcement responsibilities but it also came to symbolize the government's confidence in scientific management of environmental problems and, if necessary, court action. At least until the backlash presidency of Ronald Reagan in the '80s, the EPA epitomized second-wave resource management by setting and enforcing crucially important limits to protect the commons.

Throughout this hyperactive time, nongovernment environmental organizations played a significant adversarial role. The Sierra Legal Defense Fund, the Environmental Defense Fund, Defenders of Wildlife, Friends of the Earth, the Natural Resources Defense Council, Clean Water Action and countless other organizations doggedly lobbied for new laws and tougher regulations. When laws were challenged, environmentalists dashed to the courts, jamming dockets and elevating environmental law to an exalted new status. More at the fringe, environmental groups such as Greenpeace, Sea Shepherd Conservation Society, Citizens Clearinghouse for Hazardous Wastes, and Earth First! demanded even more from government, for they saw that government had fallen far short of protecting and reclaiming the commons. They said the people had compromised enough.[31]

The first two waves of conservation grew out of the Cartesian view of nature as partitionable and separate from humans. Wes Jackson caustically calls this "smart resource management," supremely confident in the ability of science and technology to resolve all manner of problems, highly specialized and reductionist, unable to see the big picture, unable to embrace a meaningful ecological worldview.[32] It perceived the earth "...as a collection of natural resources" and humans "as above, superior to, or at best outside the rest of nature."[33]

Resource management in the first two waves was in the hands of professionals who got their orders mostly from politicians and corporate executives and seemed neither accountable nor especially responsive to ordinary citizens.[34] They were a class of managers charged with the job of protecting the community's water, air and wildlife without infringing upon the dreams of 20th century industrial society: growth, progress, and ever higher standards of material comfort.

As America has painfully learned, second-wave resource management does not even come close to fulfilling NEPA's lofty purposes. Politics of the 1980s and 1990s and an economy that continues to operate on the assumption of unlimited resource capital seriously undermine the ecological intentions of most environmental laws. Former EPA staffer Patricia Hynes notes that, despite appearances, environmental laws and regulations do not necessarily accomplish their ends. Her critique of the Federal Insecticide, Fungicide, and Rodenticide Act (FIFRA) of 1972 (amended in 1975, 1978 and 1980), which she calls "a bellwether of environmental law and environmental law enforcement," points out that FIFRA — and by implication most other environmental laws — has a serious flaw: it "lacks an ethic of nature and any tone of high-minded idealism. It fails to implement the fundamental critique of *Silent Spring*, that chemical control is a war on nature, waged in ignorance of ecology. Rather it places a mantle of protection around the use of chemical pesticides...."[35]

Hynes sadly concludes: "The answer to the question [of] whether more environmental laws guarantee more environmental protection is no. Environmental laws, *de minimis*, give the appearance of protection and sometimes the language of protection, but not necessarily the reality of it. For the reality of environmental protection, we need laws which have ecological intentionality."[36] FIFRA was not alone in what it ignored, omitted, tokenized, exempted, and excluded. Hynes believes examination of any or all environmental laws would lead to similar conclusions. On the other hand, one would hate to imagine what our water, air, wetlands and seacoasts might be like without them.

Another second-wave problem bubbled up within the ranks of resource agencies. By the 1980s, resource professionals found themselves caught in webs of controversy. Society began to view them not as paragons of resource stewardship, as in Pinchot's Forest Service, but rather as accomplices in the destruction of the environment. The Forest Service, for example, was compromised by the institutional-corporate system of which it was a part, generally unappreciated and misunderstood by the public, an easy target for politicians, and profoundly criticized by many environmentalists.[37] The same was true of other agencies, including the EPA. Out of this caldron of controversy the third wave began to gain strength.

THE THIRD WAVE

Presently we are returning to the primordial community of the universe, the earth and all living beings. Each has its own voice, its role, its power over the whole. But, most important, each has its special symbolism. The excitement of life is in the numinous experience wherein we are given to each other in that larger celebration of existence in which all things attain their highest expression, for the universe, by definition, is a single gorgeous celebratory event.

— Thomas Berry[38]

The land ethic simply enlarges the community to include soils, waters, plants, and animals, or collectively, the land.... A land ethic of course cannot prevent the alteration, management, and use of these "resources," but it does affirm their right to continued existence, and, at least in spots, their continued existence in a natural state.

— Aldo Leopold[39]

Life and the environment are one thing, not two, and people, as all life, are immersed in the one system. When we influence nature, we influence ourselves; when we change nature, we change ourselves.

— Daniel B. Botkin[40]

Let us remember that the worldview of ecology is very much that of a vernacular, community-based society, whereas the worldview of modernism is that of a corporation-based industrial society.

— Edward Goldsmith[41]

The Ecological Way

Disillusionment awakened a third wave. Beginning in the '60s, people from all walks of life, all environmental persuasions, acquired for the first time a new view of their planet — a view from space. It was as if the global ecosystem finally popped into view. Though a number of ecologists had spoken of the interconnectedness of all living communities, few took heed. Now, with a picture of our fragile blue oasis in deep black space, many began to understand. Thinking of Earth as a living system propelled planetary science into new conceptual realms, among them geophysiologist James Lovelock's Gaia hypothesis which sees the global biosphere as a huge regulatory system maintaining ecological conditions optimum for life.

Meanwhile, the conceptual ground underlying the relationship between humans and natural resources dramatically shifted. Lest we think that the roots of this "new" thinking are exclusively products of the late 20th century, conservation writer and biographer Curt Meine reminds us of Aldo Leopold's words in the epigraph above, written a half-century ago. Meine writes: "Leopold simultaneously acknowledged the reality of human resource use and the limits of utilitarian conservation philosophy, even as he confirmed the inherent worth and dignity of 'things natural, wild, and free.'"[42] Leopold understood that "living on a piece of land without spoiling it" could not be achieved just by developing more sophisticated or powerful tools of resource management. "Success required more comprehensive ways of perceiving, understanding and appreciating the relationship between people and nature. Success, in other words, required that we not simply change the land, but that we change ourselves."[43]

This truth is perhaps most often repeated in the canon of deep ecology, whose roots date to the 1970s when Norwegian philosopher Arne Naess coined the term. In contrast to what Naess called "shallow ecology," deep ecology is fully biocentric. It advocates ecological equity, the intrinsic value of every species (irrespective of the value humans place on it), reduced human population growth, preservation of pristine places, and people's "self-realization" through simpler lifestyles and lower rates of consumption.[44] Whatever the criticisms of deep ecology, and there have been many, its advocacy of a biocentric ethic is one foundation on which a third wave of resource management is built.[45]

The same could be said of bioregionalism, a cluster of theories and practices that contend earth is best understood as a series of life territories defined by ecological verities (such as watersheds or biotic regions) rather than by political subdivisions. With help from the Planet Drum Foundation of San Francisco, bioregionalism's original think tank, the New Catalyst of British Columbia, and the widely circulated writings of Kirkpatrick Sale, bioregionalism caught the fancy of back-to-the-landers and urban environmentalists in all corners of North America.[46] Some think of it as a modern variant of old-left anarchism and utopian, nature-centered, self-reliant communities of the sort Kropotkin, Howard, Geddes and their intellectual colleagues envisioned; others view bioregionalism as a different set of propositions built around the notion of "becoming native" to, or "reinhabiting," one's home.[47]

According to Jim Dodge, bioregionalism is a blend: "a decentralized, self-determined mode of social organization; a culture predicated upon biological integrities and acting in respectful accord; and a society which honors and abets the spiritual development of its members."[48] At biennial congresses, the North American bioregional movement now draws people from some 200 constituent groups.[49] To the extent that bioregionalism brings heightened awareness of place and the need to reinhabit such places with awareness and respect for their specific ecological realities and cultural traditions, it is a key third-wave element.

Closely related is resurgent interest in rebuilding human community. The dictionary defines community as people living under a locally controlled government, having common interests, a sense of common purpose, and effective ways of resolving disputes. By this definition, it is obvious that community is largely an illusion in contemporary North America, a rare thing, says psychologist Scott Peck.[50] Despite this, community was once at the core of our republic. Jefferson thought of agrarian communities bound together by "pure democracy" as "the article nearest to my heart."[51] Nowadays, dissolution of community is widely cited as a fundamental problem and, indeed, a primary barrier to sustainability.

To fix it, Friedman, Drucker, Kemmis, Daly and Cobb, Lappé and DuBois and others argue that we must devote far more attention to local and regional economies and politics and to rebuilding social networks.[52] Herman Daly and John Cobb, in their search for sustainable economics, conclude that what's needed is "...a bottom-up society, a community of communities that are local and relatively small."[53] Friedman says we must detach communities from the market economy and rebuild political responses household by household, neighborhood by neighborhood, community by community. Drucker contends that community in the post-capitalist society will be based on "commitment and compassion rather than being imposed by proximity and isolation."[54]

Daniel Kemmis, in *Community and the Politics of Place*, argues for a Jeffersonian public policy based on "education into citizenship, the heart of which was to enable people to see (and then to act upon) the common good."[55] Understanding and acting upon the common good, "making others' conditions our own," encourages citizens to shoulder responsibilities that are clearly theirs. An even more important point, in Kemmis's mind, is the bond between people and place. Place, he says, is at the very center of a community-based political culture.

Beneath it all, communities build not from atomized individuals, "bristling with rights and choices but with no connectedness or responsibility for one another."[56] Communities grow instead when individuals "commune," "communicate," and earnestly search for "commons." Or, as psychologist Peck puts it, communities are made up of:

> ...individuals who have learned how to communicate honestly with each other, whose relationships go deeper than their masks of composure, and who have developed some significant commitment 'to rejoice together, mourn together,' and 'to delight in each other, make others' conditions our own.'[57]

Another important current bubbling beneath the third wave is what we shall call "new ecology." In the past few decades the science of ecology has undergone massive shifts in its own paradigm.[58] Classically, natural systems were believed to be closed, self-regulating, and equilibrious. The theory of ecological succession deterministically predicted phases of change, from bare ground to climax community. Deviations from this path, such as severe storms and fire, were exceptional. Humans were thought to be outside the system because "they introduced multiple states to systems, acted as disturbance agents, transported materials and organisms beyond their usual distributions, acted as external regulators,...and prevented orderly, deterministic succession."[59]

These assumptions no longer hold water. Daniel Botkin, in a troubling, important book, Discordant Harmonies, writes:

> We have clouded our perception of nature with false images, and as long as we continue to do that we will cloud our perception of ourselves, cripple our ability to manage natural resources, and choose the wrong approaches to dealing with global environmental concerns. The way to achieve harmony with nature is first to break free of old metaphors and embrace new ones so that we can lift the veils that prevent us from accepting what we observe....[60]

Lifting the veils, Botkin and others say, means abandoning the metaphor of the machine — from which we deduced the erroneous idea of "the balance of nature." Instead, an organic view of earth is appropriate, a view in which "nature disturbed" is at the core of our understanding of ecosystems and our role within them.

This new nonequilibrium paradigm — some refer to it as "the flux of nature" — recognizes that natural systems are open and regulated by things happening beyond their boundaries and are greatly affected by natural and human disturbances. Although there are stable points in natural systems, many elements of flux make it impossible to assume long-term equilibrium.[61]

Since fluctuations are the way nature works, managers must make decisions as though fluctuations matter.[62] Using nature as a measure suggests flexible, process-driven management. Practised adaptively, this sort of management sets goals using a model of the system to be managed that includes not only components and their interactions but also predicted fluctuations. It then lays out hypotheses to be tested, monitors results, checks findings against the model and changes goals and hypotheses, if necessary.[63] Management strategies must be flexible to assure diversity and persistence of the system.

While it is clear that this new ecological theory has firmly taken root, the metaphor on which it is based can lead resource managers down the dangerous path of thinking that since flux is part of the way nature works, any flux introduced by humans is justifiable.[64] This fails to take account of limits in the natural world. Natural systems can only adapt in an environment, the basic features of which have not diverged significantly from the optimum. "As their environment diverges, so adaptive behaviour becomes more difficult, and, eventually, impossible. For each particular feature of the environment there are thus limits...."[65] The same may be said of our own communities and especially of our abilities to manage them adaptively.

All these conceptual threads weave together a tapestry whose design is still unclear. The ultimate product is being called sustainability or sustainable development, terms that were popularized worldwide by the United Nations Commission on Environment and Development in the late 1980s. But sustainability and sustainable development have been used so fecklessly by politicians and their spin-doctors as to have totally lost their precision. Environmental writer Bill McKibben makes the case for substituting the words "maturity" and "mature development."[66] These too beg as many questions as they answer.

To the UN Commission, sustainable development meant meeting "the needs of the present without compromising the ability of future generations to meet their own needs,"[67] a definition we encountered more than once in our travels for this book. To believers in the present commercial system, it means integration of economic, biologic and human systems toward the end of sustainable commerce.[68] Again this begs the real meaning of sustainable.

To practitioners of resource management, sustainability has come to mean managing resources for the long run and living on income rather than depleting capital. This presumes we are able to determine environmental carrying capacities, to compute thresholds and limits, to know much more than we now know about nature's flux, and to design a steady-state economy. As David Orr notes, we are far short of these capabilities and therefore are really unable to say precisely what actions are and are not sustainable.[69] Yet we can agree on a *raison d'être*: a life of quality for generations yet born, both human and "more than human."

ल্ড

Economist Hazel Henderson calls this era of conflict between competing paradigms "the breakdown zone": a zone where obsolescent institutions and their underlying cultural and political forms are destructuring.[70] The breakdown zone, that of Copernicus and Galileo, is a zone of conflicting ideologies, a zone of "accidents" — slow-motion crises such as acid rain, ozone thinning, climate change, and toxic spills. But breakdown leads ultimately to breakthrough, Henderson argues, "a third way, a new structure, new forms, new maps, new goals and values, a win-win planetary culture."[71]

If this is so, the new forms of resource management in communities all over North America signal the beginnings of breakthrough. Place-based initiatives, which André Clewell calls "downshifting," are popping up everywhere and are profoundly different from anything preceding them.[72] They are conceived by people who understand the limits of the old culture of patriarchy and colonialism in which the government is expected to do all, who are not diverted by bureaucracy's fixation on procedures, and who know that their future depends on good care of the living resources in their neighborhood. These people, firmly rooted at home, are listening carefully to nature before taking resource management into their own hands. Their strategies derive from knowledge that nature "is full of surprises" and that the human environment and the natural environment are interlocked in labyrinthine ways. They are initiating and sticking with environmental restoration projects. They are using the marketplace to their advantage. They are engaged in collaborative, participatory community planning. And they are taking risks to find common ground with the big institutions of our day.

If the third wave flourishes, "it will be advanced by countless people working separately and in small groups, sharing only a common dream of life.... Nature will have entered their lives at an early age and will remain as a source of joy and as the measure of their best and worst efforts."[73] It will be as diverse as the communities and resource challenges of each bioregion of North America. It will be a new frontier for the American conservation movement.

Copernican change is upon us.

Practitioners and disciples of third-wave resource management are in an apparently hopeless minority and they face mountains of resistance. In Washington and Ottawa, Paris and Tokyo, Beijing and Bangkok, big bureaucracies and faceless, placeless corporations still see nature as commodity, still operate under the "tyranny of disregard" we call the global economy, still hold tightly the levers of power.[74] Backlash organizations with double-speak names like "Alliance for the Environment" and "Wise Use," under the banners of property rights, "takings," and individual freedom, belittle and sabotage an ecological worldview.[75] Like the church in Copernicus's day, they are trying to obliterate a new vision. But their assumptions no longer wash. There are too many trashed places just over the fence, too many horrors happening in slow-motion, too much dissonance, too many people who refuse to hate. We are in the breakdown zone.

Thousands of people across the continent have already refocused, have already taken up the work of living more humbly in their homes. Their examples can lead us from breakdown to breakthrough. Read on.

A COLLECTION OF NEW STORIES

∾

——————————Part Two ——————————

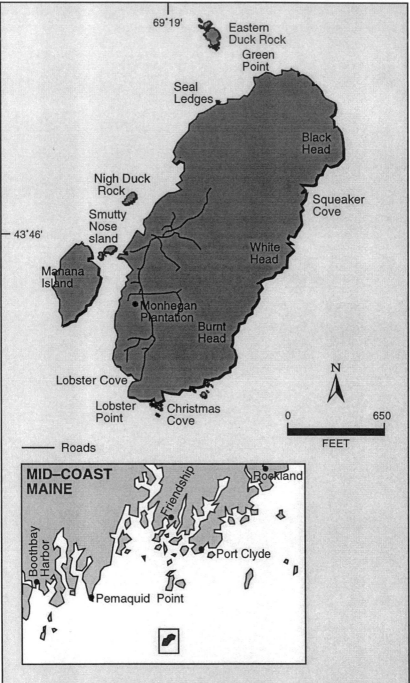

69°19'

Eastern
Duck Rock

Green
Point

Seal
Ledges

Black
Head

Nigh Duck
Rock

Squeaker
Cove

Smutty
Nose
sland

43°46'

White
Head

Manana
Island

Monhegan
Plantation

Burnt
Head

N

Lobster Cove

Lobster
Point

Christmas
Cove

0   650

FEET

—— Roads

**MID–COAST
MAINE**

Rockland

Friendship

Boothbay
Harbor

Port Clyde

Pemaquid Point

Islands Foreshadow the Future:
Monhegan Island, Maine
──────── Chapter Three ────────

Monhegan Associates [will] preserve for posterity the natural wild beauty, biotic communities, and desirable natural, artificial, and historic features of the so-called 'wild-lands' portions of Monhegan Island, Maine, and its environs, as well as the simple, friendly way of life that has existed on Monhegan as a whole.
— Monhegan Associates[1]

Who could have predicted the significance of one boy's ramblings over the headlands and through the woods of a small Maine island? Yet for Monhegan one boy made all the difference. So poignant were the childhood memories of Ted Edison, son of inventor Thomas Alva Edison, that 40 years later he would purchase and preserve for posterity "the natural wild beauty" of more than half the island. Not merely an act of extraordinary generosity, Edison's vision and philanthropy became a kind of standard by which Monhegan's natural resources would be perceived and managed. It helped the island see itself in a different light, to embrace an ethic Aldo Leopold would recognize as "love, respect and admiration for the land."[2]

Edison could not have known that his example would reinforce other forms of self-discipline and sustain not only Monhegan's "friendly way of life" but also its resource base. Thanks to Edison, fully 65 per cent of the island is zoned undevelopable. While respecting private property and business and honoring individualism and a long tradition of self-rule, the people of Monhegan have brokered important partnerships with state and federal agencies to protect the shoreline for fishers, save distinctive natural areas, avoid mass tourism, and prevent contamination of offshore waters and the sole-source freshwater aquifer. Though Ted Edison had no direct role in these partnerships, his gift of land and his dedication to a land ethic are the very foundation of Monhegan's recent resource history.

Monhegan has made tough decisions as yet uncommon in mainland communities. Little by little, the people arrived at largely self-designed, self-imposed, and self-rewarded systems to set limits. In doing this, generally without grand design, Monhegan is an extraordinary example for other islands. But Monhegan's story also speaks to the mainland. "Because islands force their inhabitants to recognize the environmental consequences of activities that seem harmless elsewhere," notes writer Philip Conkling, "island communities foreshadow the future for all communities."[3]

THE PLACE

To get to Monhegan, you need to leave your car on the mainland. Apart from the few working vehicles of residents (mostly ancient pickup trucks), cars are not allowed. At Port Clyde you hitch a ride on the mail boat, which makes the 12-mile trip the choppy waters of the Gulf of Maine twice daily in summer (three times a week in winter). You arrive at the town wharf and stroll up a rocky road toward a small village apparently frozen in time. You see no neon signs, you walk on no paved roads or sidewalks. The air is unpolluted and you hear none of the din of 20th century North America. The village is a cluster of a few dozen New England cottages, two large frame hotels, a school house, a church, a library, an historic lighthouse now a museum, a few small businesses.

Your mind takes in this scene as if it were a totally intact museum of living history: 19th century coastal New England without period costumes. But soon you realize Monhegan is authentic. It is not only in the 20th century; it is beyond. A tiny speck in the ocean (1.5 miles long, 0.7 miles wide, less than one square mile in area), Monhegan is a place where you get off the fast track.

Monhegan people are hardy, understated, and modest. They live a good life in a difficult place. Among permanent residents, there is full employment, a modest tax rate, an excellent school, above average family incomes, and a general sense of well-being.[4] They have diverse opinions on how they manage to walk the line between individualism and community. As we recorded it, their common vision includes:

- An appreciation of the slow-paced, simple and quiet island lifestyle.

- A desire to keep Monhegan roughly the way it is for as long as possible.

- Belief in the need to sustain a winter community and all that goes with it — schools, library, store, mail service and post office, etc.

- A notion that fishing is crucial to Monhegan's future in order to be a viable year-round (as opposed to a caretaker) community.

- Knowledge that the wildlands are priceless and must continue to have protection.

- Realization that the quality of the island environment is unique and fragile: sewage and septic disposal, solid waste, the impact of hikers on wildlands ecology are on-going problems.

- Understanding that the quality of the natural environment affects everyone, whether they fish, serve tourists, or simply live and garden on the island.

There are differences of opinion on many other issues. After all, this is a very small community made up of independent and self-reliant people.

Monhegan residents are one reason outsiders fall in love with this little island. Its physical beauty is another. In a very compact area, it has all that coastal Maine can offer: a spectacular shoreline of rocky promontories, high cliffs, looming headlands, and offshore islands and ledges with seals and seabirds, a classic fishing harbor — motifs inspiring landscape art for more than 100 years.

White Head, Burnt Head, Black Head, rising 135 to 155 feet above the pounding North Atlantic, are some of the highest places along the Atlantic seaboard. Manana Island, just west of Monhegan, a treeless hump rising 110 feet above the sea, partially protects the small harbor, with the town wharf at the north end. Though there is usually shelter here, the harbor is described in cruising guides as "difficult and unsafe anchorage," and there are no public moorings or marinas. Scattered along the edges of the harbor are fish houses where resident lobstermen socialize, store bait, keep their supplies, and mend nets and traps.

Monhegan itself rises safely above the surf both of normal run-of-the-mill rough weather and severe storms. The island's core is a ledge of Precambrian crystalline rocks, a quarter of a billion years old. Atop this ledge is a light mantle of glacial till, deposited about 13,000 years ago by the receding ice sheet. Small areas of emerged marine-beach deposits, beach and dune deposits, and tiny wetlands also dot the surface. At the center of the village, a bog called "the Meadow" rests atop marine sands and clay. Elsewhere soils are so sparse and shallow that the village cemetery has had to import topsoil from the mainland and water pipes are generally above ground. Tunbridge-Lyman soils cover about 55 per cent of Monhegan but rarely at tillable depths. Though people farmed throughout the 19th century, this is a challenging place to keep a garden.

About 70 per cent of the island is now covered by some kind of forest, 40 per cent of which is mature.[5] Red and white spruce and balsam fir dominate but one also sees red and mountain maple, alder, moosewood, quaking aspen and white birch. Wildflowers and other herbaceous plants lend color and diversity to the understory.[6] Of these, only the fringed gentian is threatened or endangered, though many plants once common to the island have recently been disappearing. Larry Cooper, resident wildflower expert, estimates that 64 species can no longer be found on Monhegan.[7] There are no state-listed Natural Heritage Areas but three state-listed Critical Areas (Cathedral Woods, Lighthouse Hill and Lobster Cove) contain mature forests.

Among the animals a visitor first encounters on Monhegan are white-tailed deer, the present generation of a controversial herd introduced deliberately about 40 years ago. Nowadays, their descendants (estimated at 30-40 animals) wander the wildlands and venture boldly into yards, gardens and village pathways. Many on Monhegan consider the deer a nuisance, for they harbor the tick that carries Lyme disease and they are partly responsible for over-browsing rare plants. Others enjoy the sight of deer on the island or engage in the fall hunting season. At a town meeting in 1994, a slim majority voted to "rid the island of deer and called for formation of a committee to see such implemented."[8]

As an important stop along the Atlantic flyway, Monhegan has seasonally significant and diverse populations of pelagic and passerine birds, raptors and waterfowl. Along the shoreline and on offshore islands and ledges are four colonial seabird nesting sites as well as two seal haul-outs. Seal-watching and birdwatching are favorite tourist attractions.

Monhegan's human story is likewise more fascinating than its acreage would suggest. Monhegan was long a summer fishery for Indians who canoed across the bay and camped in the present harbor area. In the 17th century Verrazano, Cabot, Gomez, Champlain, John Smith and Weymouth all made stops at Monhegan, as likely did Norse sailors much earlier. Thereafter European crews anchored near the island in summer, fished the productive waters of Muscongus Bay, and dried their catch on Monhegan's shores. For a time in the 1600s, Monhegan and nearby islands were the most important European fishing stations along the mid-coast of Maine.[9]

Beginning in 1619 Monhegan was home to two generations of European settlers, but, for various reasons including Indian raids, it was abandoned in 1676. After the American Revolution, the whole island was purchased by two families and has been continuously occupied since. In the 1830s, when Monhegan became incorporated as a Plantation, it had a population of 100, "numerous good dwellings," a schoolhouse and a church, and many small pastures for sheep, swine and cattle. (Plantations, the equivalent of villages or hamlets in some states, are the lowest level in a three-part hierarchy of "organized territories" in Maine. The other categories are towns and cities.)

Besides agriculture, fishing was a mainstay of the economy. "During the 1830s, eight Monhegan vessels were engaged regularly in Grand Banks fisheries and 9,000 Quintals (each 220 lbs.) were cured annually on the island."[10] In the late-1870s steamships began to bring tourists to Monhegan. Sometimes called "rusticators," these early tourists were city folk, like the Edisons — people having the leisure and means to escape urban America in summer. They stayed at island guest houses and inns. Many were captivated by Monhegan's beauty and quiet life. They purchased land, built small cottages, and year after year, summered there. For generations, summer residents brought new energy and ideas. "They have been...people of vision and some means," notes full-time resident Peter Boehmer; "they have been able to see the power, beauty and fragility of this place in a way that those who lived here could not."

Artists also contributed to the Monhegan amalgam. By the early 20th century, Monhegan was on its way to fame as a cherished place in American landscape art. Robert Henri's Monhegan school in the early 1900s was followed by a steady stream of brilliant young painters including George Bellows, Rockwell Kent, John Marin, Reuben Tam and Jamie Wyeth. "The island is still a mecca for artists, and there is no mistaking its impact upon their work."[11] Conversely, the impact of the artists themselves on Monhegan's economy and ambience is also undeniable. Artists open their studios to the public, conduct workshops, own property, participate in island affairs, and generally contribute to the blend of "high" culture and rustic island life.

Of course, Monhegan was not the only island settlement along the coast. A century ago, there were 300 permanently occupied offshore islands in Maine. Today Monhegan is one of just 14 offshore islands occupied year-round. Those who make it their home realize a critical mass of year-round residents is needed to keep open the school, the post office (and hence the mail run) and the store. First assessor Katy Bogel remarked: "One of my visions of the future is that we will still have a viable year-round community when our children become adults. This is very important to those in my generation who have staked out our lives here." The year-round island population has fluctuated in the past century, peaking in 1940 at slightly more than 150, bottoming-out in 1970 at about 50. Eighty-eight people were resident at the time of the 1990 census.

By contrast, the summer population of Monhegan stays steady, averaging somewhere around 400 people during the eight weeks between July 4 and Labor Day. Because of the limited number of guest rooms and summer cottages and the lack of developable land, land speculation and mass tourism are not serious threats to Monhegan. But two relatively new trends in tourism make some residents uneasy: an expanding number of day-trippers, who come to hike the wildlands trails and visit artists' studios; and rental of summer cottages and apartments to short-term visitors. Compared to Edison's boyhood, summer visitors now come and go at a much more rapid pace.

Besides tourism, lobstering sustains the current economy. Once just a small sideline to seining, trawling, and hand-lining for finfish, lobstering is now the only viable fishery. Groundfish in the waters around Monhegan have been overfished and are all but depleted, and "fishing" is now synonymous with "lobstering." Though only about a dozen lobster boats operate out of Monhegan, fully half the island income comes from lobstering. Fish houses, summer-stacked traps, colorful buoys and pungent lobster odors remind the visitor that this is a working island culture.

SETTING LIMITS

Lobstering

In the early 1940s, in a poignantly far-sighted move, lobstermen persuaded the state government to allow a closed season on lobster in Monhegan's waters. The Maine legislature passed a law in 1941 limiting Monhegan's lobster season to six months. Monhegan lobstermen don't fish in summer.

Thus, Monhegan lobstermen are fishing...when the price for lobster is very high and when they have few other economic options. They put their traps 'on the banks' in the summer, when they have alternative employment in the tourist industry, leaving the defence of their territory to the state fish wardens. The closed season keeps anyone from setting traps during July and August, when fishing for molting lobsters would result in very high mortality.[12]

Wherever we inquired about lobstering on Monhegan, seasonal limits was the first fact mentioned, and always with pride. "We give 'em the other half a year to grow. You don't see farmers killing all their chicks. You might say lobsters are our chicks," one lobsterman explained.

Monhegan lobstermen also voluntarily limited the number of traps per boat. Sherm Stanley, a lobsterman for more than 40 years, told us:

It's a shame the government has to come in and regulate when the people themselves could do it if they were a mind to. We regulated ourselves and decided on a closed season. In Monhegan we used to put in as many traps as we wanted. Then we had a meeting and decided we wouldn't fish more than 600 traps to a boat. It's been good for us and I don't think the fishermen would complain if we cut it down to 500.

Opinions vary about the rationale for these unusual self-limiting resource management decisions. Few ever argue they were acts of "far-sighted conservation." Some fishers saw it as a way of staving off greed both within the community and from afar because they cleverly used the state to keep interlopers out of Monhegan waters during a time when the territory would be undefended with traps and buoys.[13]

Others say that lobstering in summer competed with other fisheries just as important in the 1940s. By closing the lobster season, fishers were able to do both. Another reason perhaps was a need to regroup and rest. "Lobstering is a hard way of making a living," Stanley made clear. "You can tear yourself up if you try to do it all year long. We needed some down-time to repair our gear and get our strength back."[14]

James Acheson, author of *The Lobster Gangs of Maine*, sees tourism as a reason for the decision to close lobster fisheries off Monhegan in summer. Even in the 1940s, there were some fishers engaged in tourist services, if nothing more than doing odd jobs and helping open and close summer cottages. Today almost all lobstermen have a hand directly or indirectly in the summer tourist trade, so now it certainly works in their favor.

Whatever the reason — conservation, greed, protection of territory, the opportunity to do other kinds of fishing, rest and recuperation, or tourism — the lobster fishery has remained productive and profitable for more than two generations. In retrospect, the outcome of the closed season has been sustained yield of an important renewable resource. This has contributed to economic stability and community security. And today it is often hailed as a visionary act.

Wildlands

Just after the Second World War, with New England's economy booming, Ted Edison perceived the renewed threat of overdevelopment on Monhegan. He came up with a plan to counter this threat and then engaged a local leader, Sherm Stanley, to help bring greater involvement of the community. Stanley translated Edison's romantic goal of wildlands protection into language the community could accept. And, in time, the wildlands became a signature quality of the island. Because the wildlands are such an essential element of Monhegan, the Edison story is worth recounting in more detail.

Based upon land speculation of the '20s, land had been subdivided for dozens more cottages, roads, other amenities. Deeds had been issued but informal ways of keeping records made them open to question. The Great Depression and Second World War burst the speculation bubble. By the '50s, subdivided tracts were nothing more than lines on a faded map. Yet the cloud of mass tourist development hung over the island. Edison purchased as much land as he could, including several plots more than once, just to be certain he gained clear title. With virtually unlimited legal and financial resources, and great personal tenacity, Edison was able to give life to his dream of an untouched wildland park.

Island property owners responded with suspicion. The rumor mill began to churn. Was Edison behind some kind of unsavory development scheme? Or, if his motives were genuine, would a wildland park put people out of work? Would plumbers, carpenters and other tradespeople have to leave Monhegan? Edison had no intention of changing the character of the village or of altering Monhegan's unique blend of art, fishing and tourism. Yet he understood that his wildlands plan would never succeed if residents and landowners were hostile. So he invited one of the most prominent citizens of the island to discuss his idea.

One long-time Monheganite said that everyone gives all the credit for protection of the wildlands to Ted Edison but fails to recall the importance of local collaboration. It is true that Edison's foresight and philanthropy were necessary conditions. But interpreting those gifts to a sceptical island population required not wealth but political savvy. Sherm Stanley, first assessor of the plantation government at the time and titular "godfather" of the fishing community, was drawn into Edison's confidence. The importance of this friendship cannot be overemphasized:

> It was a stroke of genius for Edison to go to the head man of the fishing community. Everybody knew this. Edison spent three years working with him on the establishment of the Associates. Monhegan Associates would never have happened without the blessing of Stanley.[15]

Sherm Stanley, a hearty bespectacled man with a pure white head of hair, now in his 70s, reminisced with us about those days. We sat in the doorway of his barn on a sparkling May day, enraptured not only of his understated recollections but also with the simple beauty of the little offshore village he calls home. Stanley recalls that:

> It was in the late forties or early fifties.... I was one of the assessors at the time so I presume that was one of the reasons why he came to me.... The people on the coast of Maine tend to be a bit on the independent side; they work with their hands and they're quite self-sufficient. They might not like the idea. And so he came and chatted with me about his idea. And I guess in that particular summer we did mostly chat about one thing and another because I wanted to find out for sure just how much of the island he had in mind. I had to take into consideration the people who lived here and did carpenter work and various jobs on the island because I knew there would be quite a little bit of people raising their eyebrows, asking 'Who's this man coming in, gonna get all this property? Develop it. And ruin the island.' Naturally there was a lot on people's minds. So I wanted to be a go-between if I could, as long as I felt this man was sincere, which I believed he was.

Stanley risked his own reputation to promote Edison's idea of a wildlands park among permanent residents of Monhegan. With his help, Edison and residents from both the summer and year-round communities formed Monhegan Associates in 1954 to preserve the environmental integrity of the wildlands and also "the friendly way of life."[16] "Preserving the friendly way of life," according to some, was a code that translated roughly into: "Monhegan Associates shall not meddle in island politics."

Nonetheless, in the 40 years of its life, Monhegan Associates has acquired or otherwise put under protection about 65 per cent of the island, the vast majority of which is outside the village. Associates' land — still being acquired or bequeathed — cannot be altered for development.[17]

As the quote at the head of this chapter reveals, preserving the natural wild beauty of the island and respecting the traditional way of life is what Monhegan Associates is supposed to do. This subtly translates into sustaining the balance of power between the summer and winter communities.

> The summer people would have their place and the winter people's politics would not be interfered with. Edison's main purpose was to save the island.... He was a liberal and democratic person. The island is not. He wanted the Alliance to be inclusive but he had to compromise in order to save the island.[18]

With no further management guidelines, Monhegan Associates are seen by some as steering clear of island politics so faithfully as to be irresponsible. Cases in point are debates of the early 1990s about what to do about invasive dwarf mistletoe, which is damaging white spruce; whether to remove or control the exotic deer population; whether to limit the number of trail users; and whether to cut and clear dead trees for fire control. Dealing with such issues opens the question of tampering unnecessarily with lands that are by definition "wild." Many Monhegan people agree with lobsterman Doug Boynton who believes "the best management is no management." Thus, Maine Department of Forestry recommendations on some of these questions have never been implemented.

Though there is plenty of disagreement about how the wildlands should be managed, not one person we talked to could ever imagine opening them to development. It is unthinkable that this lovely tract of forests and wetlands — Monhegan's gateway to a wild and breathtaking coastline — would be altered in some hideous way. For two generations Monhegan residents have understood and accepted that more than half the island is off-limits to development, that the wildlands are central to Monhegan's celebration of place.

Edison's horizon for the wildlands was "forever." Perhaps that is not the investment climate among all residents today, but when you ask about the future, almost everyone responds that the ideal image of Monhegan in 20 or 50 years is exactly the Monhegan of today. And that is close to what Edison had in mind.

Land Use and Water

A distinctive form of local government operating "according to certain prudential rules" had long given Monhegan residents effective home rule.[19] One resident put it this way: "We've always had as little to do with the state as possible. If problems came up, we'd never call the state to ask if we were infringing upon this or that regulation or law. We simply took care of things ourselves in a time-honored and civil way."[20] Common law, as understood by residents and land owners, enabled Monhegan to take care of itself, largely without interference of police or courts.

With a history of successfully setting limits to benefit the community and affirm their sense of place, Monhegan in the 1960s and 1970s was able to effectively integrate new zoning ideas and changes brought by the Clean Water Acts into their "time-honored" lifeways. This arena of regulation may have seemed odd to this historically independent group, but, just like state lobster regulations, they figured out how to use it to make good decisions for the community.

Perhaps it was a shock for Monhegan to discover that it was hardly in compliance with state and federal environmental regulations promulgated during the blaze of second-wave law-making. It had neither a comprehensive land-use plan nor zoning codes required by the state. It was disposing solid waste offshore. Its septic tanks and cesspools drained into the Meadow, the town's only aquifer. It had not inventoried threatened and endangered species and habitats.

New state agencies such as the Land Use Regulatory Commission (LURC) and the Department of Environmental Protection (DEP) found their way to Monhegan. LURC required a comprehensive plan and zoning codes. DEP began to monitor offshore water quality and sensitize Monhegan to the risk of groundwater pollution. In the process, complete home rule on these matters went the way of the kerosene lantern. Land use and natural resources would, for better or worse, now be monitored and controlled by distant government agencies.

Richard Farrell, a Planning Board member at the time, explained that people had contradictory responses to the regulators:

> There were two things going on: one, some relief, because a land-use decision of my neighbor no longer needed to be approved on island but could be done at some remove. It gave me protection from my neighbor, other than going to court, which is hard on an island. It was a relief. On the other hand, ruling against a land-use

change I might want on my own property was a different matter. Here there was some opposition.

People discovered that you can't have it both ways, and reluctantly came to accept the need for a comprehensive plan, for zoning, and for special protection of areas critical to everyone's well-being.

LURC, in particular, inadvertently fostered the good social purpose of enriching the island's "social capital" by improving relationships among community members. It also helped sustain and improve Monhegan's two principal sources of income: lobster fishing and tourism. LURC thus became an accomplice in Monhegan's unique path toward more sustainable resource management.

Three land-use decisions set the tone. The first, which took place shortly after LURC came into being, gave protection to the wildlands and subdivided the village into general, residential, and maritime development districts. These districts are still the basic canon of Monhegan land use: the wildlands shall not be developed and subdivision and development in the village shall be carefully controlled.

Second, the Meadow watershed (69 acres centered around the 9-acre bog), which supplies the entire island with water in summer and includes about one-third of the developed village area, was declared "a sole-source aquifer" by the U.S. Environmental Protection Agency.[21] A hydrogeologic consultant recommended protection both from further development and from septic and sewage runoff.[22] In late 1989 LURC amended its land-use districts and standards by granting the Meadow (owned by Monhegan Associates) special protection as an aquifer and by helping the village find funds to divert some sewage.

Third, facing considerable pressure to allow subdivision of shoreline structures for summer rentals, the village actually petitioned LURC in 1988 to establish two maritime protection districts. Virtually all year-round and seasonal residents supported this petition.[23] LURC, in turn, accepted it and rezoned two areas of shoreline and the town wharf as maritime protection districts. This effectively halts development of the shore used by fishers and prevents conversion of fish houses to other uses.[24] Monhegan's fishing economy will thus not fall prey to real estate speculation and tourist pressure.

Together these decisions help to protect the natural resources Monhegan folk value most — the small village atmosphere of Monhegan Plantation, the natural beauty and wildness of the woods and rocky shores, fresh drinking water for the tourist season, and a fishing economy.

Hindsight makes the Monhegan Plantation government seem visionary. Indeed, it is possible to conclude that good leadership and consistent collaboration between year-round citizens, business people and summer residents moved Monhegan along a more sustainable path. But hindsight can be kind.

It's obvious that some of Monhegan's stakeholders were looking after their own skins — but not without enlightenment. The community has in fact been the ultimate beneficiary. For example, fishers clearly profit from LURC's intervention as they now have perpetual access to the shore. Indirectly, tourism gains too, since the village will not lose the quaintness and "lobstering ambience" people seem to cherish. On the other hand, community stability has surely also been reinforced. That 100 per cent of year-round residents and 91 per cent of the seasonal respondents opted to restrict the shoreline for fishing and maritime-related activity rather than condos or guest apartments is a clear testimony to social responsibility. Roughly the same percentages of respondents also favored state protection of the wildlands and supported the plan to safeguard the Meadow.[25] Neither individual profit motives, nor private property rights, nor politics seemed to motivate these opinions.

No one claims that LURC and other state agencies are perfect partners. Many people say that LURC's regulations, when taken at face value, and Monhegan's unique geography are a bad fit.[26] Despite this, neither LURC nor Monhegan would sever the partnership. When given the chance for full home rule, always an option under Maine law, Monhegan town meetings have consistently voted against it.

Two business proprietors lambasted LURC for holding up almost every one of their dozen permit applications in the past decade. They claim that LURC's decisions are arbitrary and capricious and heavily influenced both by the Monhegan "old boy network centered on the fish houses" and a disorganized and highly politicized village planning board. And they allege that "if people on this island don't like you or want to block your enterprise, they can use LURC to make life difficult or squelch your project, whether it makes ecologic sense or not."[27] But Bill Boynton notes that "almost everyone's had a problem of some sort with LURC. Everyone has at least one bad story." On the other side of the ledger, in 1992 Monhegan assessors, the equivalent of village council, passed a resolution praising LURC and "...expressing appreciation for specialized planning and support efforts directed toward the plantation during recent years."[28] LURC, for all its shortcomings, has helped Monhegan protect itself from itself and from runaway tourism in the process.

Many residents lament the incursion into their otherwise quiet, insular lives of not only LURC but also of the state Department of Environmental Protection and the U.S. Environmental Protection Agency. But most also realize that LURC has helped Monhegan retain its quality of life and natural environment. For instance, you can thank regulators for safeguarding the aquifer, and likely for improved offshore water quality. "For better or for worse," mused Bill Boynton, "we're wed to each other. When we look into the future, we see LURC."

Tourism

In the mid-1980s, during a particularly warm and clear summer, the number of day-trippers seemed to explode. Boat captains from Boothbay Harbor and Port Clyde made extra runs to accommodate the demand. In August, Monhegan's streets and trails were clogged. Special town meetings gave voice to heated debate about controlling the growth of tourism. As residents effectively run the tourist business, the issue was "touchy," to use the words of one person who participated in the meetings. One anti-growth advocate got in a heap of trouble with boat captains by standing on the wharf counting tourists disembarking. He and others were concerned about the impact of day-trippers on the ecological health of the wildlands. However, though the issue had certainly been squarely put on the table, no vote was taken, and nothing concrete happened.

The next summer was foggy and cool and the flow of tourists levelled off. It has never again reached that "touchy" level of 1986. Yet fear of spoiling the ambience of Monhegan and of overloading water, sewage, service, and waste capacities — not to mention the wildland's carrying capacity — forced many residents to consider extreme legal and political measures to limit tourist impacts. In 1991, resident Bill Payne asked Monhegan Associates to evaluate the ecological condition of the wildlands, asserting that they might be on the brink of ecological destruction. Monhegan Associates chose to deny his request, their view apparently in accord with that of Barry Timson, a long-time summer resident and professional geologist. In a letter to The New Monhegan Press, he wrote, "I am not convinced that the 'wildlands' of Monhegan have been defiled to the point of alarm."[29]

Until a baseline inventory is done, the state of the wildland's ecological health will be debatable as will the proper level of day tourism. At least one seasoned observer, Peter Boehmer, editor of The New Monhegan Press, sees threats on the horizon:

The present summer community has no sense of history. They are more interested in Monhegan as an investment. This has brought in a different value system. In the present scenario, the way people think of Monhegan and their connection to it is very different from the rusticators. If we are not careful, success will cause us to change this place to accommodate the tastes and meet the expectations of these short-termers. Then we'll no longer have something unique to show.

Many residents agree. They believe recent trends in tourism could undermine Monhegan's distinctive "off the fast track" lifestyle. Nobody wants paved roads, neon signs, franchised businesses, more hotels, marinas, or anything of the myriad tacky tourist elements on the mainland just a dozen miles away. However, the extent to which local tourist enterprises should expand and the appropriate numbers of day-trippers are both debatable matters. Gallery owner and long-time resident Bill Boynton put the dilemma this way: "Generally, most people here don't want to ruin what tourists come to experience or what we ourselves enjoy for that matter. But it's a hard balance because we all increasingly make our money from tourism."[30]

Leaving Monhegan

Like most who venture to Monhegan, our time was brief. We walked the wildlands, sat mesmerized on White Head as the sea crashed on the cliff below, savored sea air, soaked up 200 years of human history, enjoyed seafood, talked art and lobstering with those who make their livelihoods that way. We pledged to come again. We climbed aboard the Laura B in a raging gale. Sheets of rain, ground-zero fog, and a heavy sea made it impossible to look back. Months later, Monhegan seems almost too good to be true.

The 1991 inventory and assessment conducted for the Land Use Commission wrote: "A number of factors help to assure good natural resource protection on Monhegan. Most significant is the strong conservation ethic on the island...."[31] People of all stripes do seem to possess a kind of land ethic. However inadvertently, Monhegan's geography, its resource-based economy, its sense of place, and its long history have contributed to its sustainable lifeway. This is a path other islands and other places with tourism and resource-based economies could emulate.

Monhegan residents are hopeful. The first assessor of the plantation government at the time of our visit spoke in classically understated Maine language when she said, "My fondest hope is for an ongoing permanent and viable community on Monhegan."[32] Living year-round on a small island is the most basic tie people share. And it is a test of mettle. Another 27-year resident put it this way: "You may have big disagreements with somebody and perhaps barely speak to that guy on island, but when you meet him in Rockland [on the mainland], he greets you like his oldest and best friend. Off island, we're all Monheganites. It's a big bond."

In a letter written later by this same resident, he added: "What I think makes Monhegan a worthwhile study is that we are tarnished. We do struggle with our greed and our fouling our own nest. Even so, here we are — and it is good. This should be even a stronger message to those that think that only with an Edison can our ecology be made right. We did have a great deal of luck, and we did not blow it off while it visited us."[33]

Living here, at home on this island, is the tie that binds Monhegan people to each other and to this chunk of ledge washed by stormy seas, occasionally threatened by the rapacious American economy, and recently regulated from afar. Here is a lifestyle and a loosely clustered set of resource attitudes and practices that in total have profound lessons to teach. Few on Monhegan have heard of Leopold's land ethic and some doubt the overall influence of Ted Edison's visionary gift of land. But their love of this island radiates hope that Monhegan will be able to sustain its children and grandchildren — hope that Monhegan will always be a place to ramble the wildlands, to rusticate, to paint, to fish, and to rest on a high headland gazing out to sea, as did one small boy many years ago.

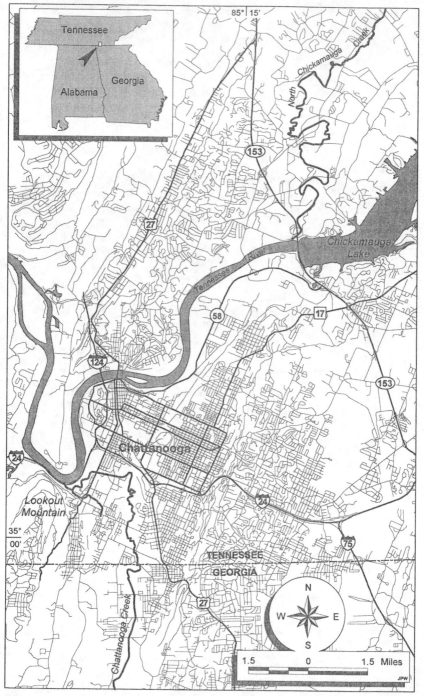

Following the River Home:
Chattanooga, Tennessee
——— Chapter Four———

Chattanooga has great natural resources. It was located here because of the river.
The river is what allowed the city to grow as a transportation and industrial hub.
The river has always been here and all we were doing is driving over it. You know
we needed to do something to reclaim this river.

— Mary Beth Sutton[1]

The Moccasin Bend of the Tennessee River has always invited
settlement. Every civilization known to have existed in this mountainous
region left some sign that they had lingered at this great river's generous
meander. Stone Age people camped here. Early woodland families honored
their dead. Spanish explorers and Mississippi Indians exchanged goods.
Cherokee peoples made a home. In 1815, John Ross founded a trading post
across the river from this bend, which in 24 years would become
Chattanooga.

Chattanooga grew from the power of the river. A finicky river, the
untamed Tennessee was tricky and tough going, but still it provided the
means for the early settlers to get their whisky, flour or salt to the markets
of New Orleans. And eventually, cotton from southern plantations would
be made into textile products in Chattanooga and shipped to New Orleans.
The river created the perfect medium for the incubation of the products of
the Industrial Revolution. Coal from the Appalachian Mountains would
fuel the factories and foundries, and smokestacks towered over the river
floodplain like a cottonwood forest of iron.

When electricity brought the promise of unlimited power, Chattanooga became the seat of one of the country's most ambitious public works efforts, the Tennessee Valley Authority (TVA). Its wild character subdued by a series of dams, the Tennessee River would be the nucleus and Chattanooga the gateway for the TVA's plan to bring prosperity to the forgotten recesses of Appalachia.

The river could do it all. It could give endless power, offer limitless access, and accept everything that no one wanted. But as the Industrial Age unfolded, the people began turning their faces from the river. The brown water smelled bad and looked worse. Those who could located their homes on Lookout Mountain to view the valley that was Chattanooga from a distance. The rest could look up at the mountains that encircled them. But by the 1960s that changed.

Almost 100 years of smokestacks pumping unfettered exhaust into this bowl of naturally humid smoky mountain air, and Chattanooga had become one of the most polluted cities in America. As one Chattanoogan remembers: "People had to turn their headlights on in the middle of the day. Daytime had turned to dusk. Particulates were so thick that your nose would blacken. Men came to work with two white shirts, one for the morning and one for the afternoon. TB sanatoriums were a thriving industry."[2]

Most days, you could no longer see the valley or look up at the mountains. And the primary motivator for the children of those who lived on the mountain was "to get a good education and leave."[3] The people who lived in the valley? Their neighborhoods were choked with the worst air in America. The creeks where their children played were toxic dumps with water running over them. But they believed that there was nothing that they could do about that. Chattanooga was controlled by those who lived on the mountain. At least they had jobs. And then two things happened. The recession of the 1970s and the passage of the Clean Air Act hit Chattanooga.

Chattanooga was told to clean up its air or no new industry would be permitted to operate in this valley. This threat was particularly ominous as the recession and ever-expanding competition from overseas production was already forcing many of the existing factories to shut down or cut back. Chattanooga was taking it from all sides and it was in serious trouble. In the words of city councilman Dave Crockett, "Chattanooga was having a massive coronary...an ecological heart attack, an economic heart attack, a social heart attack, and an urban center heart attack."

That was then. Now, 20 years later, Chattanooga has cleaned up its air but that's not all. Chattanooga is to the sustainable cities movement what Florence was to the Renaissance. Go to Chattanooga tomorrow and it's quite likely that one of the gurus of the sustainability movement, such as Peter Calthorpe or Paul Hawken, was just in town. This time they may have been consulting on the development of a zero-emissions industrial park and residential area atop the bombed out remains of an old industrial strip.

Chattanooga aspires to be the "most environmental city in America." And that aspiration is just as likely to roll from the tongue of the president of a local carpet company, the city's mayor or the director of the Chattanooga Nature Center. They are all proud that their air quality now achieves EPA standards and they want more.

Collins and Aikman, a local carpet manufacturer, is striving not only to eliminate waste in the production of their carpets, they are taking "cradle to cradle" responsibility for their product. They will accept their carpet back when the customer is finished with it and they will turn those used carpet fibres into park benches and curb stops.[4] Chattanooga's River Valley Partners want Chattanooga to become "a prime location for businesses associated with environmental products and services; a home for industries responsive to and protective of the environment."[5] Mayor Gene Roberts wants Chattanooga to be a place where "new ways to combine economic growth and environmental protection can be modelled."[6] But these community leaders aren't just promising and the pundits aren't just pontificating. Chattanooga is happening. *The New York Times* has called Chattanooga "the latest southern city to keep an eye on."

Since 1984, the people of Chattanooga have accomplished renovation of many of the downtown area's most significant historic structures. They have designed and completed the first phase of a world-class riverfront park. The sculpture gardens, fountains and walkways are the setting for the newly built largest freshwater aquarium in the country. The Tennessee Aquarium recreates the journey of freshwater as it moves from the mountains of Tennessee to the Mississippi Delta.

The city has a fleet of electric-powered buses providing free shuttle service in the downtown area. These buses were designed and built at Advanced Vehicle Systems, a firm newly located in Chattanooga. A uniquely designed waste reduction and recycling plant provides jobs for mentally challenged Chattanoogans and produces superior quality recycled stock. A children's museum, the establishment of magnet schools (Phoenix 1, 2 and 3), and a Challenger Education Center are changing the intellectual landscape for Chattanooga's children. (Magnet schools are public schools with particular emphases or themes to appeal to special needs and aptitudes of students, as, for example, a school that specializes in math and science or with an arts focus.)

A program to eliminate substandard housing in Chattanooga has provided low-interest loans to 2,500 families for the acquisition or repair of their homes since its genesis in 1987. The program enjoys one of the lowest loan delinquency rates of any mortgage lender in the country. The renovation of the historic Walnut Street Bridge as a pedestrian/bike-way and the annual Riverbend Festival have resulted in all Chattanoogans mingling in celebration of their city. Boone-Hysinger, a 1960s style public housing project, has been renamed by its residents, The Harriet Tubman. Its residents have taken on the management of this area, long considered a drug war zone, and today children are outside playing once more on the grass that is again growing in the common areas. In other neighborhoods, community gardens and co-op stores are springing up as the people are deciding what they need to nurture and rebuild a sense of neighborhood pride and community.

Chattanoogans have banded together to acquire the "Grand Canyon of the Tennessee," the Tennessee River Gorge. They have established a program to protect one of the cleanest creeks along the river, the North Chickamauga, and together they are facing the challenge and shame of harboring one of the dirtiest creeks in the country, Chattanooga Creek. They have established a local erosion control ordinance (one of the first in the state). The city has launched a program to install 2,000 stormwater cleaning devices on streets and parking lots to screen toxic metals and petroleum runoff before it gets to the river (one of the first in the country). Thousands of new trees have been planted in downtown Chattanooga and plans for new city parking areas include retaining permeable surfaces and establishing "edible landscaping" — ideas inspired by the permaculture movement.

Investment in this mid-size city has reached almost $1 billion over an eight-year period and shows no sign of slowing. Vice-President Gore claims that Chattanooga "has undergone the kind of transformation that needs to happen in our country as a whole."[7] And in this era of cynicism that seems to characterize most American cities, there is a "belief, at a very basic grassroots level, that people can effect change."[8]

Everyone will tell you that Chattanooga's renaissance has its beginnings in the process the city took to address its air pollution problem. It was both the fact that the problem affected everyone and the approach that the community took to solve it that were key elements.

When the EPA challenged Chattanooga to achieve an acceptable standard of air quality — or else, the city couldn't "pretend that the facts were still out. It wasn't a global warming type of threat. It was in everyone's face." The city responded by setting up an Air Pollution Control Board chaired by a local chemistry professor, Dr. Marion Barnes. The board was comprised of local citizens, environmental advocates, government and industry leaders. It was charged with identifying the main problems, recommending viable solutions and establishing the methods that would be used, if necessary, to crack down on those who failed to come into compliance.

Mary Walker, a newly arrived Chattanoogan at the time and a mother of young children, remembers Dr. Barnes and his committee and her recruitment into the process of helping to address the air pollution problem:

> I came here twenty years ago. It was in the middle of the summer and there was a thermal inversion. The air pollution was terrible. And I thought 'What have I done, moving my family to this place and the air is so horrible?' So I marched over to the air pollution bureau and said, 'What are you going to do about this?' They put me on a committee and then I got on the board.

> The fact that the Air Pollution Authority was local meant you had easier access to these people. You could work with them. They weren't some remote authority off somewhere else. They worked with people in a very co-operative way. If there was a problem they took the approach of saying 'let's see how we can solve this,' rather than always seeking injunctions and maximum fines immediately.[9]

Considering Chattanooga's long history of volunteerism, this approach to dealing with their air quality problem was very much in character. As city councilman Dave Crockett describes: "Chattanooga is the volunteer city in the volunteer state. We have led the country in per capita giving and per cent participation in United Way campaigns for many years. Rates of volunteer participation are very high. It is expected that people will be involved with their church, social and civic groups."

Bringing local volunteers together to address their air quality threat led to local ownership of the problem and locally fashioned solutions. In addition, the successful achievement of mutually acceptable results gave rise to the notion that co-operation between the public and private sectors of the community and the environmental and business leaders was possible in Chattanooga.

Together Chattanoogans started to see noticeable results. It was in this environment that a truly radical notion was born: all Chattanoogans might have something to contribute to a vision of their community's future.

VISION 2000

After the air started to clear, Chattanooga's community leaders began to acknowledge that the problems with their city were deeper than the mantle of smoggy air. The city was in decay, the citizens in despair. In pursuit of new ways to address these problems, a cross-section of city leaders set off on a tour of communities where new ideas for addressing urban problems were being spawned.

On one such tour to Indianapolis in 1984, these city leaders were inspired by a community-wide planning process that the city had just undertaken. They decided such a process should be attempted in Chattanooga. A community-wide planning effort would be more engaging and more representative of the community at large, it was reasoned, if co-ordinated in the private sector. Seed money from a local foundation provided the resources to implement a similar planning effort in Chattanooga. A small nonprofit, Chattanooga Venture, was established for the primary purpose of shepherding this all-city exchange of ideas.

The process was open to any who wished to participate and the decision-making approach was designed to arrive at consensus rather than majority decisions. The planning process occurred over the course of five months and involved 1,700 citizens from all corners of Chattanooga. The plan they came up with included 40 goals that they hoped would guide the city into the next millennium.

The 40 goals that they set for their community were a challenging and eclectic mix, including:

- Create a positive image for the city.
- Revitalize the downtown.
- Implement a comprehensive plan to alleviate substandard housing.
- Provide a shelter for abused spouses and children.
- Raise the community's expectations of public education.
- Promote public forums and intercultural exchanges.
- Restore the Tivoli Theatre.
- Develop more urban parks.

- Design a new government structure for the city to encourage better representation.
- Develop a comprehensive approach to resource management.

They established citizen task forces around each goal and got to work. The first thing they accomplished was the development of a shelter for battered women and children. This was something that many Chattanoogans had been trying to establish for years. Implementation of this goal happened quickly and, according to Monty Bruell, gave the community something to celebrate. Mr. Bruell was the chairman of the board of Chattanooga Venture at the time and he observed that starting out with a project that was achievable and that addressed the needs of members of the community who often feel forgotten was a powerful beginning for this new initiative. The opening of the Family Violence Shelter Center made Vision 2000 real.

The Vision 2000 committees gave rise to new nonprofit community organizations, each of which took on a piece of the vision as their principal purpose. River City Company formed to catalyze the restoration of downtown. Partners for Economic Development would focus on attracting new industry and businesses to the city. Chattanooga Neighborhood Enterprise was developed to provide a means to address the renovation of the city's housing stocks. Chattanooga Neighborhood Network helped organize active neighborhood improvement associations and train new neighborhood leaders. Partners for Academic Excellence was charged with improving public education in the community.

These and numerous other nonprofits worked with government representatives to complete the goals of Vision 2000. Together they attracted almost a billion dollars of state, federal, foundation and private investment in the city. Although Vision 2000 was developed entirely through a non-government forum, it was embraced by government officials because as one citizen described, "It was a written document that said 'these are important to this community.'"[10]

Many of these new nonprofits used Chattanooga Venture's facilities for their meetings. As Chattanooga Neighborhood Network co-ordinator Geri Spring remembers: "Chattanooga Venture was a place to focus the activities of the community. It was a safe place to do what you wanted to do for your neighborhood, for your community group. The bolder and more creative your idea, the more support Venture gave you." Venture was also important to this community because, in this town that had always been largely divided along racial and economic lines, Chattanooga Venture was neutral ground. Venture's board was one of the most racially and economically integrated in the community and this set an example for the type of representation expected in the groups that would meet to develop the Vision 2000 goals.

Chattanooga Venture also became the place where the core values of Vision 2000 would be housed. These values emphasized community involvement and participatory planning, solution-focused problem solving, action based on shared vision, and the interrelated nature of a community. Chairman Bruell described the philosophy of Chattanooga Venture in this way: "Making a great community cannot be accomplished by an individual, a group, or an organization. To be successful requires the development of a community vision and the collaboration of as many people as possible to make that vision a reality. This simple philosophy of positive community spirit represents the heart and soul of Chattanooga Venture."[11]

With Vision 2000 as the engine and Chattanooga Venture as a port of entry, these groups became the boxcars on a new Chattanooga Choo-choo. Riding on this train were several key people whose names would pop up in many of these different "boxcars." This train and these people would lead the city back to a new destination for the 21st century.

"RETURN TO THE RIVER"

The Tennessee River is, as it has been for more than a century, the lifeblood of the city. Over and over, area residents pointed to this long-ignored resource — and the natural beauty of the mountains and valleys surrounding it — as the city's number one asset.[12]

Many cities are rediscovering the marketing value of a scenic river walk. What is happening in Chattanooga transcends this level of thinking. After Vision 2000, the city turned its face toward the river with the development of the riverfront park and together its citizens slowed down enough to see it by walking over the restored Walnut Street Bridge. They learned about its origins, its life-forms and its destination as they designed and built the Tennessee Aquarium. They saw the economic potential of showcasing the river and they celebrated it together at the annual Riverbend Festival.

Chattanooga also saw that although most factories were no longer discharging directly into the river, the legacy of past dumping, stormwater runoff, and ill-designed wastewater systems remained insults to their river.

They uncovered for all to see that two streams which feed into their river are the best and worst that their community has to offer. While the children playing in North Chickamauga Creek were discovering one of the most pristine streams in any urban community in the southeast, the children living and playing along Chattanooga Creek were exposed to one of the country's most polluted waterways.

The process of rediscovery of the river led to a call for restoration and protection of the river that has become a road map for the recovery of Chattanooga. A road map that has led the city to the concept of "sustainability" and a desire to be "the environmental city." And, perhaps most importantly, to the realization that everything and everyone is ultimately connected.

As Monty Bruell observed: the "environment was important because it was a good vehicle for us to learn lessons about ourselves as a community. The environment ties us all together. Air is one place where we are all affected and bad water from Alton Park gets into everyone's drinking water. No matter how rich you are, you can't run away from it. At either end of the socioeconomic spectrum the issue is particularly felt, because the rich have high quality of life needs and the poor are dealing with the worst environmental quality problems."

Revision 2000

Chattanoogans forged Vision 2000 together in 1984. They had made unprecedented progress on almost every one of the 40 goals they set for themselves and in 1993 they came together another time for Revision 2000. Chattanooga Venture again designed a community-wide planning effort. This time they were even more fastidious about including all sectors of their community. The demographics of the 2,600 participants were within one percentage point of the city's age class and cultural structure.[13] From this body's effort emerged 27 goals and 122 recommendations and a reinforcement of the dream of Chattanooga as "America's environmental city."

The "environmental city" means different things to different people in Chattanooga. For Jim Vaughan, Chairman of the Chamber of Commerce, it may represent a way for Chattanooga to distinguish itself in a competitive world economy.[14] To entrepreneur Hamid Andalib, it may bring more tourists to the area who will stay longer.[15] For the Tennessee Valley Gorge Trust it may mean one of the world's most diverse temperate forests will be protected. For Milton Jackson, Chattanooga Creek activist, it may bring serious attention and funds to solve a terrible long-standing threat to his neighborhood's health and welfare. To Lee Ferguson, Director of Chattanooga Neighborhood Enterprise, it means developing new programs to encourage the revitalization and recycling of existing neighborhoods. To Bessie Smith, who has been fighting to protect her neighborhood of 61 years, Lincoln Park "can be kept alive and well".[16] For descendants of the Cherokee Indians, their people's great culture and loss may finally be properly remembered and communicated. For scientist, mother and environmentalist Mary Walker, it means that the city can no longer undertake any major project without "seriously considering the environmental implications."

These views are all viable, because as Geri Spring observes: "this is more than an isolated environmental message. Everything has become all interconnected. If any of this is to survive and mean anything in the long run, it has to be about connecting people in ways that will help all people. We have to do something about all the kids growing up. We have to take what is given to us in nature and use it as a model to solve our human problems. The answers to the most critical problems we face as a culture can be found in the way the natural world functions to achieve balance. And this is a process that has only one agenda really, balance and connectedness."

In 1984, Chattanooga was a polluted blue collar town in the middle of America's south land, racially and economically segregated, infected with the cancer of suburban sprawl. One of America's most "forgotten cities." It has come a long way in 20 years. The road to sustainability is longer still. Cynics say Chattanooga's efforts to sell itself as an "environmental city" are laughable. But Dave Crockett, fifth-generation Tennessean and descendant of the pioneer by the same name, has a response to those critics. "Chattanooga is a living laboratory where we can address the real challenges of our civilization. We have the best and the worst here. The full repertoire of success and challenges, you name it, we've got it. The worst and the best...both of them are assets for a city if you fancy yourself a laboratory. Papoose Creek on the Wind River Range may be pristine. But nobody lives there. If humans are to ever figure out how to live sustainably on the earth, it is in places like Chattanooga where we will find the way."

Chattanooga's renaissance may well have gotten its start from the dust of its air pollution crisis. But it was the river that opened the people's eyes to the fact that they had not lived sustainably with their lands or with each other. Discovering what they would need to do to survive as a community brought them all face to face, back to the Moccasin Bend of the Tennessee River.

Moccasin Bend holds the memories of every civilization that has lived in this valley. The future of Moccasin Bend is an unresolved controversy for this community of people. With the exception of a wastewater treatment plant, the bend is largely undeveloped. A task force has been formed to decide how a new generation will integrate Moccasin Bend into their vision of this community.

The river bends there for a reason. It hits a thousand-foot mountain and scrawls a moccasin print in the floodplain before it winds around that granite promontory. Every human civilization that has come down this river has left a print at this point as well. From the earliest hunters through the Industrial Revolution, this bend has recorded it all. And perhaps, when future generations look back, they will find that at the turning of a new millennium, the people of this valley left the blueprint for a sustainable America at the Moccasin Bend of the Tennessee River.

Fishing, Farming and Ecotourism:
The Eastern Shore of Virginia
——————— Chapter Five ———————

The Chinese character for "crisis" has two parts: "danger" and "opportunity";
we've been on a precipice between the two, teetering toward opportunity.
— Eastern Shore Resident

On a map of Virginia, the Eastern Shore is a finger of land, the 70 mile long tip of the Delmarva Peninsula that forms the eastern enclosure of Chesapeake Bay. You can get there by road via Baltimore and Annapolis or by the long and expensive Chesapeake Bay Bridge-Tunnel via Norfolk. Remoteness from the rest of Virginia and intimate connection to sea and bay make the Eastern Shore seem as much an island as a peninsula. Maybe that's why here, like Monhegan, people understand limits more readily than the rest of us.

The Eastern Shore's success in leveraging their remoteness to long-term advantage is a story worth telling. There are two sides to the story: crisis and collaboration. Partly because the Eastern Shore has responded to a series of economic and resource crises in an extraordinary way, it has attracted national and international attention. In an atmosphere of crisis, people have more often seen "opportunity" than "danger," and they have broken out of old ways of thinking.

On Virginia's Eastern Shore people have designed ways to reconstruct their economy, reinforce community, and, through partnerships and collaboration, to envision, or perhaps re-envision, a sustainable lifeway.

73

Their design, more than anything, will rise or fall on how well they succeed in pooling human resources and building community to form new institutions. To date, their collaborative ventures are not only novel; they have been embraced by a broad cross-section of people and they appear to be working. They give cause for hope.

A PENINSULA IN TIME

> Lend me the stone strength of the past
> and I will lend you
> The wings of the future, for I have them.

— Robinson Jeffers[1]

The slender landmass of Virginia's Eastern Shore comprises two counties: Accomack in the north and Northampton at the tip of the peninsula. Much of what we tell here is about Northampton County, though Accomack is clearly part of the ecologic entity we're calling the Eastern Shore. Accomack has not embraced so fully a sustainable look into the future as that envisioned by their neighbors to the south, but we sensed that the notion of sustainable development pervades the entire Shore.

From north to south, in both counties, Eastern Shore agriculture and fishing imprint the flat, sandy landscape and low-lying shores. Open fields and meadows are separated by narrow bands of forest; small fishing villages with intriguing names like Wachapreague, Oyster and Pungoteague dot seaside and bayside; pristine salt marshes and barrier islands buffer the Atlantic shore and serve as spawning and nursery grounds for fish and shellfish. In all, for a place so close to the urban bustle of the East Coast, it is an unexpectedly bucolic landscape, now occupied by 47,000 people.

Some of this is thanks to deep sandy loams that have historically supported truck (vegetable) farming, still the Shore's most important economic activity. Farms are certainly one aspect of the rural look of the Eastern Shore. Fishing is the other. Just as small family farms turned out vegetables, grains and chickens for eastern markets so also have Eastern Shore watermen, working out of little clapboard structures clustered in small villages, helped supply the demand for shell- and finfish from Boston to Atlanta.[2]

Forests dot the landscape too, though they cover less than 10 per cent of its surface. Ecologically they are very important, assuring groundwater, adding diversity to the landscape, and providing windbreaks and shade at the edge of fields. What you see in Eastern Shore forests looks more southeastern than mid-Atlantic: loblolly pines, oaks, and hickory with broad-leafed evergreens in the understory. Forests not only break the monotony of the farmscape, they are also resting, nesting and roosting places for the 250 species of resident and migratory birds of the peninsula.[3]

Salt marshes, beaches, lagoons and creeks provide still further bird habitat throughout the year. In winter, marsh hawks and kestrels soar over the marshes and woods; in spring, migrating glossy ibises, egrets, willets, snow geese, swans and a dazzling array of other waterfowl dominate the marshes in sight and sound. Ospreys return to their massive nests and the full range of songbirds, black ducks, blue herons and hawks dwell in woodland and marsh edge through the summer. On protected beaches, the endangered piping plover nests in the dune grasses along with a dozen other beach nesters and transients.[4] In fall, goose music, to use Aldo Leopold's words, echoes across the marsh as waterfowl make their way southward to the Carolinas, Georgia and Florida. The Eastern Shore, with the highest autumn bird counts in the eastern United States, is a fragile birder's paradise — a little island stopover along a coast with precious few good spots for migratory birds to rest.

The entire seaside ecosystem, in fact, is a globally significant gem, glittering amidst the tarnished American shoreline. From Key West to Penobscot Bay, no coastal area of such an extent is still so ecologically intact: barrier islands with 60 unbroken miles of sandy beaches and dunes, thousands of acres of salt marsh, coastal creeks, shallow bays and lagoons. Curtis Badger, a lifelong resident of the Shore and a descendent of original European settlers, writes: "The extraordinary thing about the Virginia islands and salt marshes is that they are today much as they were three centuries ago.... The island ecosystem is a true coastal wilderness, the last one we have on the Atlantic, providing the same gifts to humans as do the mountain ranges and canyonlands of the West."[5]

Yet the Shore has been a working peninsula since Europeans first appeared in 1620 and over countless centuries before that, for Native Americans hunted, collected, burned, farmed and fished in this diverse, food-rich habitat. As for the Euro-American presence, several small brick structures in Eastville, which house the oldest continuous court records in North America, testify not only to centuries of continuous settlement but also to the relative harmony between them and land. Indeed this is a peninsula in time where a small human population has lived long and compatibly with the ecology of marsh and bay, peninsula and sea. Long-term families are called "been heres" and they seem to have known the value of clean water and air, the limits of the natural resources that supported them.

The "stone strength of the past" on the Eastern Shore was something like a sustainable lifeway. "By tradition, human communities here are intricately bound to the land and waters," said county official Tim Hayes. "People have long relied on a clean environment for farming and fishing." Out of necessity they were good stewards. "If you intended to eat the oysters in the marsh, you didn't dump your chamber pot there."[6]

A typical life on the Shore in the 19th century might have been that of Curtis Badger's great-great-grandfather. According to family records, he cultivated a small farm, raising enough food on about 40 cleared acres to feed his family and to market some surplus. He fished and caught crabs, dug clams and oysters, hunted waterfowl and deer in the fall. His family had been on the Shore six generations so they understood that the marshes, islands, creeks and the sea were as much a part of sustenance as was his small farm. "His spirit was fed by the mystery and power of the ocean; his body was fed by fish and fowl, which in his day the land provided in great number. His eye was cheered by the warmth of winter light on slender blades of cordgrass," wrote Badger.[7] Like many before and since, home for him was a blend of land and sea.

The isolation of this unique peninsula has been both a blessing and a curse. It's a blessing that the Eastern Shore has dodged unsavory tourist development common virtually everywhere else along the eastern seaboard. "There have been more convenient places to develop on the eastern seaboard," said Northampton County administrator Tom Harris. "We were left pretty much to our own; so the villages and farmlands look much the same as they did 50 or more years ago."

Isolation fostered frugality and simple living. "You understand here that you can't just restock by making a quick trip to the mall," one resident told us. "Until K-Mart came in last year, you had to drive 60 miles for a pair of socks. So we were still darning socks long after the habit was forgotten everywhere else." For many, the charm of the Eastern Shore is a trip back in time — "a pastoral beauty, a leisured pace," to borrow the words of a tourist brochure — as well as a place where simplicity seems to be a way of life.

There is a downside, of course. The two Eastern Shore counties are arguably the poorest in Virginia. Among Virginia's 95 counties, Northampton County has among the state's highest rates of unemployment and highest proportions of people living in poverty.[8] In 1994, the overall jobless rate of 9.3 per cent was fully 3 per cent above the state average. A startling 27 per cent of Northampton County's residents live below the federal poverty line (compared to 10 per cent in Virginia as a whole). Seventy per cent of families with female heads of households and children under five live in poverty. Substandard housing abounds. The best and brightest high school graduates are forced to flee.

Former mainstays of the economy — farming and fishing — have fallen on hard times, too. Between 1990 and 1994, more than 1,500 jobs were lost in the agricultural and seafood industries as vegetable and seafood processing plants closed, farm employment declined, and shellfish were over-harvested.[9] In the face of stiff competition from "industrial strength" farms in Florida, Texas, the Midwest and California, Eastern Shore farmers have struggled mightily to stay afloat by producing small grains, soybeans, vegetables, and nursery stock. In 1993, Northampton County farms provided 450 full-time jobs (about 8 per cent of the labor force) and grossed over $68 million, slightly more than two-thirds of the total income of the county.[10] Despite hard times, agriculture is still the largest component of the Shore's economy.

These statistics conceal an even bleaker aspect of Eastern Shore life: the poor are largely African-Americans, most of whom are "been heres" since the 1600s. They now make up 47 per cent of the population. While the overall rate of unemployment on the Shore in 1994 was 9.3 per cent, 15-20 per cent of African-American males were jobless.[11] For them and others similarly shackled by a faltering economy, "island-like" isolation, "a leisurely pace of life" and "simple living" are nothing to brag about.

CRISES UNFOLD

Most people who look at Chincoteague don't see that as something we want in our future. It's a tourist area with second homes and vacation homes. It's displaced local citizens, which is not what we want in Northampton County.

— Charles Renner[12]

Like Monhegan, a few twists in recent history allowed the Eastern Shore to avoid the level of mass tourism it could conceivably have attracted — discount malls and parking lots, condominiums marching across dunes, trendy tourist resorts and golf courses, channelization of creeks and estuaries. Though just a few hours drive from Washington, Baltimore and Philadelphia, most of the Eastern Shore dodged the big tourist industry bullets.

The first bullet, aimed at the Eastern Shore in the late 1960s, opened the door of opportunity a crack. It came with completion of the spectacular 17 mile long Chesapeake Bay Bridge-Tunnel connecting Norfolk with the southern tip of the peninsula. To use Ian McHarg's metaphor, this was the firing pistol at the start of an intensely competitive race to purchase shoreland and barrier islands.[13] A 1955 national park assessment of the potential of the Shore, perhaps unintentionally luring developers, said the Eastern Shore possessed "the best remaining seashore recreational opportunities in America."[14]

Recreational opportunities would translate into big profits for the winning investor; the Shore seemed the ideal site for a resort center catering to upscale tourists and retirees. Smith Island Development Corporation, a group of New York investors, purchased land in 1969 with the intent of building communities on three barrier islands — Smith, Myrtle and Ship Shoal — at the very tip of the peninsula. At so-called King's Beach on Smith Island they planned to build more than a thousand residences, shopping malls, a golf course, airport, clubs, hotels and office buildings. A proposed causeway across the salt marshes would link these communities to the mainland.[15] As with McHarg's Jersey Shore, there would be dredging and filling, dunes would be levelled, shorelines altered, channels fashioned into straight-sided waterways. It would be Hilton Head North.

Meanwhile, people on the Eastern Shore continued to live as they always had. Tempered by the usual uncertainties in markets and climate, so long as good times offset bad times, farmers and watermen paid little attention to rumors of land speculation spawning wild visions of retirement villages and golf courses. Nor were rumors given much credence among African-Americans, the primary labor force for the agricultural and shellfish industries. In the words of Jane Cabarrus, President of the local chapter of the NAACP (National Association for the Advancement of Coloured People), "blacks never had meaningful access either to land or capital, nor were they ever fully enfranchised." Saddled with inferior education, poor housing, and inadequate health care and social services, African-Americans were "highly skeptical" about meaningful inclusion in any schemes of development.

With Hilton Head-type development on the near horizon, local real estate developers, business people and others anticipated better times. In the early 1970s the Eastern Shore was poised for a boom. But the winds changed. A recession blew in. New environmental laws and concern about property values stopped the New York investors in their tracks. The starting gun never went off.

Then the Nature Conservancy entered the picture. With help from the Mary Flagler Cary Charitable Trust, the Nature Conservancy proceeded to purchase not only the islands projected for development but also a string of all or portions of nine other islands northward. This series of purchases, gifts and bequests ultimately became the 45,000-acre Virginia Coast Reserve — barrier islands, coastal bays, estuaries, tidal flats and salt marshes — "a singular place," muses Curtis Badger, "that can give us a clue to the vastness of the great mid-Atlantic salt marshes before the bulldozers filled them and the developers paved them."[16]

As the newest and largest landowner on the Eastern Shore, the Nature Conservancy crossed the finish line first. The winner in the race for barrier island property, it turns out, had no other purpose than to preserve and protect. The prize was a wild, largely unimpacted shoreland, one of the most significant "avian funnels" along the eastern flyway. So biologically valuable was this tract that in 1979 the United Nations included it as part of the global system of Biosphere Reserves.

The Nature Conservancy suddenly found itself in the spotlight, a "three-ton gorilla capable of significantly altering the course of Eastern Shore history," says Virginia Coast Reserve Director John Hall. At first, TNC tried to keep a low profile by sticking to its original purpose of protecting a priceless natural area. It set up shop at Brownsville just east of the small village of Nassawadox, restored an historic farmhouse, and got down to work. While establishing firm protection and stewardship of the islands, TNC conducted limited tours, in co-operation with the University of Virginia ran outreach programs in local schools, landed a National Science Foundation grant for long-term ecological research, and generally tried to be a good three-ton gorilla.

Meanwhile, the everyday economy stumbled into a second set of crises. By the '80s, farmers and watermen were having an increasingly difficult time making a living. Land-rich, cash-poor and heavily in debt, farmers found it almost impossible to compete with agricultural regions that produce commodity crops. Citizens for a Better Eastern Shore member Vic Schmidt explained: "For farmers, the tax-burden has been too great and the income too small; they were tempted to put their land up for grabs. Land was fast going out of production." Phil Custis, whose ancestors landed here in 1648 and who is one of the Shore's few full-time farmers, spoke of desperation. "Farming has not been good to us the last few years. I've had to sell a farm where I spent most of my life and I've had to liquidate some assets. And that hurts. That cuts deep."

"Farmers are broke," said Steve Parker of the Nature Conservancy. "They are in worse shape than many of the landless poor people on the Shore because they are so far in debt. Farm income was okay in the '70s when corn and soybean prices were high. But when prices dropped, how could minuscule Eastern Shore farms compete with 10,000-acre operations in Iowa?"

If times were bad for farmers, they were even worse for watermen. Overfishing and disease led to catastrophic declines in their catches. Seth Rux, secretary of the Eastern Shore Working Watermen's Association, said: "We always thought as watermen that the crabs would be the last to go. They're tough rascals and they had endured a lot of pollution. Then suddenly, in 1989, every damn one of them on the seaside died. It's like a desert out there. You can't make a living on the seaside."[17]

The shellfish industry by the 1980s was a shadow of its former self. In 1950, in Northampton County there were 967 harvesters, operating out of a dozen ports.[18] In 1994, only 475 jobs, full- and part-time, were supported by shellfishing, earning $6.8 million (about 6 per cent of Northampton County's gross income).[19]

In seafood there is, however, a small shaft of light. Out of the ashes of a devastated offshore industry have risen some tentative, and so far profitable, innovative aquaculture ventures producing hard-shell clams and soft-shell crabs. If these succeed, there's potential to work with oysters and scallops as well. In 1994 aquaculture provided 95 full- and part-time jobs and, by grossing $10.5 million, outpaced offshore income by more than $4 million.[20]

Though some tourist enterprises spread southward from Chincoteague and a mini-land boom drove up land values in the late '70s, the boom crashed in the recession of the early 1980s. A small flow of retirees and second home buyers (wryly termed "come heres" by locals) dwindled to a trickle. Attempts to lure clean industry failed.

As the '80s became the '90s, the Eastern Shore was a troubling pocket of poverty, as poor as Virginia's Appalachian counties, with clusters of people living in appallingly substandard housing. "In some places, we have 15 people living in a three-bedroom house," said Northampton County extension agent Brenda Holden. "Many of these places have no running water, no indoor toilets, and the floor is the ground; 29 per cent of the houses in this county have no indoor plumbing." Northampton County administrator Tom Harris expressed shock at what he found when he arrived in 1993: "I realized that failure to properly invest in the Shore had taken its toll. There is enormous poverty and unemployment. I found a community slowly losing both its unique sense of place and its marketable assets."

The Virginia Coast Reserve was little more than an exclave. Connected by natural processes to the rest of the peninsula, it was divorced from day-in, day-out livelihood: a collapsing local farming and fishing economy, failed real estate speculation, crumbling towns and villages, abjectly poor people, few well-paying jobs. Fighting the daily battle to make ends meet, most residents knew little and cared less about the barrier island gem owned by The Nature Conservancy, an organization with a deliberately low profile, an organization that had created few jobs and had severely restricted access to the barrier islands.

"There's been some hostility out there, among a few people anyway," admitted TNC's Steve Parker. "When you're a big, wealthy outside organization in a poor place like this, you're going to be viewed with a little suspicion and distrust. There's a lot of people who simply don't understand what biodiversity means and why we should care about it."

The story to this point has two main characters: an organization primarily dedicated to preservation and a local economy suffering multiple handicaps. In time these two would converge and open the door further for crisis to be seen as opportunity.

Coming Together: From Crisis to Collaboration

We have the beginnings of a structure to confront, debate, decide, compromise, and find consensus on resources common to all the citizens of this county.

— Steve Parker[21]

We need new types of industries started here. Work on farms and the water means low-paying seasonal jobs with no benefits — the types of work that blacks here have had for generations. These types of jobs don't serve the needs of our people.

— John Nottingham[22]

The Nature Conservancy was never really indifferent to the economic plight of the Eastern Shore, it simply had its own emphasis: preservation of the barrier islands. In time, however, it became obvious to them that community and economic stability related significantly to barrier island stewardship. The Nature Conservancy came to understand that "to function over time, preserves must exist...not solely as political and geographical entities with definite borders. To provide perpetual protection, a park or reserve must be part of a larger system that is bound not only by biological ties, but by economic and cultural ones as well."[23]

A Biosphere Reserve

The United Nations conceived the biosphere reserve system in 1976 to safeguard biodiversity by integrating protection with local commerce and community. By 1994, there were 312 biosphere reserves encompassing 423 million acres in 78 countries.[24] The Virginia Coast Reserve was designated in 1979. Biosphere reserves exist in both lightly and densely populated parts of the planet; they are meant to protect mountains, grasslands, deserts, forests and coastal zones.

A prototypical biosphere reserve comprises a core zone, representative both in diversity and size of one of the world's major ecosystems. The core zone is pristine; the imprint of human activity is light. It is big enough for scientific research and for a dynamic, long-term conservation program. Multiple-use zones surround and buffer the core. As you travel outward from the core, you encounter increasing intensities of human occupance and land use. What you see in a well-functioning reserve is a variety of projects conceived by local residents to secure their own future as well as protect the integrity and stability of the whole reserve. The biosphere reserve tries to marry natural and human ecology.

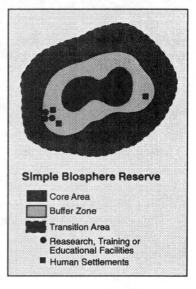

Simple Biosphere Reserve

- ■ Core Area
- □ Buffer Zone
- ▨ Transition Area
- ● Reasearch, Training or Educational Facilities
- ■ Human Settlements

By recognizing that local economy and culture are inseparable parts of any plan for protection, biosphere reserves take a conceptual leap toward sustainability, and they provide a ready model for testing in the field. Put simply, a biosphere reserve opens the door for new institutions that integrate top-down protection of biodiversity and bottom-up community-based resource management.

Not that biosphere reserves yet work as designed. Because they are often superimposed on existing protected places, the role and authority of local governments and people in the plan is often ill-defined and misunderstood. Park officials can add to the confusion. Where the prevailing park philosophy has been "hands off," officials are challenged to think differently, to figure out how to integrate humans into the regional plan.[25] On the Eastern Shore, "local people did not want to be integrated into someone else's plan, nor into a plan which had its number one priority protection and number two the people."[26]

The Nature Conservancy slowly began to comprehend the problem: here was a model with clear ecological and economic potential, a model the world would watch carefully, yet there was no way it could be imposed. By the early 1990s the Conservancy realized that preserving the wildest stretch of the Atlantic coast meant rolling up their sleeves and working in partnership with farmers, watermen, area businesses, civic organizations, and local government to develop a sustainable economy on the Eastern Shore. "Implementing the concept requires a team of different players working together to mesh preservation goals with community vitality," asserted Greg Low, the TNC Vice-President who helped bring bioreserve thinking to the Shore. "There is no way that the Conservancy or any other conservation organization could buy enough land to buffer and preserve a system as vast and complex as this. Balance between long-term preservation and sustainable human use must originate with local people and local government."[27] Neither the Nature Conservancy nor anyone else really knew how accomplish this.

Sustainable Development Evolves

A diverse range of people began to grapple with the interlocked destinies of ecology and economy on the Shore in the 1980s. The story from here is a stepwise progression of three major visioning experiences, each more inclusive than the preceding, each more expansive in its thinking, each more hopeful. The first in the 1980s was a recreation plan called *Beaches, Islands, Marshes, and Woodlands*; the second, a community look at the economic future of Northampton County — the Northampton Economic Forum; and the third, one of the first county-endorsed sustainable development initiatives in the country.

In each of these efforts, collaboration rather than confrontation was the order of the day, for it had become clear that head-butting would accomplish little. Farmer Phil Custis put it this way: "I don't see our future as a 'contest.' We all need to live and let live. I would hate to be doing something on the land that would destroy someone's living on the water. If we can get it together, it will be a win-win situation." Long had county government, federal agencies, and local organizations and businesses ignored, or worse, competed with one another, all basing their decisions on the assumption that somewhere off in the distance there would be a "big prize," a lottery ticket with a payout of good jobs, rapid economic growth, and a flood of new tax dollars. Now it was clear that none of this would happen. Something softer, more in synch with local traditions and resources was needed and seemed possible. To accomplish it people would have to come together.

Beaches, Islands, Marshes, and Woodlands: The first hint of collaboration — a realization that the Virginia Coast Reserve and the free-falling economy were opportunities rather than obstacles — came with a recreation plan in the mid-'80s. This plan, Beaches, Islands, Marshes, and Woodlands, set the tone for an array of initiatives to capitalize on remoteness and ecological integrity. It speaks of "a rare alignment of positions among several conservation agencies and the county...to guide the area's development in ways which will realize its economic potential without sacrificing its inherent values and lifestyle."[28]

The focus was low-impact tourism. The Nature Conservancy, the U.S. Fish and Wildlife Service, Northampton County, and the Virginia Division of Parks and Recreation would join forces to promote "ecotourism." It was a curious enterprise, recalls Eastern Shore National Wildlife Refuge manager Sherm Stairs. "Working in the arena of poverty here, it seemed like it would be difficult to convince people how important fish and wildlife are to their future. But, surprising as it may seem, we've been relatively successful. Historically, people here have lived with and appreciated the deer, fish and shellfish, and waterfowl. Not everybody buys into ecotourism, but many see the potential."

Beaches, Islands, Marshes, and Woodlands not only brought agencies and organizations together, it also got them to agree that remunerative tourism need not translate into flashy development. In fact, there are no resort communities or golf courses, condos, waterslides or marinas in this plan. Rather, it speaks of recreational development based on natural and cultural amenities rather than manufactured attractions, a new state park, campgrounds, bed-and-breakfast inns, and hostels rather than large new hotels and motels; it envisions low-impact recreation such as canoeing and boating, hiking and biking; it emphasizes saving "the unique natural and cultural environment...its mainland, marshes, islands, and waters."[29]

The planners pledged to improve the capacity of their own agencies to "sustain the healthy development and stewardship of the natural resources and tourism of the County" by organizing a co-ordinating group; conducting research on sociocultural, natural and archaeological elements; developing interpretive programs and literature to help educate and guide tourists; and incorporating ecotourism into the county's comprehensive plan.[30] Although the planning group never took *Beaches, Islands, Marshes, and Woodlands* to the public, in government circles and with the Nature Conservancy it became a working document.

Ten years later, many of its recommendations have become successful projects: Kiptopeke State Park is on the ground and operating, a visitor center sets the theme of low-impact tourism by drawing visitors directly off the Chesapeake Bay Bridge-Tunnel into the National Wildlife Refuge, publications promote low-key tourist activities, an annual birding festival in October at the peak of migration attracts several thousand visitors, and the Chamber of Commerce promotes many of the soft-tourism goals.

Northampton Economic Forum: In 1991, three Eastern Shore organizations — Citizens for a Better Eastern Shore, the Northampton County Chapter of the NAACP, and the Nature Conservancy — with help from the Ford Foundation, launched the Northampton Economic Forum. A group of 100 people representing diverse interests met for more than a year to engage in a collaborative effort that would take the Eastern Shore further along the pathway toward sustainable resource management. Its task was to imagine how the Eastern Shore might plan for a kind of economy that would result in an enduring blend of community, fishing, farming, and environment.

The guiding spirits were a banker, Charles Renner, and NAACP President, Jane Cabarrus, both "been heres" with a long-term commitment to the Shore. As Cabarrus remembers it, "we realized the need to plan for our young people and for our grandchildren. We didn't see ourselves as visionaries — only helpers for the generations to come." Renner said "This was one of the first times that representatives from every area of the economy, the entire socioeconomic scope of the Shore, came together."

Though everybody came to the table with institutional agendas, people participated as individuals. They were encouraged to put aside narrow interests and differences to find a way to "map out development without losing our roots." They pledged to make Northampton County a "world model community, unique in its ability to preserve its culture, history, land, wildlife, and water resources...." Northampton would show the world that a community can grow and prosper without abandoning a rural lifeway tied to land and sea.[31]

At the end of it, their plan, A *Blueprint for Economic Growth*, released in December 1992, set lofty targets: to conserve natural resources, preserve the county's rural character, pursue economic self-sufficiency for all citizens, and provide them with adequate public services. Given the Shore's recent track record, these goals may have seemed unrealistic especially since the forum had no resources of its own. Despite this, they identified strategies the county needed to take:

- Co-operative and productive partnerships between regional and local civic groups.

- More effective efforts to attract business, responsible residential development, and value-added industries.

- Career-oriented jobs in a home-grown economy that offers upward mobility and higher income for the unemployed and underemployed.

- Tourism activities compatible with the environment, rural character, and existing resource-based industries.

- Investment in Northampton's people, especially its disadvantaged people.

- Integration of local planning for conservation and development.

People seemed to like the plan, recalls Vic Schmidt, a Northampton Economic Forum participant, "especially they appreciated its emphasis on co-operation and partnerships." In an editorial, *Eastern Shore News* noted: "Crafting new partnerships between tourism and environmental organizations, between development and educational institutions, and between white and black organizations is critical...the forum itself provides a model collaboration of the best minds and most willing talent in the county...the kind of action Northampton needs."[32] On the other hand, some thought the blueprint fell short because segments of the community believed they had insufficient opportunity for input.

Special Area Management Plan: The Nation's First

Even as the Northampton Economic Forum was at work, things began to happen in the county government. In late 1991, Laura McKay of the Virginia Coastal Program approached the Board of Supervisors with a funding opportunity through the National Oceanic and Atmospheric

Administration (NOAA). The county responded by formulating a successful proposal that led to a four-year award of $800,000 to promote sustainable economic development and create new policies to protect coastal resources. As the first such effort funded by NOAA, this created a partnership between federal, state and local government. Though it would not be noted until much later, Northampton County was breaking new ground and moving along the path recommended by the Northampton Economic Forum.[33]

Sustainable Development Action Strategy: With a grant in hand and a newly formed Department of Sustainable Development, the county got right to work. Using the language of sustainable development, then emerging from the United Nations World Commission on Environment and Development, the Board of Supervisors landed a second NOAA grant in 1993 to translate plans into an action strategy. Within months, the county gathered a representative cross-section of residents to participate on a Sustainable Development Task Force. The task force would formulate a community strategy for sustainable development using public visioning sessions, workshops, and public programs.

"Even though this community strategy was in some ways new, their vision draws from roots deeply embedded in the fabric of Virginia's Eastern Shore. For more than three centuries, residents of the Shore have sustained a quality of life that fostered respect for the cultural, historical, and natural resources of the region," observed Northampton County administrator Tom Harris. "Our efforts today are quite simply the fruition of the dreams of our forefathers who diligently worked to preserve this great treasure called Virginia's Eastern Shore."

Almost overnight, sustainable development became the driving force for planning in Northampton County. Visioning sessions, which seemed to be happening everywhere, enabled people to imagine the real meaning of "long-term" and to come up with concrete ideas about how local natural resources might fit into the larger plan of community well-being.[34] Tim Hayes, Director of Sustainable Development, an environmental planner with experience and credentials one would not expect to find on an isolated spit of land, brought competing interest groups together, learned to deal with local opportunists and nay-sayers, and never lost his optimism. In working "tirelessly to bring traditional antagonists like ecologists and businessmen to common ground,"[35] Hayes and the task force helped make sustainability and sustainable development household words. Whenever he got the chance, Hayes told people: "Sustainable development is simply a plan to meet our needs now without undercutting the ability of future generations to meet their needs — an easily understood concept on this isolated peninsula, actually. I told everybody 'We've just got to figure out how to live off the dividends without drawing down the principal.'"

Tom Harris credits Hayes with convincing people that sustainable development was neither threatening nor just some meaningless new elitist trip: "He's made it clear that there's a place here for everyone. It's not a racial thing, nor necessarily a social thing; it's an economic thing. It's good home-grown economy, managing important local assets. I think that we as a community have made this connection. That's the good news. The bad news is that we made the connection because of the overbearing poverty and unemployment in this community. In retrospect, we had to make the connection. What could we do? Clearly, our economic crisis was in fact our golden opportunity."

The Sustainable Development Task Force decided to focus its attention on five resource clusters, each having the promise of bettering the regional economy and the local cultural diversity while protecting ecological integrity: agriculture; seafood and aquaculture; heritage tourism; arts, crafts and local products; and research and education. At dozens of community meetings, people engaged, much as in Chattanooga, in a visioning process. Workshops were broadly participatory and "immensely successful," Hayes believes. In the eyes of Brenda Holden, an African-American county extension agent, "this was much more inclusive than anything we'd seen before. Sustainability is a hot item. People are hearing the term. And once it's out there, it takes hold with more and more people."

The task force and its subcommittees created an action plan that blended into the overall strategy of "capitalizing on and protecting Northampton's world-class natural, cultural, historic, and human assets for the ongoing benefit of all citizens."[36] The action strategy was endorsed by the Board of Supervisors in late June 1994. As we write, task force subcommittees continue to generate ideas, continue to draw government and the private sector together. "It's one thing to have a nice plan," said Hayes, "but it's quite another to translate such a plan into coordinated actions of local government. We've made huge strides in doing just that."

In June 1994, we attended one of the task force workshops in Eastville. More than 200 people gathered to hear green business guru Paul Hawken speak and to participate in small group discussions. It was clear that virtually everyone had made the connection between "healthy environment" and "healthy economy." With Hawken's help, what they dreamed about were

Eastern Shore agricultural and seafood product lines marketed co-operatively, organic farming and orchards to play into big East Coast markets, heritage tourism, and arts and crafts that would ply to the kind of tourist who would most appreciate the Shore and its beauty. One participant at our table remarked, "I had no idea we could come up with so many good ways to make money, mostly on activities we are already doing."

Tim Hayes believes the sustainable development initiative successfully blends environment, historic and cultural preservation with appropriate economic and community development. "Despite the local tendency toward polarization and fragmentation," he claims, "we have overcome the jobs versus environment conflict. The easiest thing to understand here is the importance of natural connections. While protecting our land, our waters, our history and our culture, everyone maintains their identities yet can still be working toward goals of sustainability — even protecting biodiversity."

Grant-funded until 1997, the Sustainable Development Action Strategy is transforming plans into projects. In August 1994, it received the Presidential Leadership Award from the National Association of Counties. In April 1995, Northampton County and the town of Cape Charles hosted a three-day community workshop to create a master plan for a 570-acre Sustainable Technologies Industrial Park. This event engaged 150 residents, prospective businesses, investors, public officials and representatives of the President's Council on Sustainable Development. The partnership emerging from this workshop has so far raised $2.6 million for planning, land acquisition, and construction of infrastructure. A Swiss-based photovoltaic panel manufacturing firm will be its first industry.[37]

Another funded effort growing directly from the Sustainable Development Action Strategy is the Eastern Shore Heritage Trail, which has received $750,000 in federal and state funding. It will wend its way along the peninsula, linking historic sites, such as the Eastville Inn and the Nassawadox sawmill, both to be restored as part of the plan. The broad goal of ecotourism, set two decades earlier in *Beaches, Islands, Marshes, and Woodlands*, is now being successfully translated into low-impact heritage tourism.

Other accomplishments flowing from the Sustainable Development Action Strategy lead one to the conclusion that the strategy is not a plan collecting dust in the county library:

- Zoning ordinances have been proposed to preserve compact villages and towns, minimize runoff, preserve vegetation, and cluster development to protect water quality.

- A preservation strategy has been initiated for historic villages and towns.
- Annual birding and county heritage festivals are being staged.
- A county geographic information system has been initiated.
- Expansion of the aquaculture industry is being promoted.
- Niche-marketing of locally grown produce and seafood is being promoted.
- Artisans and craftspeople are being encouraged to develop products to serve the heritage tourism market.

Meanwhile, the Nature Conservancy — ever goal-directed, project-driven, and results-oriented — is moving forward on a number of fronts. "We have a 'no surprises rule' with the county," explained Virginia Coast Reserve Director John Hall. "We don't spring anything on them without laying the groundwork and vice-versa."

As a high profile project for the Nature Conservancy, the Virginia Coast Reserve still draws lots of money — priming the pump for a range of new initiatives. For example:

- A sustainable development corporation to develop and market products of the Eastern Shore.
- Long-term ecological research on the reserve and surrounding waters.
- Stepped up interaction with local educators.
- Partners on several Sustainable Development Task Force subcommittees.
- Partners in the Virginia Eastern Shore Economic Empowerment and Housing Corporation.
- Seaside farms conservation easement program.

"We are entering a very significant era," claims Hall. "The challenge in the years ahead will be to distinguish activity from progress, to balance excitement and terror, to prevent the community from getting disillusioned. We need a bunch of small successes."

Whatever might happen to the Nature Conservancy's initiatives, the key point is that the people of the Eastern Shore now embrace the sustainability initiative as their own. The real story here, the story that the President's Council on Sustainable Development comprehended well, is that the biosphere reserve is now part of a comprehensive plan conceived by "we the people," in Tom Harris's words. Harris says the Sustainable Development Action Strategy "is being implemented not by an outside force but by Eastern Shore residents through locally elected and democratically responsive officials." Northampton County now can claim a nationally impressive class of initiatives to its credit. "Sustainable development is understood to be our future," concludes Director Hayes. "We have consensus to go forward."

IN SUMMARY

The world watches this bold attempt to put sustainable resource management on the map. Some on the Eastern Shore are optimistic. "What we've got here is very hopeful," said Tom Harris. "You don't sell the factory, you sell the products. Our factory is the seaside and these beautiful pristine creeks and lovely farms and open space and our culture. That's our future and we want to market it by selling our products and not destroying our factory." John Hall of the Nature Conservancy agrees: "This place has a chance to get it right."

There are nay-sayers, of course. A businessman at a County Board of Supervisors meeting we attended in 1994 lashed out at the Sustainable Development Action Strategy: "We don't need any of this," he said. "We don't need a sustainable development initiative for economic development of this county. What we need is a cut in taxes and for the government to get off the backs of existing businesses. If you do this, you'll be surprised what might happen." The poor people, who have been disappointed many times, wonder too. President Cabarrus of the NAACP put it this way: "We've been promised the moon before and we didn't even get decent housing with indoor plumbing. Sustainable development must take account of our impoverished situation."

Indeed Virginia's Eastern Shore mirrors the tensions abroad in our land: tensions between individual gain and community welfare, between warring special interests and finding common ground, between short-term opportunism and long-term stability, between resource extraction and ecological sustainability. If the tension suggests opportunity more than it stirs up fear, if it draws people into partnerships and collaborations, if it breeds hope, then all the initiatives on the Eastern Shore will sustain not only sealife and birdlife but also "been heres" and "come heres" in a long-term blend of restorative economic activity and ecological conservation.

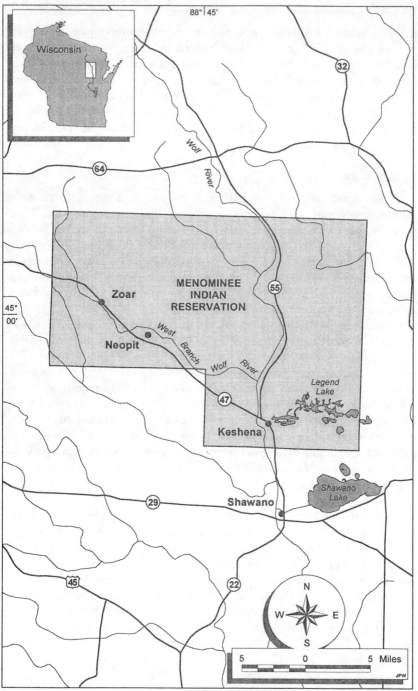

Listening to the Forest:
Menominee, Wisconsin
———— Chapter Six ————

When the Creator made this world, the first thing He made were the trees. As He had much work to do, He asked the trees if they would watch over the land. The trees promised they would be steadfast and watch until the Creator returned. The trees waited and waited; as they waited they grew sleepy and sleepier still. It was a very long time that they waited. And finally all of the trees went to sleep except one. Only the evergreen was left still watching over the Earth. When the Creator returned He found the trees sleeping and He was very upset. He told them because they had broken their promise they would all lose their leaves in the winter. Only the evergreen would keep their leaves as a reminder of the sacredness of a promise.
— Iroquois Legend[1]

Anyone interested in the concept of sustainable forestry will probably hear about the Menominee Forest eventually. Located in the center of Wisconsin, Menominee County, Menominee Reservation and Menominee Forest are all essentially one and the same: rectangles of green nestled away among rolling wheatfields. The week after we visited the Menominee Forest, noted author and naturalist Wendell Berry was there. He was looking for ideas for making his own homeland in Kentucky more sustainable. Over the next two months foresters from Sweden, South America and students from 27 countries would visit the Menominee Forest.

Marshall Pecore, chief forester for the Menominee Tribal Enterprises (MTE), claims so many come to Menominee because "we still have lots of the things that there's a shortage of everywhere else. Hawks, songbirds, bears, butterflies — every time they come looking for them they find them here. These are the things we're kind of proud of." The Menominee are proud of their forest. It is something they guard and treasure. But make no mistake, it is a working forest and has been for 140 years. The Menominee derive 28-30 million board feet of timber a year from their 220,000-acre forest. This keeps their mill active year-round and, between jobs in the woods and mill, it makes the forest a major source of stable employment in the community.

The Menominee forest is nothing short of a miracle. Eleven of the 16 major forest types found in northern Wisconsin flourish here. The Wolf River that flows through the reservation is a designated National Wild and Scenic River. State heritage ecologist Eric Epstein claims "the aquatic features of the Menominee Reservation could rightly be held up as ideal." Rare invertebrate species are regularly found in the rivers; the fish fauna is diverse and representative of the historic mix of species. Deep-woods-nesting birds like the hooded warbler are still found here. There are few invasive exotic plant species problems. According to Epstein, the Northern Hardwoods portion of the forest is the largest relatively unbroken example of this forest type in Wisconsin. Here, unlike most of the remnants of this forest type in the state, the native yew, cedar and hemlock are reproducing effectively. Cedar and hemlock 350 years old can still be found. Epstein believes that the understory composition, tree species mix, age and size class structure closely resemble the way the original uncut forest must have appeared.

In addition to these ecological riches, the Menominee forest yields a sustainable product of high-quality veneer oak and curly maple. Their lumber makes baskets, flooring, furniture, cabinets and pallets. They are a major player in the pulp industry of Wisconsin. And it's a Menominee-grown white pine tree that will form the mast of the Milwaukee schooner being built by the State of Wisconsin to be a center for environmental education and a floating ambassador for the state.

Still, "the mill cuts what the forest has to give us," according to the mill's manager, Matt Ottravec. "And we never modify our cut for the market." The cut is marked at least two years ahead and the mill will know what the forest will yield at least one year in advance. This gives the mill and the marketing department time to prepare for the product.

"WE CALL IT SUSTAINED YIELD"

Almost anyone you talk to in Menominee country will tell you "we practice sustained-yield forestry." But this isn't sustained-yield cellulose production, it's sustained-yield forestry. Marshall Pecore explains it this way:

> Sustained yield to the tribe has meant long-term continuous development, caring and nurturing of this forest resource. Not to exceed the harvest and to stay within the permanent confines of the forest resource. We know to have a healthy stand of maple, we have to have all the other attributes of the forest, all the age structures, all the other components. Rather than assuming if we tamper with this we won't have to worry about that. We'll never understand all of the interactions. One thing we do know is we have to keep as many of the pieces as we can in our little quarter of a million acres. We may not know how it all works but we know if we keep all of the pieces, all of the interrelationships will be strongest. Some people call what we are doing ecosystem management or sustainable development; we call it sustained yield.

Maximum quality, quantity and diversity of like tree species is what they strive for in the management of the forest; "this is what the tribe wants," according to Marshall. "It's our job to figure out what blend and how to achieve it." Until recently, the formula for cutting was derived from directions given by 19th century chiefs: "Start with the rising sun, and work toward the setting sun, but take only the mature trees, the sick trees and trees that have fallen. When you reach the end of the reservation, turn and cut from the setting sun to the rising sun and the trees will last forever." With these instructions over the years, the foresters got "a feel for what species fit best on the land and they would take a stand in that direction."

All-age single-tree selection was the principal cutting regime. Every 15 years, timber markers would return to an area of the forest and mark the dead or deformed trees. These would be cut first. Individual trees under some kind of competitive pressure would be marked in the second pass. These would be cut only when the target volume was not met in the first pass. Using this method, two billion board feet of timber has been removed over the 140 years of cutting history. Yet the standing timber has remained constant and saw timber has increased since the first measurements were taken in 1914. The value of the forest has clearly been maintained. But because of some errors of the past, Marshall estimates that about 50,000 acres do not "fit the tribe's objective of right species and best quality and quantity." In addition, this form of cutting is favoring maple reproduction and the forest is changing towards maple dominance. "And that's not bad," Marshall is quick to say. "But when you look at the 150-year trend we will have mostly maple. We will be putting all our eggs in one basket. If there is a disease that kills the maple like Dutch Elm did to the elm component of the forest, then some generation — I don't think it's going to be this one — will suffer."

Menominee foresters have become even more motivated to understand as precisely as possible which natural community type is best suited for the different conditions that exist across the 220,000-acre landscape. To maintain the early successional forest community types such as aspen and jackpine and to promote the reproduction of native pine stands, Menominee foresters have introduced some practices that have caused concern among the community. The reproduction of aspen requires sunlight and white pine requires bare soil. To achieve these conditions foresters have added clearcutting, herbicide application, and mechanical soil disturbance to their suite of potential treatments. These applications have required considerable dialogue between the foresters and different members of the community. As a result the people have come to recognize the value of maintaining some of these disturbance-dependent community types and the foresters have been inspired to be extremely cautious in the use of these procedures. Clearcuts are always less than 30 acres and never on a steep slope or next to a river and herbicides are never broadcast.

"WITH NEW INFORMATION WE WILL ADJUST OUR MANAGEMENT"

Menominee foresters believe that the development of a new forest stand typing procedure constitutes a real breakthrough as they steward their forests for the next generations. This procedure uses small ground-cover species to define the overstory species most likely to flourish best on that site.[2] Marshall Pecore is genuinely excited about this new method for stand typing. "Now we can make site decisions based on thousands of years of evolution and plant succession." Approximately 50 per cent of the forest has been typed according to this new system and these data have been input into a computer mapping system.

The Menominee are very concerned about reducing the secondary impacts of logging. Loggers who want to operate in this forest are required to attend training sessions every year during the wettest portion of the spring when the woods are off-limits for cutting. They also need to accept certain rules and restrictions that are well beyond the expectations of other forest owners in the state. Each sale of timber is carefully watched and excessive damage to standing trees, failure to restrict movements to designated trails and roads, or the use of unauthorized equipment will result in a fine to the contractor. In spite of these high expectations, loggers compete for the opportunity to work in these woods. One state forester has remarked that the Menominee are at least 50 years ahead of the rest of the state when it comes to forestry techniques.

Perhaps this progressiveness is the result of what ecologist Epstein describes as the Menominee's "greatest asset — their openness to new ideas and input." Menominee Tribal Enterprises President, Larry Waukau, puts it this way: "With new information we would adjust our management. We are interested ultimately in the best possible scenario for human, plant and animal sustainability." Some evidence for this rests in the fact that the Menominee follow the fate of not only the tree species but also the shrub and ground layer component in their 900+ permanently marked monitoring plots. Marshall Pecore talks enthusiastically about how this plot information will influence their ability to integrate the new method of stand typing. He also sees as hopeful technical breakthroughs new approaches to felling trees and other procedures recently developed in Sweden that reduce logging impacts on the forest. Additional evidence is found in the fact that the Menominee are dedicating some of the new-found wealth brought by the establishment of casinos to the development of a college with special program emphasis in natural resources.

The two-year-old College of the Menominee offers Associate Degrees in forestry and the college's new Institute of Sustainable Development has been established to attract researchers to the forest and the community. Baseline inventories for breeding birds, amphibians and raptors are some of the projects that are under way in co-operation with the college and the Wisconsin Department of Natural Resources. College instructor George Howlett remarks that the most significant achievement of Menominee forest management "has been the discipline to try to really understand and systematically relate to the forest and integrate new information."

"THE FOREST IS THE MENOMINEE"

There is absolutely no doubt that there are dedicated and intelligent people committed to management of this forest resource, but we couldn't help but believe there was something more than meets the eye here. How is it that the Menominee had the will, the discipline to preserve this forest through times of incredible poverty and suffering, through the exertion of enormously powerful forces that rendered almost every other piece of this state profoundly changed? Why is it the Menominee can look at over a billion dollar asset and not see economic salvation first? There are so many communities where meeting the present economic need is much more important than the environment. What is different here?

We asked this question in one form or another of everyone we encountered. Perhaps the answers are best summarized by Verna Fowler, President of the College of the Menominee.

> We are one of the few tribes east of the Mississippi that has their own indigenous land, one of the very few. Not as much as we used to have, but we still have part of it. And as an Indian tribe, we have always held our land in common. That's very strong for us. We've been here thousands of years and it's that sense of belonging.

> The forest is the Menominee people. You look over there — that's Shawano county, that's a farmer's field. The forest is gone and so too are the Indians. The forest is here and so too are the Indians. The Menominee are here. Our history lives here. We have always tried to hang on because this is where we belong. This is where we've always been.

For hundreds of years the Menominee have defended their forest against seemingly impossible odds. When all other indigenous people were being deported to unfamiliar grounds hundreds or even thousands of miles away, they held on to a tiny corner of their ancestral lands. When the powerful timber barons exhausted the primeval forest around them, they went after Menominee lands from every possible direction. Hungry and fighting adversities of all kinds, somehow they managed to hold on to their forest. Efforts to make farmers out of the Menominee and teach them the European successional process of primeval forest to cows and wheat failed over and over. The forest persisted. When the children were deported to boarding schools, they survived the near loss of their language and values. They resisted allotment of their lands and most recently they overcame the attempt to terminate the tribe completely.

The survival of the Menominee forest is much more about the people than it is about forestry. Some may want to say it's a story of accidents of fate or magic and miracles. Either perception has its romance. But the story of how this 220,000-acre remnant of a once vast forest biome persisted is a tale of cultural wisdom, commitment to place and, like the evergreen of Iroquois legend, vigilance.

"We Have Always Been One With the Environment"[3]

The Menominee tribe once occupied an area of over 9.5 million acres, covering parts of northern Michigan and Wisconsin from Lake Michigan to the Mississippi River. This primarily forested landscape was blessed with productive lakes and rivers. The people who made their home here speared the giant sturgeon, made sugar from the maple trees, prepared herbs for medicine, picked strawberries and blueberries, and gathered wild rice, each in its time. These and other products from the land and waters gave them sustenance, healed the sick, and formed the rhythm of each year for over 5,000 years. Menominee language for the months of the calendar reflects the pattern of their year: Sturgeon month, sugar-making month, strawberry month, rice-threshing month.

"The people were always forest people and we have always been one with the environment," remarked David Grignon, Historic Preservation Director for the tribe. Menominee myths, stories and language buttress this observation. Their name means "wild rice people." Their origin myth describes the first Menominee as a great white bear who emerged from the Menominee River and took human form. Eagle, beaver, wolf and thunder spirits joined the bear. And the legend that foretells the end of the tribe states that when a specific rock, the Spirit Rock, crumbles, the Menominee people will cease to exist.

The Menominee's first encounter with European people was along the shores of Lake Michigan in the area now known as Green Bay. Here, in 1634, the French explorer Jean Nicolet received some furs and information from a people he described as handsome, prosperous and healthy. Over the next 200 years these people, who had so successfully navigated the North American wilderness, struggled to understand and cope with the strangers who brought ever-changing rules, new diseases and new beliefs to their ancient homeland. But the 200 years of contact and exploitation by French, British and American settlers reduced the Menominee population threefold and resulted inexorably in a series of treaties that ceded all but 0.03 per cent of their lands to the United States.

Still, the white farmers and loggers wanted the Menominee to go farther west. The United States government suggested that they go to the Crow Wing River of Minnesota. Chief Oshkosh and other leaders of the tribe visited this new place and declared it unfit for Menominee. "Even the poorest land in Wisconsin is better than the Crow Wing," Chief Oshkosh said. He went to Washington, D.C., and pleaded that his people be allowed to stay on a part of their homeland. This visionary act of stubbornness is perhaps one of the greatest legacies the legendary Oshkosh gave his people.

Washington conceded and, in 1854, what was left of the once "hearty and prosperous" woodland tribe loaded their belongings in birch canoes and paddled up the Wolf River to a remote section on the edge of their once vast homeland. This hungry, sick, dispirited band of 2,002 "enrolled tribal members" had hardly landed at what was to be called Keshena when the timber barons of the new frontier were realizing the mistake the U.S. government had made. There was ancient white pine on those lands. In the economy of the times, these trees were gold.

Perhaps the more cynical interpreters of Menominee history might say that the events of the next century were contrived to take the gold of the forest from the Menominee. Some may say "No, it only looks that way. Previous generations really believed they were acting in everyone's best interest." But no matter what motives you assign to the interaction of white civilization with the Menominee, no one can deny the game of brinkmanship that has been played with this forest since 1854.

"WE WANT TO SELL OUR TIMBER FOR A FAIR PRICE"

From the beginning of the establishment of the reservation, loggers pirated the white pine that grew along its edges and surveying teams tried to lay claim to Menominee lands. U.S. Bureau of Indian Affairs officers struggled endlessly to convert the Menominee from woodland people to farmers. Urging them to clear their forests for grazing and crops, agents provided seeds, tools and livestock. They advised the Menominee to divide their lands into allotments to encourage the development of individual farm units. Droughts and fierce winters brought failed crops and dead livestock. The Menominee went back to the forest, to what they knew had always sustained them. They tapped maple trees, sold berries, fished and hunted. But this land was not vast enough to provide for all the people and by the 1860s the Menominee determined that they could perhaps derive some value from their forest without destroying it by selling the dead and down timber on the reservation.

The Bureau of Indian Affairs office agreed and, in 1863, white loggers were invited to harvest the "dead and down" timber. The Menominee knew their forest and they carefully watched the cutting. It wasn't just the dead and down trees the contractors were taking. Menominee complaints to Washington led to the dismissal of four local officers in six years and some believe to the purposeful setting of the great fires of 1866. Fire-damaged timber would mean more dead and dying white pine available for harvesting.

By the late 1860s the "Pine Ring," as the timber barons of the region were then called, were getting desperate for Menominee's pine stands. Through their influence, Congress passed an act in 1871 allowing the sale of Menominee lands if the local council approved. Up to this point, the Menominee themselves were engaged in infighting and had polarized into two groups, the traditionalists and Catholics. The threat of the sale of their land brought them together in 1871 as it would again and again over the next century.

The Menominee were "unwilling to part with any portion of their lands," the council stated. In the next year, with the assistance of a sympathetic Bureau of Indian Affairs agent, the first Menominee lumber camp was established. By this time, white pine was virtually gone everywhere but on the Menominee lands. The effort to "civilize" the Menominee — make them farmers and gain control of their forest resources — escalated. The mills conspired to pay less for the forest products the Menominee delivered. One Indian agent decreed that only Menominee who farmed and cleared land in the summer could log in the winter. Local schools were closed and children were sent to boarding schools where their language was forbidden. Still the Menominee carefully watched their forest.

By 1878, increased pressure by timber interests to release Menominee lands for sale or increase access to white pine led to orders from Washington that all logging cease on the reservation. This, the "Pine Barons" hoped, would force Menominee to sell the richest timbered areas of the reservation. In a letter published in a local paper, Chief Neopit gave the Menominee's response to this latest strategy:

> I desire to make the following statement...a general council of the Menominees...fully and unanimously disapproved, and in the strongest terms protested against...the sale of all our pine and agricultural lands. We want to sell our timber for a fair price.... But we will not consent to the sale of any more of our land. We want it for our children and grandchildren. We accepted our present reservation when it was considered of no value by our white friends. And all we ask is to be permitted to keep it as a home.[4]

The local Indian affairs officers pleaded with Washington to allow the Menominee to continue their logging program and Congress reversed its decision in the same year. Over the next years, the Menominee would continue to develop their skills as foresters. Lumbering would become the main source of revenue. According to the BIA agent of the time:

> Every able-bodied Indian who so desires, can find employment during eight months of the year at good wages cutting and banking logs and driving them to their destination. There is considerable work peeling hemlock bark. During the berry season the women and children earn considerable money picking berries. Hunting, fishing and trapping all yield some revenue.[5]

But still there was no opportunity to rest from the watch.

In 1888, a ruling handed down by the U.S. Attorney General's office stated that "the right of Indians on an Indian reservation is one of occupancy only" and the "title to the timber is absolute in the United States." Under this ruling, lumbering became illegal and would be stopped. In response, in 1889, the Department of Indian Affairs promoted a special act through Congress allowing the logging enterprise to resume.

Over the next few years there would be endless accusations between white logging interests and the Menominee and among different factions within the tribe itself, each alleging some misconduct or mistreatment toward the forest or each other. Finally, after over a generation of battling for their trees and their right to cut them, in 1890 the Menominee, the Bureau of Indian Affairs and the newly formed U.S. Forest Service agreed on a plan for the Menominee's forest resources. Together they convinced Congress to pass an act authorizing the tribe to cut the forest according to a strict, controlled regime under the supervision of the U.S. Forest Service. The act established an allowable cut of 15-20 million board feet per year with profits distributed as follows: 1/5 to the hospital and the poor and 4/5 to a tribal fund held in trust by the U.S. government. The Menominee had the first legislated sustained-yield forest in the country.

Over the next half century, the Menominee became one of the wealthiest tribes in the country. A modern mill and electric power plant were built on the reservation. Schools, hospital, a clinic and a community center were established. The Menominee people achieved a 95 per cent literacy rate. A small garment factory and sewage treatment plant were in operation. Thirty to 40 per cent of the adult male members of the tribe were employed in logging or mill-related jobs. During the Depression, even with many people in surrounding communities without work, the Menominee were employed.

Through this period of relative prosperity, never more than 20 million board feet a year of timber were cut. And during this time tribal members were ever vigilant, ever concerned that the "growing heart of the forest" remain intact. They watched the activities in the forest. The tribe took exception to many of the decisions of the non-Indian management. Thirteen different lawsuits were filed against the U.S. government during this period detailing their concerns over logging practices, management of funds, loss of land, and absence of Menominee in decision-making positions. Eight of these lawsuits were resolved in favor of the tribe and the settlements, coupled with mill profits, resulted in a $10 million tribal fund and an increased number of Menominee in administrative positions.

By 1953, the majority of civil service and administrative jobs were filled by Indians and paid by the federal government from an operating reserve derived from tribal funds. Total federal and state assistance to the tribe was less than 11 per cent of the tribe's annual operating budget. Household income for tribal members was comparable to white communities in the surrounding area. It was this prosperity that brought the next great threat to the forest, the Menominee Termination Act of 1954.

"A POLICY DESIGNED TO MAKE MENOMINEE PEOPLE NON-INDIANS"

In the 1950s, the U.S. government conceived of a strategy to finally achieve full "assimilation of all Indian tribes and individual members." The policy of termination was summarized in House Concurrent Resolution 108, 1953. It resolved:

> ...as rapidly as possible to make the Indians within the territorial limits of the United States subject to the same laws and entitled to the same privileges and responsibilities as are applicable to other citizens of the United States...[and] that it is the sense of Congress that, at the earliest possible time, all of the Indian tribes and individual members thereof...should be freed from federal supervision and control.

But, as Nicholas Peroff points out, this policy meant that the federal government would "dismiss all of its promises pledged in a long series of treaties" and it would usher in "one of the most ill-considered congressional experiments in the history of the national Indian policy." Precisely because of the Menominee's prosperity, they were the first tribe slated for termination.

On June 20, 1953, the champion of Indian assimilation, Senator Arthur Watkins, made a visit to the reservation. Watkins made an offer to the group of Menominee that met with him that if they agreed to withdraw the reservation from federal protection and supervision, a settlement payment of $1,500 would be given to each enrolled Menominee. One hundred sixty-nine of those gathered (less then 10 per cent of the enrolled tribal members) voted to accept his proposal. Ourada speculates that few of the voters understood what they were voting for or realized that the "policy was designed to make the Menominee people non-Indians, at least from a political point of view." But, armed with that vote, Congress passed the Menominee Termination Bill of June 17, 1954. In August of 1954, every enrolled man and woman received their payment and payments belonging to children and incompetents were held in trust by First Wisconsin Trust of Milwaukee. The Menominee then began to prepare a plan for their termination which was to commence within seven years.

Over these seven years the reality of the termination of the tribe and the treaty agreements with the U.S. government began to settle in. The federal government had discontinued any support to the tribe except for some funds to develop the termination plan. If the Menominee would successfully navigate the termination, there would be untold issues and questions to be addressed. Questions such as: Should the reservation be ceded to one of the adjoining counties or should the reservation be its own county? Would there be sufficient tax base from this population to maintain the services of a county? The Menominees had resisted allotment; they owned most of the land in common. Would they now distribute the land to individuals? If so, what would they do with the forest? How would it be managed? The mill had always been managed primarily as a source of employment, not as a for-profit business and had never paid taxes. Operating the mill to make money and paying taxes on profit would be a completely different set of conditions. Would they be able to effectively shift to these new terms of operation? What about individually occupied home sites? Would they just be deeded to the residents? Could the county government rely on people who have lived thousands of years with the ethic of tribal ownership to pay taxes on individually owned properties?

The Menominee decided by vote to create their own county. With considerable input from state and federal representatives, they also determined that they would keep the forest whole by creating a jointly held business corporation, Menominee Enterprises Incorporated (MEI). All enrolled Menominee would receive a $3,000 bond interest in the corporation and 100 shares of common stock. Again, the interests of minors and incompetents would be held by the Wisconsin Trust Company of Milwaukee. MEI would be run under a private trust agreement with the State of Wisconsin. The majority of the new Menominee Enterprises Incorporated board of directors would be nontribal members.

Shortly after the termination bill, most Menominee grew suspicious of the concept of termination. As the development of the plan for termination proceeded, disenchantment with the concept increased. Attempts to forestall the termination escalated. The composition of the corporation's board and the fact that the First Wisconsin Trust Company would hold considerable interest were very contentious issues. They meant that it was conceivable that sale of Menominee lands could proceed without the full participation of the Menominee people. One extension was granted but pressure by the State of Wisconsin and the Interior Department led to the submission of the termination plan. The termination of the Menominee tribe was consummated on April 30, 1961 with these issues and many others still unresolved.

The period of termination was a time of incredible bleakness. The termination plan hugely inflated anticipated tax revenues for the new county. At the same time, expenses for the new county were grossly underestimated. The trust fund that had given the tribe security before termination had been distributed to the tribal members in 1954 and was all but gone. There was a depression in the timber market and the reduced revenues, coupled with bond payments, taxes and lack of resources to invest in maintenance and modernization brought the mill from a thriving concern into a state of decline. All occupants of home and farm sites were expected to purchase the land from MEI. Shortly after termination, they received bills for the cost of the lands and for the taxes to the new county. People with money used it to secure their dwellings, those with no money surrendered their bonds as payment for the land. With these bonds returned to the corporation and the bonds held by Wisconsin Trust Company, the Menominee people's interest in the corporation further diminished.

The hospital closed, most of the educated Menominee left the county, unemployment rose, health and alcohol abuse problems increased. Before termination, combined federal and state support to the Menominee was never more than $160,000/year. By 1971, ten years after termination, federal and state aid had increased to almost $2,000,000/year. Forty per cent of Menominee-held bonds had been forfeited to the state or other non-Menominee concerns to secure welfare and other services. The county had the highest unemployment, lowest family income, lowest number of high school graduates and most substandard housing in Wisconsin. As Patricia Ourada points out, "In a matter of years, the government's decision to terminate the tribe reduced the proud, independent, self-supporting Menominee Nation to a poor, disorganized group of citizens dependent on federal and state support."

What brought this "disorganized group of citizens" together, however, were the actions of the failing Menominee Enterprises Incorporated. In 1968, in an effort to keep the corporation from going under and to increase the tax base of the county, MEI entered into a joint venture with a private development company. On 5,000 acres of pristine lake and riverfront lands, they drained a swamp, dammed a small lake and created a recreational development area called Legend Lake Estates. Menominee lands went on the market, the forest was threatened. This action spawned deep reactions as this poignant testimony demonstrates:

> Must the next thing be our land?.... All over the state land is owned by counties, the state and the federal Government. Develop those lands first before you take any more from us. Our values are different. Your values are, when you see trees, your first thoughts are, 'Boy, what money could be made from those trees.' Our old people taught us, 'Do not put a hatchet in that tree unless you are going to use all of it.' And when you travel through this reserve, you can well understand the poem by Joyce Kilmer, 'Only God can make a tree.' As the Indian parent travels through this land of ours, we are grateful that we still own it and pray that the Great Spirit will keep it so. We think of our children who helped us to plant some of those trees and we...like to think that the Great Spirit held their grubby little hands in His.[6]

Educated Menominee who had left the reservation and were living in Milwaukee and Chicago; young people emboldened by the events of the '60s; elder tribal members who had stayed close to the reservation and more traditional ways — all united to fight the conversion and loss of their forest. They formed several grassroots groups, the most visible of which was DRUMS (Determination of Rights and Unity for Menominee Shareholders).

DRUMS advocated restoration of Menominee control over the corporation (MEI) and its assets; cessation of the sale of land to non-

Menominee; and development of socially and economically sound programs that would not destroy the land and culture of the Menominee.

There were some elements of Menominee society that were experiencing gains under the new policies. And there were Menominee who did not agree with DRUMS and who were suspicious of DRUMS as a radical group of "outside agitators." However, the vast majority of Menominee agreed with the goals of DRUMS and had begun to view them as the most hopeful path toward protection of their lands and to tribal reinstatement.

DRUMS used many of the nonviolent tactics of the civil rights and peace movements to further their positions. In addition, they employed sophisticated lobbying techniques. DRUMS' mission expanded to include reinstatement and formal recognition of the Menominee tribe. Their efforts attracted the attention of nationally prominent figures concerned about Native American issues. Tribes all over the country began to support the Menominee as did other socially conscious, mainstream entities, such as the League of Women Voters, the Lutheran Church, the Kennedy Youth Action Coalition, and the Friends Committee on National Legislation. By 1971, major Wisconsin newspapers wrote editorials in favor of reinstatement of the Menominee tribe and restoration of Menominee lands "without which," *The Milwaukee Journal* stated, "the current tragic chapter in Menominee Indian History could be the last chapter" (Milwaukee Journal, 7 November 1971.) In this same year, President Nixon, the governor of Wisconsin, and both U.S. senators from Wisconsin would each express support for the reversal of termination.

In addition to the national political campaign, DRUMS worked to secure elected positions in county government, they obtained majority shares in MEI, and they eventually achieved a majority of the positions on the MEI board of trustees. Their legal efforts to halt the sale of Menominee Lands at the Legend Lake Resorts led to a Wisconsin Supreme Court decision in 1972 in support of their position. This decision was reversed a year later by the federal Supreme Court. But by this time DRUMS had achieved majority on the MEI Board and the sale of Menominee lands was stopped.

One year later, with almost unanimous support, Congress voted to reinstate the Menominee tribe. On December 22, 1973, the bill was signed by President Nixon. This bill officially ended the policy of termination. Of the 60 tribes and bands terminated during this 20-year period, only the Menominee were able to achieve reinstatement and of the 1,365,800 acres of tribal lands removed from federal trust status, only the Menominee lands remained largely intact.

Ada Deer, one of the leaders of DRUMS, commented that this fight had shown those people who believe that nothing can be done in this society "that it just isn't so. You don't have to collapse just because there's federal law in your way. Change it!"

"They Watch the Cutting"

During the period of termination, the people had never forgotten their watch over the forest. Although the practice of sending all of the forest product cut on the reservation to the Menominee mill was changed, strict adherence to sustained-yield harvest was not.

We asked Jim Heinz, President of Menominee Enterprises Incorporated during the period of termination, what kept the managers from just liquidating the highly valuable veneer and old-growth stands of white pine during this time? If they had done so they could have stayed within the 20 million board feet limit and dramatically increased their return. Heinz answered: "I'll give the credit to the Indians. There are a few here who go fishing or gathering or whatever all the time. I swear somebody is on every road on the 'rez' every day and they do watch the cutting. They know there should be so many trees standing. They know how the forest should look after it's been cut. That's the discipline here. The Indians become the discipline."

The language that spells the tribe's new agreement with the U.S. government bespeaks this discipline and vision. This agreement grants the Menominee maximum self-determination and protection, not dominance, as long as they practice "sustained-yield forestry." The interpretation of this mandate is the genius the Menominee bring to this relationship. Their absolute commitment to the forest is what provides them the wisdom of restraint and is the source of their indomitable vigilance.

Menominee Tribal Enterprises (MTE) is now the arm of the Menominee community entrusted with management of the forest and milling operations. It is overseen by a 12-member elected board of directors and answers to the Menominee tribal legislature. Twenty years after reinstatement, MTE is still struggling with some of the residue of termination. At the point of reinstatement, they inherited an old mill and considerable indebtedness. Renovation and modernization of the mill is a continuous challenge and they are still working to purchase the outstanding bonds and repurchase the properties that fell into private hands.

"WE HAVE TO MOVE TOWARD SUSTAINABLE DEVELOPMENT"

The current president of Menominee Tribal Enterprises, Larry Waukau, doesn't spend too much time on "if onlys" when he talks about MTE today. And caring for the forest is an absolute given. What he thinks about are ways to expand the profitability of the forest without increasing the cut. The mill has always been treated as a major source of employment. "And that's good," Waukau believes, "but the Menominee can be more sophisticated than that. We can find ways to get more profit out of our product. You know the guy who grows potatoes gets one price for his crop. But that potato is worth much more as a french fry."

Waukau is bringing Menominee Enterprises into the 21st century. He is working to build a company where the employees derive quality salaries and benefits, where their green practices give them an edge in the market, where increased capital goes toward asset replacement and increased modernization, and where new products are constantly being developed. "Right now," Waukau says, "we are good at sustained-yield forestry. We have to move toward sustainable development."

The Menominee are making impressive strides in their efforts to re-create a strong community. Income from a recently developed casino is helping make progress possible. Unlike some tribes, Menominee have resisted dispersing gaming proceeds to the enrolled members as direct cash payments. Rather, they have used proceeds to rebuild medical, school and community services. They have developed a college and created curricula at all levels of their schools to teach newly repatriated Menominee their history and the value of the forest. They have also continued to show their commitment to the forest. With revenues derived from the gaming industry, the tribe recently purchased a 2,000-acre adjacent tract of cleared agricultural lands to accommodate the housing and infrastructure needs of the hundreds of Menominee wishing to return to the reservation. Carving space out of the forest for the new community of Middle Town was not acceptable to the tribe. In a sense, according to Marshall Pecore, "the forest boundaries represent something of a land-use policy."

Still, there are challenges for the people of the Menominee Nation. Many of the newly repatriated Menominee have brought urban problems and habits that are strange and threatening to the traditional values. There is still poverty and unemployment. And there are squabbles that plague any small community, only in some ways more so because as Waukau points out, "this is like running a family business." Much is riding on the leaders of this generation. When asked if he found the responsibility frightening sometimes, Waukau responded: "I keep my mind open and clear and I listen to the forest. I ask it what I can do. How can I leave it better than I found it? I look to see, do the berries still grow? Do the birds still sing? Some of what I look for is spiritual. I have no fear. What I have is concern. What I have is hope."

"LOOK WHAT WE HAVE"

There is enormous cause for hope in Menominee country. There is an unmistakable feeling of growing prosperity as you travel through this rural landscape. The people in the county offices are busy and lively. And there is a profound pride in the accomplishments of the tribe and the beauty of the forest. The forest management program is gaining international attention and received a Presidential Award for Sustainable Development in 1996, and one of the first Green Cross Certifications in the country by Scientific Certification Systems (a non-profit organization which certifies that wood products were derived from a forest managed for ecological sustainability). In the words of David Grignon: "When our people go off the reservation or to other reservations, they see places that may be more successful with economic development. But what else do they have? They have nothing like this. This is a beautiful place. Menominee see that. And they say, 'Look what we have! Look what Chief Oshkosh and the rest of the chiefs left us.' We have to keep it. It's part of our culture. We have to teach our young the values of our culture, our language. And the forest is key."

Larry Waukau and Marshall Pecore are profoundly aware of the trust vested in them in their roles with Menominee Tribal Enterprises. They know they work for the good of the forest and the tribe. No matter what, Larry is confident that, given good information, the tribe will always make the right decision and he is committed to the tireless pursuit of this information. These leaders are aware and listen to the wishes and opinions of tribal members. For most assuredly, someone will always be watching and if the tribe does not like what is being done, they have the courage to change it. That courage has worked time and again.

The first time we heard about the Menominee, someone was saying that when you look at a satellite photo of Wisconsin, the Menominee Forest stands out like a deep green oasis surrounded by a desert of plowed fields. Now, having been there, we know it is fitting that those who have kept watch over the forest are leading the rest of us who fell asleep.

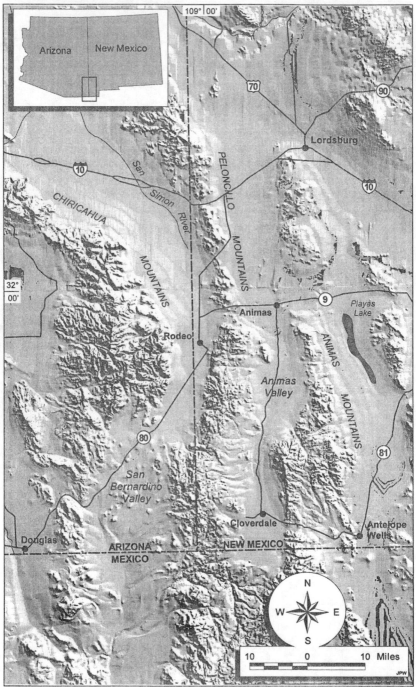

Finding the Radical Center:
The Sky Islands of the American Southwest
───────────── Chapter Seven ─────────────

A healthy, calmly self-confident government can only be developed by turning adversarial factions and interests into problem-solving citizens.

— Daniel Kemmis[1]

The Malpai Borderlands Group is named after the Malpai Ranch, the place where the group held its first meeting. Everyone is always telling Wendy and Warner Glenn that they have misspelled the name of their ranch. The correct spelling of this Spanish word is M-A-L-P-A-I-S. But the Glenns changed the spelling. Malpais is Spanish for "bad land." Wendy and Warner liked the sound of the word "Malpais" for their ranch but they didn't want to think of their land as bad.

But it is bad land. The heavy clay soil is rocky and the range is covered with plants so mean you dare not think to ride without your chaps. The palatable grass is sparse. You're lucky if you can raise a cow on 50 acres. It wasn't always this way. A little more than 100 years ago observers decreed this area the promised land. When Bartlett came upon the Glenns' valley in the early 1850s he described it as "a patch of green eight or nine miles long, resembling a luxuriant meadow."[2]

A valley just north of the Glenns' ranch was described in 1872:

...a beautiful grassy meadow, spangled with wild flowers of every hue. Everywhere on the more open areas those fine stock grasses, black, blue and hairy gramas, grew luxuriantly. Here and there...sacaton [grass] touched my stirrups...large areas were covered with another useful forage plant, known to the Mexicans as galleta, one of the earliest to 'green up' in the spring. There were practically no banks to this stream. It simply flowed softly and quietly.[3]

The Glenns live within a million-acre region of southern Arizona and New Mexico bounded by the Mexican border to the south, the Gillespie Mountains to the east and the Chiricahua Mountains to the west. The community of Douglas is the only town of any size in the region. The business of Douglas has been largely related to copper mining and other activities that characterize life on the Mexican border (some legal, some not). The million-acre region to the east and north of Douglas is vast and open. It is the domain of 35 ranching families and the federal and state government. This region was part of The 1853 Gadsden Purchase from Mexico. It was a good buy. The north-south ranging mountains were rich in timber (ponderosa pine, oak, pinyon). The foothills and valleys that surrounded the mountains were covered in "copious grasses."[4]

Many of the rivers flowed year-round and were lined with gallery forests of cottonwood and willow. Cienegas (marshes) formed along the runs of springs and seeps. Here tall sacaton grass meadows were dotted with tree-sized mesquite. Elevations range from 3,800 to more than 8,400 ft. These elevation changes resulted in the establishment of 179 different plant associations and a rich diversity of animal species. Deer, grizzly bear, bighorn sheep, beaver and a distinct species of elk, the Merriam elk (now extinct), were all plentiful.[5]

After the Civil War had ended and the U.S. army successfully convinced Geronimo that this would not be the Apache homeland, the valleys and mountains of the New Mexico and Arizona borderlands would be opened to the settlers. Some Mormons came from the north and Mexicans from the south. But it was primarily soldiers, leaving the overgrazed ranches of west Texas, who left the biggest mark on the borderlands. No other resource users before or after the Texas cattle ranchers of 1870 had landed with so many feet at once on these desert grasslands. Sure, these valleys had been grazed by the Apache and the Spaniards before them and they'd been farmed by the Hohokam before them. But it was the Texas ranchers with their massive herds of cattle and sheep that changed this landscape surely and inexorably.[6]

The trail across southern New Mexico to Arizona was all cluttered up with herds of longhorns, slowly but steadily grazing their way west. Under the old 'open range' conditions, these great herds were devastating.... It was a mad race to get the grass first. No one was there to say to them nay; no one seemed to care what the results of the overgrazing and overstocking process might be.[7]

Maybe they thought these were inexhaustible grasslands. But probably they, like their ancestors before them, were prepared to move on should their approach to land use happen to not be self-perpetuating. Within one decade every permanent water source was claimed and "practically every acre of range was occupied."[8] The supply of beef was so great that by 1885 prices dropped more than threefold. This put an additional strain on the range because the ranchers who could afford to do so held their cattle longer, hoping to ride out the depressed prices. With no fences to control their movements, the cattle clustered intensively in the areas of permanent water. Soon the grassy banks of water courses were barren and the gradual slopes aggressively deepened.

A major earthquake that struck the area in 1889 resulted in altered stream flows and the loss of numerous springs and seeps.[9] This put added pressure on the remaining wetlands and water sources. By the time the droughts of 1891 and 1892 hit, the ranges were severely stressed and the market so thoroughly saturated, they could hardly give cattle away. By 1893, one-half to three-fourths of the region's cattle would be found dead on the open range, "sun bleached bones and horns" the only remaining product.[10]

In the course of this 20-year period, the rich, arid grasslands watered by artesian springs were replaced by woody brush and cactus with names that speak to the disdain that the early namers felt for these tough survivors: snakeweed, burrowweed, cat's claw. "Wide expanses of drifting sand" were common.[11] Shallow, perennial, cottonwood-lined streams became fast, down-cutting, seasonal "waterways...cut from the hills to the river bed. There [was] now nothing to stop the great currents of water reaching the river bed with such force as to cut large channels and destroy much of the land."[12]

Leopold wonders about this landscape and its changes in his essay "The Conservation Ethic." He compares the response of the desert grasslands to the settler's occupancy with the response of the Kentucky cane lands to similar abuse. He recognizes that the Kentucky soils were more forgiving and accepting of the weed species that came in the seed bags of the European settlers. The succession from rich cane grasses and forests to the immigrant bluegrass was in a sense an act of serendipity. But how could the settlers have known that the desert grasslands could never be as forgiving? There was nothing in their bag of tricks that could replace the desert grasses once they were gone. Nothing from Europe had ever seen anything like the soils, winds or droughts of the American southwest. How could they have known that the "ecology of the southwest was set on a hair-trigger?"[13]

There were other types and decades of misuse since those cattlemen. Electricity didn't really come to these parts until 1960 and wood was the major source of fuel for 80 years. In addition to selling saw timber, wood was cut for almost every imaginable household use and for the mine shafts and smelting furnaces of the great copper mines of the region. Homesteaders tried their hand at farming and the period of the 1930s was another age of unrealistic and dashed hopes.

The range was hit hard by the practices of the 1880s and the forces that might have helped the range recover have been hamstrung since that time. Fire would have been a natural part of these desert grasslands. Fire serves to stimulate native grasses and retard the vigor of woody plants. But fire has been misunderstood and subsequently suppressed these last hundred years. Subtle changes in the amount and seasonal distribution of rainfall have had their impact on range recovery as well.

However you choose to weight the role of history or climate, you can't escape the conclusion. Today this land is "malpai." And, as a result, Wendy and Warner and most of their ranching neighbors work very hard to sustain a relatively modest lifestyle. After the grasses were depleted, those who chose to live their lives in the borderlands region accepted that it meant hard work but recently things have been becoming more troublesome than ever.

All of these families rely on leasing some portion of the 43 per cent federal and state lands that are braided within their family-owned lands. There had been talk of increasing grazing fees. With a growing unfriendly national sentiment toward grazing on public lands, there was a constant question as to whether their leases would be "pulled out from under them" at any time. The largest, most productive private range in the region, the Gray Ranch, had just been purchased by the Nature Conservancy and there was talk that it would be sold to the federal government for intensive recreation. The cattle market had been steadily depressed. With the range deteriorating, cattle prices going down and grazing fees going up, some of their neighbors were selling out to subdivision. These "ranchette" subdivisions result in increased traffic and domestic animals, increased trash and trespass, less opportunity for the use of prescribed fire, and more fences and roads to restrict the movement of wide-ranging wildlife species.

Of all of their concerns the neighbors were most disturbed by the conversion of the open landscape to fragmented 40-acre homesites, their inability to use fire to resuscitate the range, and the loss of the Gray Ranch as the heart of their rural ranching community. The neighbors had begun meeting regularly to discuss their mutual problems and, during the course of their front porch conversations, they had decided that the traditional ways of dealing with their problems, lobbying and fighting, were not likely to yield results, especially with these concerns. Fourth-generation rancher Bill McDonald recalled:

I'd testified in front of the legislature, written letters to my congressmen, attended rallies, meetings, done strategies on how to stop this and that. And it's a defensive, reactionary mode that in the long run was leading to a negative, depressed outlook on things. And that's no way to live.

McDonald wanted something different. He wanted a more positive, proactive way to take control of their problems. He was looking for a way to move ahead with more assurance that the progress would be lasting. Often solutions derived through the political process only seemed to be as lasting as one legislative session or one four-year term.

Bill was one of the first ranchers who met at the Malpai Ranch to discuss these concerns and together with a half-dozen of his neighbors they decided to form a new type of group. The group would be dedicated to dialogue and problem-solving in a positive, consensus-based way. They would invite agency people, scientists and environmental groups to help them understand all sides, to build new approaches, to seek common ground. As rancher Bill Miller put it: "we decided we would stop talking among ourselves about how to stop the Bureau of Land Management from doing this or that. Rather we would go to the BLM and say 'Hey, why don't you sit down with us and plan together rather than make plans in Washington that affect us without our involvement.'"

Since that first meeting the Malpai Borderlands Group, as the ranchers now call themselves, has realized encouraging and intoxicating successes. And along the way, they have formed a caravan, eclectic and bold enough to be worthy of the pioneer spirit.

∽

The ranchers felt that the heart of their homeland has been the

322,000-acre ranch known as the Gray Ranch. The Gray changed hands in 1990 from a private rancher to the Nature Conservancy, a nonprofit organization that routinely purchases natural areas for conservation purposes. This ranch represents a full third of the borderlands region. The group feared that the Conservancy would be too distant to ever understand their community or their issues and that they would transfer the Gray Ranch to public ownership and take a significant resource out of the private sector.

The Gray Ranch is a remarkable ecological treasure. As a result of a less intensive grazing history and less accessible mineral resources, the Gray contains some of the largest and most exceptional examples of the native grassland and riparian communities of this region. The Animas Mountain range, which is contained entirely within the 322,000-acre ranch, adds considerable topographic and soil diversity. One of the Gray's vast ranges is the floor of an ancient Pleistocene lake that once stretched across the border to Mexico. These distinct soils, landforms and relatively intact valleys coupled with the sheer vastness of this unfractured wild landscape provide the conditions for maintenance of 106 different plant associations and an animal species diversity unparalleled in North America. Many of these species are restricted to this area and are at risk of extinction.[14]

The job of the Nature Conservancy is to find and protect these precious vestiges of our nation's natural history. The Conservancy is good at its job. When it found the Gray Ranch, it was for sale and the Conservancy borrowed the $18 million necessary to purchase it.

While the Conservancy celebrated this "rescue," the community viewed it as another example of the work of powerful outside forces bent on changing their community. Fear, suspicion and rumor abounded. The Nature Conservancy assigned John Cook, Vice-President for Major Programs, the job of determining how to retire the debt it accrued in the purchase of the ranch while not compromising the conservation goals of the project. John was totally unprepared for the attitudes of the community toward the Conservancy. He thought the Conservancy's technique of acquiring lands at risk of development and conveying them to public agencies or retaining them as nature sanctuaries was mom-and-apple-pie material. John worked primarily in the eastern U.S. where the Conservancy had been generally viewed as a positive partner with the local communities in which they had worked. He had no idea of what he would encounter as he took over the job of deciding the long-term fate of the Gray Ranch.

John understood his goals. "I work for the Nature Conservancy. I want a full complement of living native systems in living native environments and that's what I am here for." But John realized that he needed to understand more about the larger landscape in which the Gray Ranch is found in order to really achieve his goals.

John listened. He learned new words but he also heard his interests being described in language different from what this Rhode Island career conservationist had ever spoken. What he was beginning to hear was that the ranching lifestyle absolutely requires "open space." The antelope, Coues deer and mountain lion he cared about also require "unfragmented landscapes." He started to understand and see some things in which he had a shared interest with the ranching community. Ranchers need grass. The natural grassland communities are the linchpin community in this landscape. If the grasslands were not rehabilitated and protected the larger ranging animals could not survive long-term.

Grasslands need fire. Fire stimulates the reproduction of native grasses and reduces the woody species. Natural lightning-strike fires were a given in this landscape and the use of fire by aboriginal Americans is well documented. But fire had been routinely suppressed ever since settlement times. The ranchers and the Gray Ranch all needed to have prescribed fire introduced if they were to have flourishing grasslands again.

Ranchers need water year-round. Riparian wetlands are the single most threatened natural community in the West. John could see that restoring the grasslands and native riparian systems was the goal for both a good conservationist and a good rancher. John was learning these things as he was trying to unravel and understand the fear and paranoia that characterized the community's feelings toward the Conservancy and, by association, him.

John and many of his Conservancy colleagues were also starting to see that the government would never have sufficient moneys to protect and manage all of the lands that must be secure if the character and quality of America's native landscapes are to be saved for the next generations. New strategies for more integration and co-operation between public and private land managers would be essential to protect and revive the ailing lands of the West especially.

Two ranches to the west of the Gray Ranch, an unusual borderlands resident and rancher was also noticing all the changes in this community. Drum Hadley had come here 30 years ago, taking leave, in a sense, of the privileged eastern lifestyle that characterized his childhood. Like Teddy Roosevelt before him, he sought to capture the western spirit; and, as a young man, Drum apprenticed himself to a Mexican-Indian cattleman. Through his guidance, Drum learned from direct experience about a more ancient approach to living in the harsh borderlands.

In 1973, Drum bought a badly run-down ranch on the Mexican border, the Guadalupe Canyon Ranch. Everyone remembers what it looked like when Drum bought it, its destroyed riparian areas, its rocky exposed bones. Naturalist Frederick Gehlbach had visited this ranch ten years earlier and he described the "sunbaked aspect of the Guadalupe's slopes." "Grass is sparse," he continued, "the soil is heavily compacted — what soil there is. When the rains come...water runs off the slopes instead of percolating through them, and a two-inch downpour causes major flooding."[15]

Using knowledge he gained from his mentor, Drum set out to revive the Guadalupe ranch to a healthy, productive cattle operation. He raised his family there and made it his life's work to restore this gateway to Mexico. His efforts have been rewarded and today the restoration of Drum's Guadalupe Ranch is recognized in the Malpai area.

Drum Hadley is a man of extraordinary energy, creativity and wealth. He could have chosen to live anywhere and could have pursued almost any life's work. But Drum had chosen to live in the West and he valued the traditional resource-based lifestyle of the region. Although to some of the borderland's third- and fourth-generation families Drum Hadley is an outsider, to Wendy and Warner Glenn, Drum Hadley and his son have "paid their dues. They are ranchers, they understand the land. They love the land." Drum had been taking part in the front porch meetings at the Glenn's Malpai Ranch, and had been watching with as much interest as any of his neighbors to see what would become of the Gray Ranch.

In 1992, Drum Hadley determined that the fate of the Gray was too important to leave to chance. Drum set up a meeting with John Cook. Drum and John took the measure of each other. They found similar passions and earned each other's trust. Drum expressed his interest in buying the ranch. For over a year, John and Drum worked out the terms of a "deal" for the Gray Ranch that would address both their individual and mutual concerns.

Ultimately, Drum Hadley formed a private operating foundation, the Animas Foundation, which purchased the Gray Ranch from the Conservancy with certain restrictions. These specified that the ranch could never be subdivided and the use of the lands for cattle or hunting would be limited so that the native wildlife, grasslands and riparian systems would be preserved in perpetuity. A respected ecologist was hired to manage the Gray

Ranch and a plan for the management of the ranch was approved by all parties.

Drum introduced John to the Malpai ranchers and John introduced them to the Nature Conservancy's goals for the Gray Ranch. The Malpai Group convinced John that protecting the Gray Ranch was more than just deciding the fate of that 322,000 acres, it was also about ensuring that the rural neighborhood of the Gray would not become a place so fractured and riddled with subdivisions that the ranch would be an isolated island. The Malpai ranchers put John on a horse and showed him what it really takes to live on this land and John introduced them to foundation fund-raising and conservation land protection strategies.

The Gray Ranch secure as part of the community, the ranchers of the Malpai Group embraced John as one of their own and the Conservancy encouraged John to work as one of the Malpai Group's co-executive directors.

The Malpai Borderlands Group is now a private nonprofit organization with an elected board of directors and co-executive directors, fourth-generation borderlands rancher Bill McDonald and career conservationist John Cook. The group describes its purpose in this way:

> Our goal is to restore and maintain the natural processes that create and protect a healthy, unfragmented landscape to support a diverse, flourishing community of human, plant and animal life in our Borderlands Region. Together, we will accomplish this by working to encourage profitable ranching and other traditional livelihoods which will sustain the open space nature of our land for generations to come.

The board of directors of the Malpai Group is comprised of land owners and Dr. Ray Turner, former director of the desert lab at the University of Arizona and a well-respected range ecologist. Decisions are made on a consensus basis and the board actively invites participation from all their neighbors and local interests to help them all "reason together." But, as Bill McDonald puts it, to be an effective participant, one "needs to have within themselves the capability of changing the way they think. Not by denying what they knew and thought before but by accepting that and also accepting something else that wasn't there before. Something that they may not have had the opportunity to look at and use." Bill wonders whether everyone is capable of doing this but he is quick to add "I wouldn't say they aren't. I've seen some people that I would have sworn we wouldn't have gotten to first base with, who are now enthusiastic about what we are doing."

The Malpai Group has developed co-operative working relationships with all the federal and state land-holding agencies in the region. The Natural Resources Conservation Service (formerly the Soil Conservation Service) and the U.S. Forest Service have each dedicated a scientist to the Malpai region to work with the Malpai ranchers to develop a co-ordinated plan for range improvement and management that crosses all different land ownerships. The U.S. Forest Service has provided a grant to help derive and map baseline data for the planning region.

The Malpai Group has developed a wildfire response plan for the entire region according to the wishes and needs of all landowners. They executed the first interagency prescribed burn of a six-thousand-acre grassland that crossed two states and four different ownerships. They implemented a 310-acre pasture restoration project. And they are working with a biologist from the University of New Mexico on a long-term study to better understand the changes and causes of change in the rangeland vegetation of the region. They are held up as an example of hope by every level of government and frequently asked to share their progress and methods.

The Malpai Group and the Animas Foundation have also developed a concept for using the Gray Ranch in such a way as to reduce the threat of subdivision of other ranches in the region. The Gray Ranch has exceptional grass reserves. Many of the adjacent ranches have severely degraded range conditions in desperate need of rest. But many of these ranchers are caught in a vicious cycle. They cannot afford to take the cattle off the range. Cattle prices are so low that there isn't enough value in their stock that they could sell their cattle, give the range a rest, and still have money left to repurchase stock when the range is sufficiently improved to restock it. As a result, third- and fourth-generation ranchers who have no desire to leave their lands may be forced to go out of business and sell out, usually for subdivision and second home development.

Understanding this dilemma, the Malpai Group and the Animas Foundation decided to work together to use the Gray Ranch as a "grass bank." Under this scenario, grass from the Gray Ranch could be made available to another rancher if that rancher were willing to convey a conservation easement to the Malpai Group that restricted his or her ability to subdivide the lands in perpetuity. The value of the subdivision rights of an interested rancher's lands are appraised and the rancher can trade that value to "buy" access to a certain amount of grazing time and acreage on the

Gray Ranch at current market leasing rates. While the ranch is resting, the rancher agrees to work with a Conservation Service range manager to develop a grazing plan for his or her ranch. The grass bank concept has resulted in easements over 19,500 acres of land to date.

Although every community has it's "nay-sayers" (and this community is no exception), among most of those ranching families not directly involved there is a feeling of "cautious optimism" about the work of the Malpai Group. The grass bank concept, however, has sparked some criticism from the skeptics. They contend that the Animas Foundation and the Malpai Group are taking advantage of desperate ranchers whose backs are against the wall to gain rights over their lands. The Malpai Group counters that the concept is entirely voluntary. It enables ranchers to keep their family ranch and improve their ranch's productivity and gives ranchers a second chance to make their business profitable without the need for additional cash outlay by an already financially strapped rancher. It also reduces the threat of subdivision of the land, which hurts all of the ranchers in the area.

Members of the Malpai Borderlands Group are encouraged by their success. As rancher Ed Roos says, "There isn't anything we can't do." Brian Power, District Ranger with the U.S. Forest Service, is equally enthusiastic. He realizes that even though the Forest Service's goals and the Malpai Group's goals may not overlap entirely, there is much they do share. He recognizes that the government can't own and manage all this land, nor would they ever want to, and also that the conversion of ranches to "rural subdivision slums" creates enormous problems for the protection of public lands, wide-ranging wildlife, and public land managers. "Ranching needs vast open spaces and so does wildlife. The rancher and the conservationist should be natural allies," Power observes. He values the Malpai Group's approach of looking for shared interests and working on mutually beneficial projects.

"In all ways it's better now than it has been at any time since the 1890s," soil conservation scientist Ron Bemis is quick to tell you. Ron's work with the ranchers in the region leads him to believe that the longer a family persists here, the better stewards they become. "They start to understand what the land can and can't endure," he claims. "They get better with every generation." Ron believes that maybe "now that we have third- and fourth-generation ranchers we have a chance to really understand how to manage these lands sustainably." The way Ron sees it, "there isn't a rancher involved with the Malpai Group who isn't passionately, intimately and romantically in love with the land." Wendy Glenn agrees but she also recognizes that it's the lifestyle that the ranchers are fighting for as well.

> We have to take care of the land so we can stay here. We want to be ranchers. We want the open space lifestyle. It's not like in the past when people ruined the landscape or [when] the place got overcrowded they moved west. Well, there is no more West. We are the West. So we've got to take care of what we have.

These ranchers are starting to use words like "ecosystem health" and "prescribed fire" and "natural processes." Even some like Bill McDonald are entertaining the question of whether cattle are the only or best way to achieve the goals of the group he helped found.

> When I first took over this ranch from my grandfather I wanted to be a cattleman. I wanted to fit in with the cattlemen. That hasn't changed, but I now no longer look at the place only in terms of cattle. I'm more concerned about maintaining the open space. If cattle ranching is the sustainable activity that supports open space, that's great. I want to stay focused on the big picture — the open space. For the sake of future generations, I want to be open-minded about what it takes to maintain it.

The Malpai Group was the result of a coming together of a few ranching families. All devoted members of local cattlemen's associations, none of them were strangers to the rhetoric and rancor that represent the traditional ways of fighting the range wars. When facing new battles, these ranchers met together and, as Bill Miller describes, "revived the traditional practice of neighboring." But in this case they were ready to acknowledge that their neighborhood had changed. To really "neighbor," they had to include the interests and ideas of people and agencies with vastly different histories and experiences. And they had to try to understand these people's rights and needs just as they wanted theirs to be understood and respected.

As Bill McDonald notes, "it is time we set the traditional ways aside and move to the radical center." It's tradition to defend one side or the other without listening or trying to understand the other side's concerns. It is radical to attempt to ferret out the truth on both sides. This, plus action on the landscape, is what the Malpai Group is dedicated to facilitating. The Malpai Group believes it is only through this new form of "radical" interaction that they will achieve their goals.

The Malpai Group acknowledges that whether they like it or not they are married to the government; 43 per cent of the land is state- or federally owned. Many of the mountaintops are federal lands but a plat map of the valleys is a maze with state, federal and private lands hopelessly intertwined. No rancher lays claim to fee simple ownership of all of the lands that he or she uses. It's not uncommon for a rancher to have leases with the state, Federal Bureau of Land Management, and the U.S. Forest Service or for a single pasture to include three different ownership parcels, each owner requiring different things from the lessee. These arrangements do not make for easy marriages. Trust and good communication are things that constitute a good marriage and the relationships between state, federal agencies and private ranchers have not been characterized by this form of interaction.

Suspicion, fear and lack of understanding have been the norm and they run deep on both sides. Consequently, one of the key objectives of the Malpai Group has been to improve communication. The efforts of the Malpai Group are providing encouraging results. Among the agency representatives and the ranchers there is a type of euphoria emerging from the fact that for the first time they have begun to listen to, understand and respect each other. The ranchers are starting to see that the agency staff do have an interest in them, care about their future and are, in fact, human, not just indifferent bureaucrats. The agency managers are starting to see that there "is a lot of commitment to the land here. There are ranchers here who really care about the land and want to stay here...who are willing to listen and learn."[16] In joint problem-solving sessions, agency and rancher participants are starting to ask what is right for the resources of the region first, not "What is your position?" or "What is the policy?"

ෆ

The Malpai Group is young, their projects still very new. It is hard to say whether they will succeed in protecting this great rural wilderness from the ravages of our culture's appetite for space. And it is much too soon to tell whether they will stumble on the right path home to those grassy meadows and spring-fed *cienegas*. The protection of the Gray Ranch, the acquisition of conservation easements, the rehabilitation of the Guadalupe Ranch, the emergence of new ideas, the acceptance of new information, and the co-operation between public and private land owners are all favorable omens. And the fact that the region's land owners and users are striving to build connections in a place that has always prided itself on fierce individualism is cause for hope.

Daniel Kemmis in his essay "The Last Best Place: How Hardship and Limits Build Community," discusses Hegel's theory that America would never be able to contribute to the development of a truly civilized society until it had exhausted its frontier.[17] As long as the frontier existed, Americans could escape the really tough challenge of forging societal norms that allow individual freedoms but not at the expense of the rights of other members of the biotic community and the needs of future generations. Here lies the true challenge facing our culture. And here in the Sky Islands along the strained border of two nations, some brave and visionary neighbors are trying to face this challenge. They are trying to face their limits together without losing the beauty and spirit of the American frontier.

At first glance it seems an irony that the power of community collaboration is being discovered here. One of the last places settled in the great American frontier, this is a country that selects for the toughest individuals. Yet, perhaps it is fitting. For it is exactly the power of America's wilderness that is inspiring this discovery. This is the power that has inspired the explorer in us, the conqueror in us, and the soul in us. And, maybe, now, if we let it, it can inspire the wisdom in us.

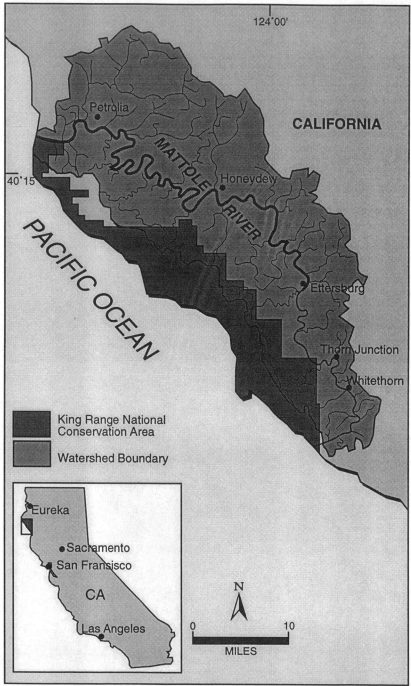

What We Have in Common is the Salmon:
The Mattole Watershed, California
—————————— Chapter Eight ——————————

Reinhabitation means learning to live-in-place in an area that has been disrupted and injured through past exploitation. It involves becoming native to a place through becoming aware of the particular ecological relationships that operate within and around it. It means understanding activities and evolving social behavior that will enrich the life of that place, restore its life-supporting systems, and establish an ecologically and socially sustainable pattern of existence within it. Simply stated it involves becoming fully alive in and with a place.

— Peter Berg and Raymond Dasmann[1]

The valley is alive. The river sings and swells with life. The land struggles towards health, against odds, always producing marvels. There are other valleys but none more beautiful.

— David Simpson[2]

The Mattole River empties into the Pacific just south of Point Mendocino, the westernmost protrusion of California into the Pacific. Flowing northward for 62 miles, the river is tucked into a compact watershed of 300 square miles in the still emerging Coast Ranges. Seismically the most active place in California, three major fault lines join here, making it the epicenter of numerous quakes. Nonetheless, it long has been a lush and productive home for humans.

129

There are no cities or towns in the Mattole Valley. To get to the tiny villages of Petrolia and Honeydew takes an hour of careful driving on some of the most spectacular of North American roads, wending their way over the Coast Range. When the builders of Highway 1, the coastal route north from San Francisco, encountered the Mattole's mountainous and tectonically alive terrain, they gave up and turned the road eastward to join interior Highway 101. The Mattole makes Virginia's Eastern Shore seem readily accessible. It's an isolated place, strangely sequestered, a lost coast and a valley of incomparable beauty.

Athapaskan-speaking Mattole and Sinkyone peoples occupied this valley at the time of first encroachment in the early 1850s. Little is known about them, for they were quickly obliterated by settlers, culminating in the massacre of Squaw Creek in early 1864. Survivors were sent to Round Valley Reservation a hundred miles south where they and their language became extinct. "In the span of eleven years, a culture and people which had been in place for hundreds or thousands of years was completely decimated."[3]

Settlers brought cattle, sheep, hogs and a market-driven economy to the valley. Isolated though they were, they found ways to respond to the needs of fast-growing California. Oil wells near Petrolia in the late 1860s raised hopes of quick money but oil deposits proved insufficient and the boom fizzled. A bustling agricultural economy — based on crop agriculture, orchards and stock rearing — emerged in the valley by the 1870s. Fertile soils and ample rainfall brought good harvests. Mattole settlers prospered in a kind of rough-hewn way. They built a school and churches, engaged in a diversity of businesses such as sawmills and gristmills, a slaughterhouse, and, all in all, fashioned a diverse and relatively self-sufficient economy.[4]

At the turn of the century, they briefly shifted to tanoak bark, an early source of tannin for curing leather. Typical of the extractive economy of the day, tanoaks were cut much faster than they could grow back. With diminishing raw material, the tanning factory closed, and the people returned to agriculture, livestock, trapping and, of course, fishing.

Abundant runs of salmon and steelhead handsomely supported offshore commercial fishers, local river fishing and sport anglers who would converge on the Mattole in winter. The size and scale of seasonal runs were fabled, especially of the king or chinook salmon that returned to the river after four or five years at sea, resplendent 30- or 40-pound adults. During their exuberant runs, horses spooked at crossings and men could simply scoop salmon from the river using pitchforks to load their wagons.[5] Salmon brought to the valley their "utterly exotic intelligence," each and every year.[6]

After the Second World War, loggers moved into the valley. In 1947 more than three-fourths of the watershed was still forested with old-growth — redwoods at the headwaters, Douglas fir in the lower valley. Newly developed bulldozers gave loggers access to steep slopes and serious logging and milling began in the '50s. Between 1950 and 1970, eight sawmills operated out of Honeydew alone. It was a feeding frenzy:

> It came out fast...all in the space of [a] single generation. No one paid any attention to what anyone else was doing. There was no awareness, really, that a whole watershed was being stripped of its climax vegetation all at once.... The trucks taking timber out of the valley were so numerous and frequent that their drivers had to agree on one route out and another one in.[7]

According to rancher Sanford Lowry, the logging boom was partly the result of an ad valorem tax on standing timber levied by California in the 1940s. Lowry's father was burdened with more than $1,000 additional taxes each year. "This was ample incentive for everyone to sell off timber as fast as they could." So it was sold, cheaply, at about $2.50 per 1,000 board feet (compared to $400 per 1,000 board feet now), and this opened the Mattole for the expansion of ranching.

Lowry says "gypo loggers," mostly from Oregon and two or three times removed from the buyers, did the cutting. Working on a very narrow margin, they logged badly, cutting roads with their 'dozers up and down slopes, skidding in the creeks, trying to do the job cheaply. To the ranchers' dismay, they left the landscape a wasteland, and virtually all the logging took place before the passage of the Z'berg-Nejedly Forest Practice Act of 1973, California's reforestation law. Once the timber was cut, the land became "stump meadows" for cattle and sheep.

Logging provided good jobs. A generation of men made their living in the woods and mills, and many of them came from ranching families. By the late 1980s the big stands of big trees were largely gone: 91 per cent of the old-growth forests had been cut.[8] Loggers moved on and took most of the jobs with them. What they left behind was an exposed, steeply sloping landscape, subject to frequent tremors and quakes, in one of the wettest places in North America. "For anyone who knows anything about accelerated erosion, this was a formula for disaster," said geomorphologist Thomas Dunklin. The soils quickly found their way into the Mattole.

To make matters worse, in the '60s and '70s many ranchers, especially in the headwaters, subdivided their holdings into 40- to 80-acre tracts for newcomers. Each property required a road or long driveway, most so poorly designed they would annually wash out. By the late 1980s, geologists estimated that 76 per cent of the Mattole's most serious erosional disturbances had some connection to roads.[9] Roads were contributing tons of sediment to the river and its tributaries.

THE SALMON GOT OUR ATTENTION

Salmon now need, more than ever, a strong, informed constituency.

— David Simpson[10]

The Mattole River, once prime salmon and steelhead trout spawning habitat, was choking with sediment. Severe storms in the '50s and '60s literally changed the river "from a cold, stable, deeply channelled waterway enclosed and cooled by riparian vegetation to a shallow, braided stream with broad, cobbled floodplains, warm in summer, flashy in winter."[11] This new river made mockery of the historic Mattole, the one the native people called Clear Water.

Places where salmon and steelhead lay eggs and pools where young fish develop — cool, clean gravel beds — were buried in mud. Trees that once provided shade along the riverbank had been cut. Modern Mattole inhabitants, who had in living memory been part of the "dramatic spectacle of life in valleys where salmon run,"[12] were alarmed. "Sure, we could see that the rivers here were in trouble," said rancher Lowry. "We blamed commercial fishermen. We could see their boats anchored off the mouth of the Bear River. They used nets and they bragged that they caught their biggest fish at the mouth. Lack of shade for cool water, poor logging practices, a destroyed estuary, disastrous floods in 1955 and 1964, a sea lion population that is out of control, and drift net boats...finished the fish off."[13]

David Simpson, new to the valley in the '70s, told us that king (or chinook) salmon runs, which were reckoned by the Department of Fish and Game to be more than 30,000 in the mid-'60s and were probably a few thousand when he first arrived, had dwindled by the late '70s to a few hundred at most. "The absence of big numbers of fish really got our attention," he said. Though there were forces at sea undoubtedly contributing to the decline, Simpson and a group of newcomers were convinced that the river's bad health was a primary contributing factor. Without places to spawn, they reasoned, the salmon would have no chance whatsoever.

In 1981 Simpson, Freeman House and others formed the Mattole Watershed Salmon Support Group (now called Mattole Salmon Group — MSG) and pledged to restore the run. With help from fisheries biologist Gary Peterson and a variety of other experts, they became "a volunteer cottage industry in salmon propagation."[14] Peterson, who conceived of himself as "working for the fish," was the perfect technical advisor.[15] He contributed not only expertise but also boundless enthusiasm, dedication and "chest wader endurance." Tending fish traps near Ettersburg in 1987, Peterson once stayed in waders for 41 consecutive hours.[16]

"We knew the salmon were leading us into uncharted waters, and we were all novices," said volunteer Rex Rathbun. "But we also knew we had no choice." This was, after all, one of the last vestiges of the original wild mosaic of the valley and a small but perhaps significant component of Pacific salmon genetic diversity. Our response, wrote co-founder House,

> was to take it on, to attempt to puzzle it through, to learn whatever needs to be learned in order for people who lived in the valley to do what was necessary to make the king salmon population viable once more.[17]

The Salmon Group soon realized their naivete. The salmon had many lessons to teach. Among the most important was that salmon are an integral part of the entire riverine ecosystem that actually extends to the outermost edges of the watershed.

Though the number of king salmon spawning in the Mattole was 1000 or less, perhaps genetically a hopeless bottleneck, the Salmon Group conceived a plan. They would try to boost hatch-to-fry ratios without endangering the natural imprint of the river upon the salmon. Using techniques perfected in British Columbia, they captured a small number of adult fish as broodstock in winter. They extracted, fertilized and artificially hatched their eggs, then reared salmon fry to fingerling size in hatchboxes carefully lined with selected clean gravels and fed by filtered water directly from tributary creeks. The ecological conditions of the Mattole would thus be firmly imprinted in the salmon fry.

With experience, they consistently achieved egg-to-fry survival rates of 80 per cent or more, compared to less than 15 per cent in the river.[18] Since incubators could accommodate 30,000 fish, they believed they could significantly enhance the spring outflow of salmon to the sea. In theory, four or five years later, after these juveniles had matured in the North Pacific, fall runs would improve considerably. Unfortunately, it wasn't this simple.

For one thing, it became obvious that the Mattole estuary, which closes in spring behind a huge sandbar at its mouth, was contributing to high mortality of juvenile salmon. They were either being sent to the ocean too small and vulnerable or they were trapped in the estuary, which in summer would fatally "cook" them.[19]

After tries at trapping naturally spawned juveniles in the headwaters failed and an attempt to create deeper, shaded pools in the estuary proved inadequate, they devised a "rescue rearing" strategy, just as ingenious as the original hatchboxes. In spring MSG volunteers net up to 6,000 naturally spawned downstream migrants, then release them to rearing ponds at Mill Creek near the mouth of the river. These naturally imprinted fish are carefully tended through the summer in cool freshwater pools. There they grow to 120 mm or more, the optimum for ocean survival. When the bay mouth sandbar opens, they are released to the lower river.[20] The Mattole Salmon Group also learned something about centralized resource management, for it seemed to them that bureaucratic blockades were thrown up at every turn. The lesson here is not to be discouraged, for in the long run what may emerge is an improbable, though thoroughly amicable, partnership. It would not have appeared so at first.

Officials of the California Department of Fish and Game (DFG) denied permits to nonlicensed civilians trapping and incubating wild fish.[21] One prickly bureaucrat even insisted that only qualified fisheries biologists could drive vehicles transporting live fish. Ultimately, enthusiasm and knowledge overcame official doubt and the Salmon Group was not only given permission for the hatchbox program and other stream-centered work but also DFG funding and praise.

"What we have accomplished in partnership with agencies is remarkable, but we and they can do more," asserts David Simpson. "We have to recognize that these agencies have spent 20, 30, up to 100 years doing their thing. They're not going to suddenly deconstruct just because grassroots organizations are doing some stream work. But they can start to listen and they can develop mechanisms to incorporate grassroots input. Then we will have accomplished something." Simpson's wife, Jane Lapiner, adds: "It seems like the agencies at the top want change and a lot of people in the field want change. But there's this whole middle level in the offices who don't know how. I'm not exactly sure how either, but it is the crucial level to influence."

Between 1981 and 1994, in addition to Department of Fish and Game grants, the Mattole Salmon Group also received funding from foundations and memberships as well as from a unique Salmon Stamp Program devised by the Pacific Coast Federation of Fisherman's Associations.[22] In this program commercial fishers levy a tax on themselves, or more precisely on each pound of salmon caught offshore. Revenues from the stamp program are then poured back into salmon restoration projects — an economic device that ensures nature is being paid for its service, as neat an arrangement of this sort as we've encountered in our travels.[23]

Not counting thousands of volunteer hours (many contributed by out-of-work commercial fishers), the Mattole salmon rescue program costs about $40,000 a year, most of which goes directly to trapping, surveying, spawning, and raising juvenile salmon. In the fourteen years of the program, more than 500,000 king salmon have been released, a per fish cost of less than a dollar, which besides being far below the cost of raising salmon in high-tech hatcheries, maintains genetic purity in the run.[24]

In spite of uncertain funding, the Mattole Salmon Group continues its work. At least as important as hatching salmon, everyone agrees, is making people aware of their watershed identity. By involving school children each year to help raise juvenile salmon and release them to the river, a whole generation of kids now knows about the biological, ecological and cultural significance of salmon to people, who, like themselves, have the good fortune to live alongside a free-flowing natural river that empties into the North Pacific. "With the children, many good seeds have been planted," said Jane Lapiner. "Who knows where this will lead?"

One of the obvious advantages of building a restoration ethic through hands-on work "is that working together provides people with...common experiential information," Freeman House told the editors of Turtle Talk.[25] While this is certainly true of Salmon Group volunteers, they still represent a relatively small slice of people who live in the watershed. Though ranchers were never systematically excluded, most were never included either. Consequently, some ranchers still think of the Mattole Salmon Group as an exclusive environmental club.

Has all this salmon work actually made a difference? In the first ten years of the hatchbox program, numbers of both chinook and coho salmon declined. Less than 200 chinook salmon spawned in the entire Mattole in 1990. However, recently salmon numbers seem to be on the rise. In 1995, 750 to 1,000 king salmon made it upriver, the biggest run since 1987-88.[26] The numbers of large salmon observed and the average size of fish trapped both increased too. Yet short-term trends will not determine the survival and good health of salmon runs here or anywhere in the North Pacific.

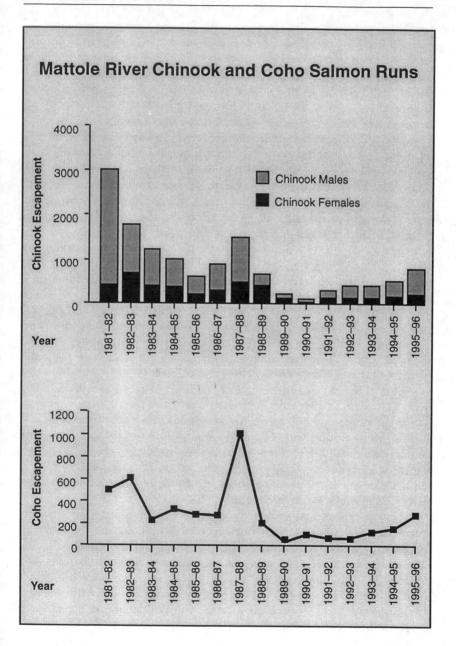

Mattole River Chinook and Coho Salmon Runs

Many residents believed that saving our salmon runs was simply a matter of a few years of operation of a few hatchboxes. This was never the expectation of the Salmon Group. We felt right from the onset that making a difference in a watershed that had been as heavily impacted as the Mattole was going to require work not of years but of decades, even generations.[27]

The fate of salmon that spawn in the Mattole also depends significantly, as rancher Lowry asserted, upon what happens once they swim to sea. Salmon in the North Pacific are under extreme pressure from trawling and incidental catches, international gill and drift netting, weather, disease and water pollution. As a consequence, in the 1990s salmon fishing regions in California have become economic disaster zones and sport fishing has been severely curtailed.

In spite of all this, "the Salmon Group's hatchbox program has been very important," concludes Freeman House. "Without their efforts, the salmon would probably be gone." For Mattole salmon who, in their time at sea manoeuvre around gill- and driftnets and avoid trawlers at every turn, the end of their journey is now somewhat more reassuring, though their muddy home river continues to be far less than ideal.

Gary "Fish" Peterson cautions, "While we celebrate the gains that Mattole salmon are making, we must keep in mind that only by exercising the utmost care in our land-use practices in this watershed do these gains have any prospect of continuing."[28]

BEYOND THE HATCHBOXES

The Mattole Restoration Council is a coalition of community groups, landowners, and individuals in the Mattole River watershed seeking to restore and sustain the healthy functioning of the watershed's natural systems, such as forests, fisheries, soils, flora and fauna. The council is founded on the idea that the people living here are the ones best suited to work toward these aims.

— Mattole Restoration Council Brochure

By the mid-1980s, it was clear that restoration needed to reach beyond the hatchboxes, beyond the estuary, and beyond the mainstem and tributaries. A larger, watershed-wide organization was needed that would pull together small groups that everywhere in the watershed were beginning to be engaged in restoration and convey to them and their constituencies the need for a Mattole-wide watershed identity. In 1983, the Salmon Group helped launch the Mattole Restoration Council (MRC) — a coalition that defined its purpose as restoring and sustaining the healthy functioning of all the watershed's natural systems.

Over the decade of its life, the council has engaged a broader cross-section of watershed residents (though mainly still "back-to-the-landers" rather than ranchers), has taken controversial positions on logging and logging practices, has been a timber-watch group, and has engaged in a wide range of river restoration activities. These range from serious study of geomorphology and the sources of erosion to in-stream erosion control and tree planting, seeding, and slope stabilization. Recently, the MRC has also been a "watershed witness," monitoring and mediating forest harvest plans in the still uncut reaches of the Mattole, and engaging in road improvement and decommissioning on Bureau of Land Management property.

∽

When we first visited the Restoration Council's office in December 1992, what most impressed us was their dedication to serious study of the watershed. Freeman House, our guide that day, told us that putting restoration projects on the ground forced them to systematically map the entire watershed. "In mapping it and in seeking professional assistance, we learned the essentials to begin our work of healing," he said. "What was most shocking was the lack of information organized by watersheds, especially how much old growth was left and where. When it comes to good data, watersheds are really unclaimed territories."[29]

In 1989 the Restoration Council published *Elements of Recovery*, an extraordinary local geography, rich in cultural, historical, ecological and geomorphological detail, a handbook for watershed restoration. The Mattole is subdivided into 12 units, each a grouping of tributaries covering 50,000 acres or less. A small battalion of resident surveyors, trained by Redwood National Park geologists, then went into the field to plot sites and sources of erosion in every reach of the river. This information and an earlier survey of salmonid habitat form the basic templates for MRC work.

Topographic maps and aerial photographs plaster the walls of the Restoration Council office. In imagining how a new kind of resource management will actually be put into force, this is reassuring testimony of the importance of local geography in any community-based initiative. "It's clear that you can't begin to work without detailed knowledge of the place," said House. Janet Morrison, Council Director in 1994, said that Freeman House's co-ordination of mapping the Mattole for the erosion survey was the very base upon which everything else has been built.

Among the most impressive maps is a two-color poster comparing forest cover in 1947 with that of the late 1980s. Besides graphically portraying the post-Second World War timber splurge, the map and the act of its creation empowered the MRC with information to tackle both the most seriously scarred landscapes and to protect the remaining small patches of old growth. By 1996, dozens of high priority erosion scars had been healed and about two-thirds of the small area of remaining old-growth forests had in some way been protected.[30]

These impressive accomplishments would not have been possible without a base of verified data. Fervently committed to the concept of "watershed identity," the MRC tagged all other information — salmonid habitat, land ownership, roads, building sites, land cover, forest harvest plans — to drainage units. This locally conceived and controlled manual geographic information system itself speaks volumes about the importance of local geography in reconnecting humans to the ecological systems they inhabit and reinhabit.

Freeman House puts it this way:

By spending the time to reorganize biotic, geologic, and demographic information into a watershed context, we are ritually reanimating a real place that had become totally abstracted. Our maps of salmonid habitat, of old-growth distribution, of timber harvest history and erosion sites, of rehabilitation work, our creek addresses for watershed residents, become, when distributed by mail to all inhabitants, the self-expression of living place.[31]

✧

The Restoration Council goes from season to season with part-time directors and staff. They receive funding from the state, the Bureau of Land Management, foundations, and direct marketing companies who donate trees for planting to offset the paper they consume (another economic device to pay nature for services rendered). In 1995, they took in $336,000, mostly for contract work. From this they paid almost $48,000 in wages and $217,000 to independent contractors for rental and operation of heavy equipment and for consultation.[32]

The council has been going through growth pains — but "good growth pains," according to Janet Morrison. In 1995 they signed a memorandum of understanding with the Bureau of Land Management that will open doors and release funds for a wider range of restorative activities, especially in Honeydew and Bear Creek watersheds. As a start in this new relationship, in 1995 and 1996 the Restoration Council decommissioned 3.5 miles of "a road to nowhere" in the King Range, a road that had the potential to contribute significant amounts of sediment to the river.[33]

Besides transacting partnerships with government, MRC also crossed the bridge in 1994 to a new kind of collaboration with rancher Sanford Lowry and Pacific Lumber. At Lowry's invitation, MRC did a baseline survey for his timber harvest plan. Sierra Pacific, which did the logging, and MRC monitored river-borne sediment and road-related erosion before, during and after the cut, for in Lowry's opinion, it's important to know what the salmon can tolerate.[34] As the first tangible partnership with a big landowner in the ranching community and with industrial timber, MRC believes it is breaking new ground.

In the last analysis, the MRC has taken major strides in repairing the wounds of the watershed. Though there is still some logging and associated road construction, there are now more jobs in the valley in restoration than in logging.

FROM CHAOS TO CONSENSUS

The basis of consensus, the ground on which it rests, is trust. Without trust, consensus really hobbles along. But it also engenders trust. It's a sort of circle.
— Caroline Estes[35]

Consensus has discouraged us. After all, we are not all Quakers.
— Sanford Lowry[36]

Fifteen years of salmon enhancement, erosion control and tree planting had not prepared the most stalwart of reinhabitants for the storm brewing in the late '80s. Despite years of living together, there was neither much interaction nor serious polarization between ranchers and homesteaders, the two main Mattole subcultures. As homesteader Dan Weaver put it, "We were neighborly but we mainly hung out with people like ourselves; people who agreed with us."

When the endangered spotted owl virtually shut down the California timber industry, "brushfires of emotion" swept through the community, culminating in Redwood Summer of 1990, a series of rallies, blockades, tree-sits and the like, protesting planned cuts of the last big stands of big trees.[37] As the summer of 1990 drew nigh, everyone along the north coast of California became tense. People in the Mattole, base camp for Redwood

Summer, remember cordiality turning to hostility. "It was nerve-wracking even to go to the general store in Petrolia," remembers Freeman House. Fuelled by the concept of "zero net sediment," the brushfire in Mattole exploded into a major blaze.

Here's how it happened.

In the highly-charged atmosphere following Redwood Summer, the California Department of Forestry called a series of public meetings to air new regulations requiring zero net sediment from logging operations. These regulations, prompted by sister agency, Fish and Game, made the connection between deteriorating salmon habitat and careless logging practices. But agency timing could not have been worse.

On a cool, foggy day in January 1991, 150 people gathered in Ferndale at the second of two meetings on "zero net discharge of sediment." According to Dan Weaver, a homesteader who would soon play a large role in the watershed: "everybody wanted to protect his own stake, fearing that the meeting's outcome might be detrimental to his own property. The atmosphere was highly charged; clearly there was a feeling among ranchers that 'hippies,' who had been associated with MSG and MRC, were 'pointing fingers.' The timber companies were skittish too."

The meeting started calmly but soon became tumultuous, recalls Weaver. "It was a long meeting with lots of angry tirades and people threatening to walk out or settle things in age-old ways." Though the meeting came close to dissolving in chaos and resentment, at the very end, a small ember for dialogue glimmered. After most of the ranchers had walked out in protest, the meeting's facilitator, a University of California extension forester, called them back saying, "Hey, you can't leave us. Why don't you just form an agenda committee, leave the government out, decide yourselves what you want to deal with." "Leaving the government out" apparently appealed to some. Hard-core rancher Anne Smith suddenly grabbed environmentalist Rondal Snodgrass's hand and held it high above her head. "We'll be on the agenda committee," she shouted, much to the surprise of Snodgrass. That's all it took. The agenda committee, comprising Smith and Snodgrass and a cross-section of other volunteers, promised to lay out a plan for another public meeting. People who an hour earlier were virtually at war went home with hope in their hearts.

గ

As a retired navy pilot relatively new to the valley, Dan Weaver had both leadership and mediation skills and experience. He and his wife, Tally Wren, had even crossed lines in their short time in the Mattole — they had friends among both ranchers and homesteaders. Wren remembers that "everybody felt comfortable with Dan. He had already volunteered to be on the agenda committee; he became the logical choice as facilitator." A couple of weeks later, the committee met and "was a little tight at first," said Weaver, "but we just basically kept talking. By the end of the third meeting, we got beyond hearsay and found some common ground and we were excited. With the help of Freeman and others, we broke through the polarity fence and started talking about how to make the Mattole a healthy and productive place."

> There were 11 of us, representing all shades of opinion. Anne Smith, a woman born and raised in the Mattole, from an old family, hosted the meetings. She was very open-minded and played a significant role, when most people had not really developed trust in one another. Among others, were Rondal Snodgrass and Freeman House, who have always been associated with the environmental community; Richard Bettis, from Pacific Lumber, a key figure because he was able to see the value of working with diverse interests; Russell Chambers, a rancher in his eighties who made eloquent statements on how degraded the river had become; and Sanford Lowry, a pivotal figure.

"You have to have people from each of the poles of opinion," Weaver explained, "people who are trusted by their communities and are willing to come to the middle." Lowry was such a person.

෩

In spring 1994, we met Sanford Lowry at a noisy roadside coffee shop in Fernbridge. As orders and aromas of country breakfasts filled the air, we settled into conversation. To easterners like ourselves, he fit our image of a California rancher: a handsome, burly man, sixtyish, wearing a big leather stetson, jeans, cowboy boots, talking straight and sincerely.

It quickly became clear why he was pivotal. He's been chairman of the Wool Growers and Cattlemen's Associations, has been active in community and church, is an officer in the Farm Bureau. He's a respected third-generation rancher. But he's also uniquely a bridge person; on his own volition he's attended a sustainable futures conference at Humboldt State University, participated in California bioregional forums, and is a board member of the Mattole Restoration Council.

When we got to talking about the "agenda committee," he said he volunteered to participate partly on the neighborliness principle, partly on the notion of "tending home." "When you get right down to it, everybody who lives here — the ranchers, the enviros, fishermen, the timber companies — are neighbors by virtue of sharing the same place," Lowry said. "If we don't manage our own affairs, someone else will. As a landowner, I've got to be involved. I don't want to stand idly by. I want some say because I expect to keep my ranch intact and the land is important to me and to my children."

ა

The agenda committee prepared a consensus statement and called a public meeting on April 21, 1991. Well attended, the meeting had the cordial air of collaboration. Those present, again representing a cross-section of opinion, accepted the statement, officially appointed a co-ordinator (Dan Weaver with help from University of California extension forester Kim Rodriguez), and, a month later, gave birth to the Mattole Watershed Alliance: "a diverse group of residents and landowners working together to improve the health of their watershed and their quality of life through communication, co-operation, and education."

Without bylaws or official structure, the Alliance has met regularly at different sites around the watershed, making all decisions by consensus. So far the Alliance has primarily made recommendations about resource use in the valley. Among these:

- Sport fishing regulations (which were accepted by the California Fish and Game Commission).

- Estuary restoration for summer "overrearing" salmon in partnership with Bureau of Land Management, timber companies, the Mattole Salmon Group, and the Mattole Restoration Council.

- Changes in driftnetting and offshore fishing (position statements were produced).

- Restoration of Mattole Salmon Group's funding through the salmon stamp program and the Department of Fish and Game.

- Bureau of Land Management road repair and decommissioning.

- Paving a Mendocino County road, paralleling the Mattole River headwaters, which was contributing sediment to headwaters.

- Helped convince county road crews to haul landslide spoils to stable sites rather than pushing them into the nearest waterway.

These accomplishments are primarily advisory and tend to skirt around the tough issues. The alliance has never really been able "to cut to the chase," says salmon activist David Simpson. "Consensus begins to break down when logging practices and land-use issues come up." Freeman House remembers the hard-won consensus document of 1993 on "habitat characteristics and biological functions important in maintaining forests, associated plants, and wildlife for the sake of watershed health and productivity." However, when it came to whether the consensus document should be mailed to residents and property owners, consensus vaporized. The document has yet to see the light of day.

Whatever its shortcomings, the alliance is the first truly cross-cutting coalition in the Mattole. It includes not only all land users and interest groups but also representatives of industrial logging (Pacific Lumber and Sierra Pacific Industries), the Bureau of Land Management, and the University of California Co-operative Extension Service. The California Departments of Fish and Game and Forestry have so far been invited only as consultants.

Like most new collaborative efforts of this kind, the Mattole Watershed Alliance is fragile and clunky. "The alliance sometimes resembles a cart with 16 wheels, four of which are always flat. A different four on different occasions. It's a slow process."[38] Sanford Lowry is similarly discouraged, both with the slow process of consensus, and with the ongoing impression he senses that ranchers, timber owners and timber companies are the villains. "My dream of us all working together because we are all neighbors sometimes looks impossible," he wrote in May 1996.[39] But so far he has not dropped out. Perhaps because of its fragile state, the Alliance did not meet from late 1993 to mid-1995.

"Once we got away from the salmon, we were on thin ice," Weaver said. Discussion of post-fire salvage procedures caused some attenders to walk out and file suit. A timber company representative then stayed away for more than a year. Richard Bettis from Pacific Lumber, who feels so strongly about the alliance that he would continue to attend even if his company told him to pull out, defended industrial timber's paranoia: "What do you expect? We got blindsided by a suit after a forest harvest plan was discussed at an Alliance meeting."

Seth Zuckerman, a journalist who has written extensively about the

Mattole and who now chairs the Mattole Restoration Council board, countered by saying, "Unless they give up the right to log without the alliance's approval, they shouldn't expect participants in the alliance to give up our right to bring suit to enforce the law." He went on to tell how limited the alliance can be:

> As soon as you start talking about forests and sediment, it gets personal. It's coming off everybody's land, everybody's roads, everybody's building sites. These are matters of people's everyday lives and livelihoods. Consensus disappears. Another reason for this is people's concept of private property values here. Everyone agrees that the salmon is common property, but people can't see the trees as everybody's forests.

Perhaps Simpson is right. The alliance so far has not been able to take on the root issues.

Tally Wren believes that a lack of tangible projects stalls the Alliance. With a few small successes, Wren thinks the Alliance would be stronger. Its most successful endeavor, she believes, was the estuary project in 1992, a time of remarkable collaboration:

> Lots of ranchers, the BLM, a timber company, the Salmon Group, the Restoration Council, and the Alliance — all spending a weekend working on improving salmon habitat. It was almost comical to see the ranchers competing for the driver's seat of the Cat, almost knocking down one another to work on the project. There was lots of donated material, equipment, food; when it was done, everyone felt good.

Another common effort that may pay dividends, according to Wren and Weaver, is the consensus training many people went through in 1992 and 1993. Weaver believes that consensus is especially helpful to the ranchers who, because they dislike attending meetings, will always be in the minority. "Ranchers do care and do want to talk about watershed issues," he says. "To keep them in the mix, consensus is valuable, even essential."

At the end of the day, everyone credits MWA with raising consciousness and helping chill-out the emotions of Redwood Summer. At alliance meetings, people are more likely to perceive each other as good human beings and to listen to each other's viewpoints. Linda Roush, area manager in the Bureau of Land Management's Arcata Resource Area Office, thinks of the alliance as "a great avenue to get to know people well and also to put some fears to rest that the government may be doing something that they don't know about." Lowry thinks the alliance has "cleared the air" for the Mattole Salmon Group and the Mattole Restoration Council to do their work. In other words, it has enabled the ranching community to understand that their work accomplishes community good rather than threatens private property rights.

As to the future, Freeman House thinks that the new California Department of Forestry designation of "sensitive watersheds," which some residents of the Mattole advocate, may re-energize the alliance or may cause it to come unstuck. Sanford Lowry fears that sensitive watersheds will just add another layer of bureaucracy that people who make their living from the land will have to pay for.[40]

"We don't need 1991 all over again," said Dan Weaver in 1994, "but some of the crisis-driven energy has dissipated." The alliance has survived both a hiatus and some "fairly divisive" lawsuits. "There are still fears out there," he concludes, "but most would rather be making decisions locally. We have not been able to take on tough issues like timber harvesting practices, yet we've developed a common language and with each meeting trust builds. We need to go on."

FROM WATERSHED ALLIANCE TO REINHABITATION

Times have changed and the salmon seem to be coping.

— David Simpson[41]

Our time in the Mattole convinces us that this is about a different kind of resource management based neither on political constructs nor resource warfare, but rather on the way nature actually works. It centers around a unit of inordinate natural significance, the watershed, and on mutual concern for the health not only of this watershed but also of the human economy. This kind of resource management is home-grown and mindful of the need to sustainably use natural resources — rangelands and timber specifically. It welcomes partners, particularly folk who for generations have made their living from the land and waters, and it strives to make decisions on sound scientific information and local knowledge of place. It respects the web of living things and perceives that human well-being depends on the well-being of ecological processes.

Counting children, maybe a quarter of Mattole residents have so far engaged in this experiment, inspired by the salmon as a powerful symbol of reinhabitation. "It turns out," says Freeman House, "that no one is antagonistic to salmon. If you can make people aware that salmon is what you're helping, almost no one can say no."[42] That people are doing their own resource management rather than leaving it to agencies in Sacramento or Washington is testimony to the power of "home." Out of such work comes confidence that the valley may again become good salmon habitat and continue to be a healthy environment for people, too.

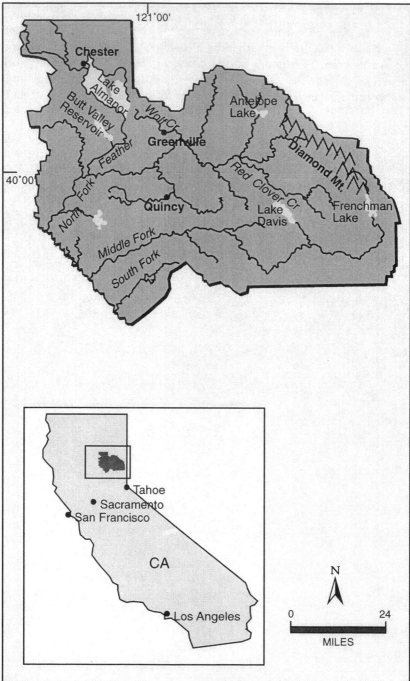

A Restorative Economy:
Plumas County, California
———— Chapter Nine ————

The restorative economy comes down to this: We need to imagine a prosperous...culture that is so intelligently designed and constructed that it mimics nature at every step, a symbiosis of company and customer and ecology.

— Paul Hawken[1]

Tucked into the eastern edge of northern California, Plumas County is rugged and beautiful. The Sierra Nevada Mountains dominate the landscape with elevations as high as 8,400 feet. Canyons and jagged formations guarantee nothing is easy about navigating the roads in and out of this region. The 20,000 residents who make this county their home share the challenges that the terrain offers them with the same grit one always comes to expect from the rural American West. There's no complaining about the fact that winter storms can close the canyon roads to the outside world for months at a time. Electricity can be down for weeks. Melting snows can flood the valleys and wash away the always tenuous mountain roads.

The western slopes of these mountains interrupt heavy clouds moving inland from the Pacific, and 60 inches of average annual precipitation falling on rich soils yields one of the most productive forests in the world. Cellulose fibre grows like bamboo in the tropics, resulting in forests where 80-year-old trees take on the stature of ancient sentinels. The 1.2 million acres of National Forest grow over 400 million board feet of timber every year. Few places in the world can boast similar productivity.

These forests are also the headwaters of the Feather, a river of inestimable value to California's urban and agricultural fortunes. The deep canyons and narrow openings have made it relatively easy to trap the rains that fall on this county into reservoirs. As a result, this watershed supplies water to over 10 million people living in areas as far away as Los Angeles. The fast-moving streams also power a series of hydroelectric dams that together produce as much electricity as an average nuclear plant.

This is a community whose livelihood has always been inextricably linked to the county's abundant resources. With a seemingly endless supply of natural resources and a small population providing products in high demand to ever-expanding markets, how could it have happened that by the end of the 20th century, this community and its resources were poised at the brink of disaster?

The evidence was incontrovertible. The reservoirs that captured the melting snows and translated them into water for southern California were filling with sediment. Streams that once boasted trout so thick you could walk on their backs now had populations of two fish per stream mile. No one could remember how long it had been since ducks gathering in the valley wetlands were so loud they kept them awake. The rich mountain meadows, where at least three generations of ranchers had made their living, were eroding away in great chasms. Many of the once magnificent forested mountain slopes reminded one of a "dog with mange." After a century of fire suppression, everyone — homeowner, logger, forest service employee, and environmentalist — lived with the constant fear that catastrophic fire would send their interests up in smoke. In the span of four years the school district went from one of the wealthiest in the state to one of the poorest. And in a place where people seldom locked their doors, someone's bullets twice pierced the office window of a prominent member of the community.

It is in this climate that the residents of Plumas County collectively arrived at a new vision of the future for their community. Wilderness advocates, timber mill operators, loggers, forest service personnel, cattle farmers and ranchers, environmentalists, soil conservationists, members of the chamber of commerce, school teachers, wives of loggers, elected officials — all found common language and common goals and expressed their new vision in a manifesto called the Quincy Library Group Proposal. Their manifesto and the process that produced it has the potential to put this little community at the epicenter of one of the most important shifts in resource management in the history of this country.

Their home-grown proposal blended what is known about the ecology of the landscape with what is believed to be necessary to restore perturbations of the past effectively and move the natural and human communities towards health and stability. Like all revolutionary documents there is hope written here and a history of struggle that led to this point.

RESOURCE HISTORY

The people of this region have always been intimately entwined with the resources of the land. Their story begins with the Maidu Indians, who fished the streams and hunted in the alpine meadows and forests, kept open by regular ground fires. When John Muir walked through the area he likely encountered immigrant shepherds from the Basque region of Europe summering their vast flocks of sheep on the abundant forage of the mountain meadows and grassy understory of the open forests. With the coming of European settlers, the fires were less frequent. The native grasses and meadow flowers were grazed heavily. In no time, like the native people, many of the native plants were replaced by new varieties transplanted from the European continent.

The gold rush of the mid-19th century diverted the livestock keepers and drew prospectors from all over the world. Any easterner who wasn't nailed down came west to find her or his fortune. The great rush was most profound in these Sierra slopes. With no law and no prior claims, everything was fair game. The thousands of newcomers needed food; the abundant game was a ready source. They needed timber for housing, mineshafts, flues and fire. Everything that could be reached was cut. Massive hydraulic cannons shot water across the slopes, washing whole sides of mountains to release precious metals locked in the loosened rock.

It was against this free-for-all backdrop that Teddy Roosevelt conceived of the designation of a sizable portion of these lands as the Plumas and Lassen National Forests in 1905. The early handful of forest rangers had more than enough work just trying to understand the boundaries of the newly designated forests. They also had to identify who was doing what on government land and create some kind of order out of the lawless mess that was our western frontier. Their focus wasn't to stop use, but rather to document and control use and suppress forest fires.

When the gold had been mostly tapped out, and every stream had been panned, most of the miners moved on. Timber became the resource of choice on the mountain slopes and a ranching economy settled in the valleys. By the 1940s, fire suppression was in full swing and grazing, timbering and mining were under a system of public permit. Then the Second World War broke out. Wood for the war effort and the post-war housing boom that followed all meant considerable product was extracted from these forests. At this time, another critical event happened in the history of this community. E.S. Collins, a successful timber mogul from Minnesota, purchased 92,000 acres of land in the region. Collins had a notion that there was a better way to manage forests than he had witnessed in the East. He believed it was possible to "ensure a perpetual supply of timber for a mill that would never close centered around a stable community."[2] He was interested in practising "sustainable forest stewardship." With input from the best foresters and scientists he could find, Collins began a quiet course of timber management whose aim was "forest health first, not what they wanted to bring to the sawmill."[3]

As the century hit mid-point, work in the woods and mills was the mainstay of the economy. Seventy-five per cent of the county was National Forest land and the principal use of this forest was timber production. It was also at this time that Plumas County's water resources came into play. With California's population growing tenfold in the first half of the 20th century, Californians turned their thirsty attention toward the Feather River. Dams and plumbing works were designed that would eventually supply 30 per cent of the water needed by Central Valley farmers and 25 per cent of the water used by the state's sprawling southern cities.

By 1980, technology became more sophisticated and multinational timber companies replaced local home-grown logging companies. Logging practices shifted from cutting single trees to massive clearcuts. In the "prime years" of the 1980s, over 240 million board feet of timber were cut per year from the Plumas National Forest alone, making it one of the three most productive forests in the entire National Forest system.

Here, as elsewhere in the West, logging roads pushed ever more aggressively into the roadless areas and the last stands of old-growth forests. The heavy rains and melting snows ran fast across the exposed slopes and hundreds of miles of freshly bulldozed logging roads. These faster streams incised deeper channels and carried ever-increasing sediment loads, which they would eventually drop behind the dams that blunted their journey to the sea.

Still, multinational timber operations with sophisticated new mills and American consumption of timber products all resulted in a greater push to "get out the cut." As late as 1991, 243 million board feet from big trees in the Plumas were coming to mills in northern California.[4]

In their rush to claim the big trees, the logging companies and the Forest Service ignored the expanding stands of white fir and other small trees that had grown as a result of almost a century of active fire suppression. Huge amounts of dry branches had accumulated on the ground. White fir and other small, brittle trees were crowding the understory of every forest. These were competing aggressively for nutrients and soil moisture, rendering the remaining larger overstory trees more susceptible to disease and insect damage. The low branches of the white fir were creating a ladder of highly flammable materials capable of carrying catastrophic fires into the crowns of the already stressed large trees. The fires that were foreshadowed threatened to be expensive and terrifying beyond anyone's experience.

Meanwhile, throughout the '70s and '80s, new people drifted into these mountains: back-to-the-landers and urban refugees from San Francisco and Los Angeles. The newly-established Feather River Community College attracted teachers and students. Entrepreneurs started developing a modest but promising tourism industry. A greying population from the more fast-paced and congested south found the area's safety and low cost of living attractive for their retirement years. These were people with different expectations of the local resources. They were outsiders with different viewpoints and affiliations. They were members of the Sierra Club and Audubon Society. By the early 1980s they were a noticeable presence in the Forest Service's planning process. These concerned newcomers were increasingly dissatisfied with the Forest Service's stewardship, and they aggressively demanded change. For the first time in the region's history a local chorus was chanting the same refrains that were being sung by the urban environmentalists. "No more clearcutting." "No more logging old growth."

What these people didn't know was that most of the loggers didn't like the clearcuts any more than they did. In a much quieter way, they, too, were complaining to the Forest Service. Although more trees would be cut, the people who made their living in the woods believed that this policy would be disastrous for them as well. Clearcutting was faster and required less skill than single-tree selection. They reasoned that this would result in fewer jobs in the woods and the most skilled loggers would no longer be able to demand a wage equal to their experience. In addition, they feared the public's reaction to clearcutting. As one logger's wife remembers, they told Forest Service officials "this is the worst thing you can do and we operators are going to get the blame."[5]

A COUNTERCURRENT

John Schramel had taught school in Plumas County since 1959. An outdoorsman and father, John and his children had become increasingly concerned over the years by changes they were observing in their favorite haunts. As John recalls it, "I was a real fisherman and I could see where the streams were degraded." In 1985, John ran and was elected to the Plumas County Board of Supervisors. When he assumed his role as County Supervisor, John was hoping there was something he could do "even on a small scale, to fix things." He remembers feeling "a little at sea wondering how to start things up."

The first winter of John's new term as supervisor was a hard winter in the mountains. Heavy snows resulted in severe flooding. This was causing a serious problem at Pacific Gas and Electric's (PG&E) hydroelectric works on the Feather River. An increase in sediment caused by increasing upstream erosion was resulting in siltation of PG&E's reservoirs. This, in turn, was leading to operational problems with their equipment. As much as four million cubic yards of sediment had accumulated behind the Rock Creek dam alone. At $16/yard to remove, this was a problem that could get very expensive.

One afternoon in his kitchen, John and some of his neighbors were talking about the problem. It seemed the more they talked, the more excited they became. They decided that there was something that could be done at the local level that could have lasting value. It might be possible to direct attention a little closer to the source of the problem and even create some new jobs in the process. They could restore some of the more drastically damaged stretches of streams to slow down flow, reduce erosion and therefore reduce sedimentation. They reasoned, also, that if they could hold the water longer in the upstream reaches of the watershed, it would help the ranchers by keeping the upland meadows moister longer, thereby improving the growth of forage. And as a side effect it would clean up the streams for fish and rehydrate the meadow's wetlands for waterfowl.

They decided they needed some partners and investors in their idea and for that reason, in May of 1985, they called a public meeting that attracted 20 different local, state, federal, private and public entities, including Pacific Gas and Electric. The partners that gathered quickly embraced the germ of the idea and added their own slant. Collectively, they determined that they would implement a co-operative restoration project.

The group chose a private stretch of the Red Clover Creek for their first demonstration project. John described the area as a "hard mountain valley...kind of a high desert like you might find in eastern Colorado. There was lots of sage brush intrusion and the stream was horrible, hot and full of algae. The stream banks were all broken down. Nothing was there. I think we found three fish in a mile and half stretch." John recalls people saying "it would take 50 years to get anything done on this."

Ten different entities, including PG&E, agreed to pitch in funds, time and material. Students, ranchers, agency bureaucrats and environmental activists all participated in the work. Plumas Corporation, a nonprofit subsidiary of the Chamber of Commerce, supervised the project. The work was completed on November 9, 1985, in five months.

The restorationists all held their breaths through the severe winter of 1986. When the weather cleared, however, their work had held up valiantly. Within two years, monitoring results indicated that the rate of erosion had significantly decreased and there was a marked increase in the trout fishery and waterfowl usage. John describes the results as "a paradise compared to what it looked like. We got more wildlife up there than you could shake a stick at. Even an osprey nested. I thought, my God, the Lord is pretty good letting us have all of this here."

A CO-ORDINATED APPROACH TO RESTORATION

The success of this first project led to the formation of a formal Memorandum of Agreement between 17 different public and private entities concerned with watershed improvements in the region. The group agreed to identify erosion sources; develop a regional erosion control plan for the watershed; design, fund and implement erosion control measures; and co-ordinate with private and public landowners. The work of the consortium was co-ordinated by Plumas Corporation and the group established themselves as a formal entity under an existing but little-known co-operative framework called the Co-ordinated Resource Management program (CRM). This framework allowed for the pooling of funds and the use of personnel from one land ownership to another.

The East Branch Feather River Co-ordinated Resource Management Group, as the group called themselves, decided on the following goals and principles:

- They would work on shared economic and environmental problems that have cumulative watershed effects.

- They would not duplicate or interfere with the activities, agendas or roles of polarized interest groups or agency mandates relating to current resource management practices.

- They would work on demonstrations of innovative watershed restoration techniques, patterned after natural processes as much as possible.

- The projects would be undertaken only on lands voluntarily offered by the landowner.

- The projects would be chosen by consensus, funded co-operatively, and the landowner would take the lead on individual projects.

- And they would work together on projects that could demonstrate tangible ecological success and avoid "laying blame."[6]

As John Schramel describes it, "We decided we would make decisions by consensus. Boy, we can argue and argue and argue. But one of the neat things about it, we've approached the point where no one blames anyone for what took place in the past. That's history, under the bridge and gone. We forget. We start at ground zero and realize that our job is to reach consensus and get something good done for the watershed. And by, golly, we get there one way or another."

The group consciously wanted to develop a process for encouraging local initiative and local control over resource issues. They were starting to see that leaving everything to federal and state government could lead to "either total exploitation or exhaustion of the resource base or no use of the resource base."[7] They believed both paths were anathema to having a healthy local community. Theirs was a hands-on activism that was based on the principle that more trout and waterfowl, more jobs and less sedimentation were goals around which ranchers, loggers, government bureaucrats and environmentalists could all rally. As CRM member Ray Stine observes: "When we go out and do stream restoration projects, we've got the environmental groups going, 'Ah, that's what we need to be doing.' And we've got the local folks, the people who have been raised in this community, looking at the improved streams and the ducks and things coming back, and they say, 'Ah-ha, that's the way it used to be around here!'"

From 1987 to 1993, the CRM implemented 33 restoration projects and studies; $2.7 million new dollars had been directed to these projects from the member groups and tangible results were being documented. The project areas were showing increases in waterfowl populations of 20-700 per cent. Trout populations had increased from 50-500 per cent and stream bank erosion had decreased 90-150 per cent. Feather River College had established a certification program in watershed management. A wholesale native plant nursery opened that specialized in species that would be used in the restoration projects. And two local high schools became involved in a sophisticated program of monitoring for several of the restoration units.

The projects were showing real results. Technically, streams were healing. Economically, new money was creating new jobs for local contractors and recent graduates, and new challenges were spawning new small businesses. Socially, they had drawn together an improbable cross-section of people to work on locally designed and locally controlled solutions to shared problems. People were working together and seeing each other and the resource base of their community in a new light. In the words of Ray Stine:

> The reason the CRM works so well is the individual members have over the years been able to take the blinders off and see other people's perspective on things. As a result we now look at the environment and the watershed as a whole rather than the part or the thing that narrowly concerns us or our agency.

So impressive were the results that Plumas began to get national publicity and a steady stream of outside inquiries. It's not that the work itself was that unusual; similar restoration projects were happening in other places in the West. What was really drawing the curious was the collaborative approach that was being taken to get the job done. Old hippies and fourth-generation ranchers, high school students and resource agency professionals, backhoe operators and college professors were coming together to get something done for their community. They were laying the foundation for a profound cultural change. One that would help them in the increasingly dark times that lay ahead.

THE WORST WAS YET TO COME

The CRM projects may have started to heal a few stream miles of the watershed, but the lifeblood of Plumas was still hemorrhaging. Clearcutting continued and local and national discontent with the logging practices became increasingly sophisticated. Almost every major timber sale on public land was being tied up in court and this tactic, plus increasingly complex requirements and regulations, was tying the Forest Service in knots.

In 1993, the Forest Service issued an interim plan to prevent the California spotted owl from becoming endangered like its northern cousin.[8]

At the same time, downsizing rolled through the Forest Service. Just when the local economy was in greatest crisis, the pre-eminent resource manager in the region was forced to pull its own plug. Between 1991 and 1994, Plumas National Forest headquarters and the ranger stations in the county lost 200 permanent and temporary jobs.[9] This effectively shut down logging operations in the Plumas. Output dropped from over 243 million board feet in 1990 to less than 60 million in 1993.[10]

The economy and community were in free-fall. Fear and despair led to finger-pointing and denial. Outraged locals railed against anyone not of their persuasion. Loggers charged that their jobs were endangered because of some worthless bird and some bleeding-heart liberals backed by big money suits in Sacramento and Washington. Friends of Plumas Wilderness argued that the spotted owl was just a last gasp indicator of the sorry despoliation of Sierra forest ecosystems by greedy yahoos who couldn't see the forest for the trees. California Women in Timber alleged that men in far-off office towers — timber magnates and environmental elitists alike — were undercutting families whose livelihoods depended upon work in the woods and mills. And everyone blamed the Forest Service. Mike Jackson, an environmental lawyer in Quincy and one of the most prominent critics of forest practices, had bullet holes in his office window. The war had begun and the battle lines were drawn.

THE CALM IN THE CENTER OF THE STORM

Then emerged a thoughtful leader, a conservative county supervisor and small business owner, Bill Coates, long a friend of the logging industry. Coates realized that unless something was done, his community would be "wiped out." He quietly asked two key community leaders to meet with him: Jackson, the *de facto* leader of the environmental activists, and Tom Nelson, an official from Sierra Pacific Industries, the largest logging operation in Plumas. Their meeting was furtive. These "three veterans of the Timber Wars" had a long history of bitter disagreement and mistrust but on two things they agreed. They wanted to see their community survive and the Forest Service's management had failed them all.

Soon these three leaders began to meet openly at the Quincy Library, a neutral place. Anyone who desired to participate in drafting a consensus plan for the management of public forests that would lead to "community stability" and "forest health" was invited to join them.[11] The Quincy Library Group (QLG), as they came to be called, drew almost every sector of the community. Friends of Plumas Wilderness, timber companies,

California Women in Timber, the Feather River Alliance for Resources and Environment (a "wise use" or resource development advocacy group), natural resource professionals from many agencies, members of the Sierra Club and the California Sport Fishing Protection Alliance, and cattle ranchers — all met semi-monthly at the library.[12]

Key to these meetings was participation of those who had been working together for almost a decade through the projects of the Co-ordinated Resource Management group (CRM) and foresters from Collins Pine Company. Those who had the experience of the CRM knew something about the ecology and health of the watershed and about collaboration and consensus-based decision-making. Collins Pine foresters brought 50 years of experience and data that could tell the group something about managing a forest for more than the trees.

The group took a good look at Collins Pine's lands. The forests they saw still had 200- and 300-year-old trees. It was an open forest of mixed ages and mixed species growing together with a much reduced threat of wildfire. For 50 years they had cut only those individual trees that were in ill health or starting to fail. They consciously left snags and trees with active nests. What the group found was a forest with bald eagles, black bears and California spotted owls. They also saw that under this approach, the forest had managed to provide a sustained yield of timber to their mill. Yet the forest still had as much volume today as it did when Collins started cutting in 1941. As Collins Pine's forest manager puts it, "After we get through logging, there's still a forest here."[13]

The people of Quincy also saw that in the battlefield of western timberlands, where everyone was sniping, Collins Pine was a demilitarized zone. Outside critics weren't criticizing Collins Pine. They were recognizing their forestry techniques as exemplary. Collins Pine produced the first wood product to be awarded the "Green Cross" by Scientific Certification Systems, an independent agency that evaluates a company's impacts on the environment.

Like Dorothy returning from her terrible adventure in Oz, the citizens of Plumas County learned that the answer to their problems was always right there in their own backyard. They borrowed some of Collins Pine's techniques. They used the co-operative approach of the CRM to hammer out details. They incorporated suggestions from an alternative management plan written by the Friends of Plumas Wilderness during the Forest Service's 1985 planning process. They acknowledged their common experience of living in this place and they embraced a new language of community stability and forest health. The Quincy Library Group used all these ingredients to create a consensus document they called a "Community Stability Proposal." The document sets as its goal, community and forest health. To accomplish this they recommend a program driven by the need for forest restoration, not timber quotas. Their "desired future condition is an all-age, multi-story, fire-resistant forest approximating pre-settlement conditions."

The plan calls for a diversity of age-classes and species of trees rather than single-species domination; individual and group selection forestry rather than clearcutting; stream restoration and protection rather than grazing and logging to the banks. It recommends planning and management by watershed rather than by ranger district. It endorses immediate implementation of fuel reduction recommendations outlined in a set of interim guidelines established to protect the California spotted owl. It calls for recognizing the role of fire in the ecosystem and for the Forest Service to seek to "create a forest that will more closely mimic the historic natural landscapes of the Sierra." It recommends roadless, sensitive and riparian areas be off-limits for harvest. It calls for the creation of a "northern Sierra working circle," a proposal that would require that most of the felled trees be sent to local mills. It also advances the recommendation that progress be measured in ecological terms: miles of stream restored; reduction in sedimentation; increases in spotted owl, trout and waterfowl populations; and acres of reduced fuel hazard, not just in board feet harvested.

The Quincy Library Group proposal was not a watered-down compromise hammered out in an adversarial process, where everyone, including the resource, leaves a loser. The Quincy Library Group proposal was an innovative concept based on a vision of ecological and economic health. It dared to recognize and place limits on human activity and to direct that the Forest Service and the community start thinking about their choices and options in terms of forest health and sustainability, not in terms of timber quotas and regulations.

Here was a plan developed by the consensus of a broad cross-section of the community, heartily endorsed by the most extreme elements. Here was a plan that was fashioned in an open and collaborative process and forum where all sides were heard and all thoughts encouraged. Forest Service employees participated in crafting this proposal, side by side with the presidents of the local Sierra Club, California Women in Timber, and the Cattlemen's Association. Surely this was what the framers of the Forest Resource Act had in mind when they created the Forest Service planning requirements. However, when the enthusiastic coalition signed and presented their Magna Carta to the U.S. Forest Service in November of 1993, they hit a bureaucratic brick wall.

Forest Service personnel readily admitted that it was developed by a representative forum. They saw it as consistent with their new mandate for "ecosystem management." They believed that it would fit the state's interim guidelines for protection of the California spotted owl.[14] But the local office claimed that they couldn't just shift their operation in the direction laid out by the QLG's plan. They had to be absolutely certain the proposal conformed to federal laws and policies. They had to follow procedures and that would take time. Their personnel had been so badly pared that there were few people to make the necessary evaluations. With the omnipresent threat of law suits from every faction, they couldn't risk doing anything too hastily.

The Quincy Library Group would not be daunted. They took their proposal to Forest Service officials in Sacramento, to the service's Western Regional office and ultimately to Washington. In February 1994, a delegation of 40 members of the group took their plan to the wizard himself, Jack Ward Thomas, chief of the United States Forest Service (USFS). They informed Chief Thomas that they had done what President Clinton instructed local communities to do. We settled "our differences locally in the conference room, not the courtroom. We created a plan which seeks to approximate pre-European settlement conditions. Our proposal is ready to go. All we are waiting for is USFS authorization and the funding to go forward."[15]

The delegation received acclaim. Their plan was applauded and held up as an example by every level of government from local agencies to the President himself. Their process was mentioned in House and Senate reports.[16] It took two long years, but the Forest Service's own formal assessment of the Quincy Library Group proposal proved the group's assumptions to be valid. Based on that assessment, in November of 1995 Plumas County National Forests received a direct appropriation of $4.7 million from the Secretary of Agriculture to implement part of the fire hazard reduction recommendations and other restoration activities. When the Draft California Spotted Owl Management Guidelines were published in 1995, the QLG quickly evaluated them and recommended a new approach to protect the owl without sacrificing the forestry provision of the QLG proposal.

THE ECONOMICS OF RESTORATION

In spite of some hopeful signs, at the time of this writing full implementation of the community's Plan for Stability is still hamstrung by the inability of the Forest Service to respond. The local Forest Service administrators contend that availability of funds remains the chief impediment. Plumas Corporation restoration projects co-ordinator Leah Wills believes it's much more than that.

> If you're really serious about this new democracy and a reinvented government, it's going to take a whole different structure. It's a huge shift. Every step of the way from planning, to rules and regulations, to bookkeeping, the whole system is set up for individuals to act individually in a hostile environment. Even if people's hearts are in the right place and everyone's desperately trying, you will hit so many walls it will take your breath away. And they're not intentionally placed walls but the walls of the old way of doing things.

Leah is no stranger to these walls. As the project co-ordinator for Plumas Corporation's restoration work, she has had to scale many. Leah has been there since that first day in John Schramel's kitchen. Since then, she has been a visible spokesperson for the work and philosophy of the CRM.

She and others in Plumas County see an obvious source of funding for implementation of the Quincy Library Group proposal. "In ecosystem management the ecosystem is the capital and you get to live off the interest. When you begin to realize that, you see that capital maintenance is the obligation of the people using the resource. Taxpayers alone shouldn't be paying for this watershed. This is a working watershed. This watershed provides water for ten million people and a third of the farmers in the Central Valley. Pacific Gas and Electric and the state water authority make millions and millions of dollars every year off this watershed. And until recently it was one of the top ten timber producers in the country. Who ought to be reinvesting in the restoration of this watershed? It sure isn't just the taxpayer in Idaho; it's also the consumer in Los Angeles."

Leah believes the benefits of investing in the ability of the watershed to produce and store water would be obvious to the consumer. Restoration would reduce sedimentation, giving the reservoirs a longer lifespan. Additionally, large storms and snow melts would not result in frequent major runoff events causing the reservoirs to fill quickly and excess water to be released. Instead, water would be held longer in the mountain meadows and upper reaches of the watershed, guaranteeing flow into the reservoirs throughout the summer.

Under this investment strategy, city dwellers in southern California would have more water longer into the summer. The high mountain meadows would be saved from desertification. Soil would be kept in place to grow 300-year-old ponderosa pines in the forests and trout in the streams. By investing in the removal of the heavy fuel buildup, the soil would maintain more moisture. This improves timber quality and reduces the threat of wildfire. The investment would surely pay off in the reduction of catastrophic wildfires. In this region, the alternative is clear: if you don't actively manage fuel loads, eventually "you will pay dearly to put the fires out." Put this way, it isn't difficult to see the connection.

A shareholder understands when a corporation makes capital investments. This isn't a tax or a fine, it's just good business. And this is a "CRM way of doing it. You build on something people will understand, where they will see the direct benefit."

Plumas County representatives have been discussing this funding concept with the state water authority for some time. On April 14, 1994, John Sheehan, Director of Plumas Corporation, introduced this idea to the California State Senate Agriculture Committee. To date, there has been no response.

There is no dispute among economists that the market has not adequately determined how to assess the costs of things like pollution and loss of soil and species diversity. Neither does the market understand how to value restoration or maintenance of the natural capital that underlies its business interests and our communities' health. In these times, when the free market dominates global exchange, the world must determine a way to correct these errors in the system.

In the United States, we have attempted to correct these problems with regulations or government subsidy. Yet rivers and estuaries continue to degrade and salmon face sure extinction. Regulation alone will not level the playing field on a global basis. It will not inspire the logger or timber company to develop a long-term view when they need to bring dinner home tonight or show a profit to a stockholder tomorrow. Government spending alone cannot begin to redress the profound debt that has accumulated in hundreds of years of exploitation. And as Paul Hawken points out, as long as environmental protection is "carried out at the behest of charity, altruism or legislative fit...it will remain a decorous subordinate to finance, growth and technology."[17]

In the Feather River Watershed, good forest management and restoration of the integrity of the system will result in a more sustainable yield of water. If the people of Plumas County can improve the area's capacity to provide a high quality, sustainable supply of water and the market can learn how to best reinforce their work, the whole ecosystem — including the human part — will flourish.

A RESTORATIVE ECONOMY

Plumas County is asking that the principal users of the Feather River's water invest in the restoration of this watershed. "A couple pennies a month by each user" is what they estimate it would take.[18]

The change to a restorative economy based on sustainable forest management and restoration of a healthy ecosystem is profound. It requires new skills, new ways of projecting and pricing the products and the levels of productivity derived from the forest. It requires flexibility, creativity and a commitment to change. All of these things are very difficult, especially for large bureaucracies like the Forest Service. Still, as difficult as it is for our government to change, when the people achieve true consensus, the government must respond.

Reasonable people got together in the Quincy Library. They forged a concept that is truly innovative and based on a vision of ecological and economic stability. It isn't perfect. But the people of Plumas are trying to steer a course for their community and the resources they steward by a new understanding of the destination. The measurable goals speak about forest health and not commodities. Instead of "talking timber quota, [we are talking] acres treated."[19]

The Quincy Library Group and the Co-ordinated Resource Management team are proud of what they have done. They know they have something worthy of their continued commitment. They are prepared to persevere. What some people claim is most remarkable about what is happening in Quincy is not really the plan they created or the stretches of stream they have healed, but the sense of community they have found. As one school teacher put it, "Perhaps one of the most important things that is happening for the kids is that they are seeing adults put aside their differences and solve their problems for the good of the whole community."

When asked what this community will be like in 20 years, everyone saw vastly improved forests and rivers, less threat of fire, a stable and predictable flow of resources from the National Forest, a more diverse economy and more trout. In sum, the members of this community are now armed with a potent vision of a new kind of relationship with their resource base. They have successful experiences with collaboration and partnership. They possess a renewed sense of place. They are hopeful for the future. Their optimism is warranted. Perhaps they will in fact realize their collective vision, for as environmentalist Mike Jackson points out, "This is a community that hopes and understands that its best days are in the future."[20]

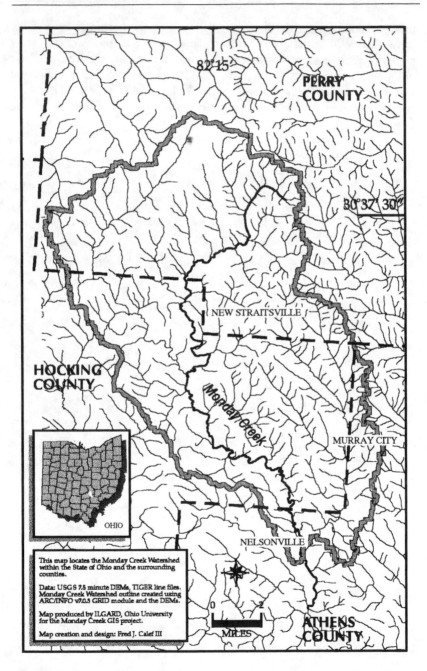

PERRY COUNTY

82°15'

30°37'30"

NEW STRAITSVILLE

HOCKING COUNTY

Monday Creek

MURRAY CITY

OHIO

NELSONVILLE

This map locates the Monday Creek Watershed within the State of Ohio and the surrounding counties.

Data: USGS 7.5 minute DEMs, TIGER line files. Monday Creek Watershed outline created using ARC/INFO v7.0.5 GRID module and the DEMs.

Map produced by ILGARD, Ohio University for the Monday Creek GIS project.

Map creation and design: Fred J. Calef III

0   2

MILES

ATHENS COUNTY

Restoration at Two Extremes:
Monday Creek and Chicago's Forest Preserves
──────────── Chapter Ten ────────────

The hope of ecological restoration has begun to produce a subtle Earth change in my sense of the future. It all depends on our consciousness, on an informed and deliberate willingness to proceed into a millennium in which our long-accustomed relationships to Nature are reshaped, and in which we ourselves are reshaped by our dealings with Nature. One still hopes for a liberatory future, a far gentler, indeed a happier future. I believe restoration will help us there.

— Stephanie Mills[1]

As it turns out, our nine stories tell of only a small subset of community-based conservation initiatives, all with the same hopeful prospects, the same fragile infancy. The list of places we have not visited is long and getting longer. Clinch Valley, Virginia; Applegate Partnership, Oregon; Gila Valley Covenant, Arizona; Willapa Bay, Washington; Swan-Seeley Valleys, Montana; the Sand Hills Initiative, Nebraska; the Greater Kitlope Ecosystem, British Columbia are just a few of the many we have heard or read about.

Our purpose has been to tell a few of the many possible stories well, not to conduct survey research. Two other stories, which we tell briefly in this chapter, show that collaborative, community-based resource management is happening across a very broad spectrum and often centers around a distinct element of the third wave: environmental restoration. These communities have discovered, as many others have, that one of the best ways to enter the

167

new resource management era is through the doorway of what Leopold called "land doctoring."[2] As people participate in environmental restoration, they engage themselves in their native landscape, perhaps for the first time. This, in turn, enriches their appreciation of place, brings a new sensitivity about its diversity, resilience and mystery, and helps them come to terms with their own and nature's limits. As restorationists, Stephanie Mills notes above, they reshape nature and are reshaped themselves in the process.

Although the antecedents of environmental restoration reach back at least a century, it was not until the 1980s that it moved to the foreground of resource management.[3] David Brower observes that the restoration movement seems to have jump-started itself, perhaps in direct proportion to the destruction of earth's ecosystems.[4] Recently it has swept the continent as thousands of professionals and amateur environmentalists have waded into wetlands and streams, put their backs to tree plantings and prairie recovery, helped populations of birds, animals, fish and toads recover.[5] Restoration tries to knit back the tattered edges of the world, to rehabilitate natural communities and functions. William Jordan believes that restoration involves the techniques and attitudes of agriculture and medicine practised with full ecological consciousness.[6]

Restoration also reaches deeply into human consciousness, for it puts peoples' hands in the earth, gives them an evolutionary view, teaches them that nature is not "out there" but is habitat for them and the community of life around them. Restoration helps them make a contribution that might create a bridge between lands past and people future.

Another gift of restoration is that it enables people to touch the artistry of the native landscape. In places very near their homes they find pieces of the previously painted canvas: a small wetland along the edges of a country road; prairie grasses hovering around toppled graves in old cemeteries; a narrow creek that flows through their subdivision; a tiny tract of never-cut or once-cut forest. Seeing such possibilities is not only restorative, it's close to the heart of the ecology of hope.

Consider these two places, at opposite ends of the spectrum of wealth and urbanity: a sparsely settled, Appalachian Ohio watershed where people have been poor for generations and where they have recently plunged into cleaning up acid mine drainage and other forms of stream despoliation; and forest preserves in wealthy, metropolitan Chicago, where thousands of urban and suburban residents now engage as volunteers in prairie and savanna restoration. While it may be unwise to make too much of the common thread here, we observe that restoration has quickened the pulse of neighborhood and community resource management, has attracted people to the work of healing, and has given each place a new definition of home.

THE MONDAY CREEK RESTORATION PROJECT

As local legend goes, when European explorers and surveyors arrived in this part of the country from the east they arrived along the banks of a substantial creek in a narrow valley on a Sunday. Thus is named the stream Sunday Creek that begins near Oakfield.... The next day the party journeyed another 15 miles or so west and found the drainage channel for the next major watershed. Thus was named Monday Creek.

— John Winnenberg[7]

Our goal is to return Monday Creek and its tributaries to fishable and swimmable conditions. That's a tall order and we expect it to take a long time.

— Mary Ann Borch[8]

Trimble, Ohio, is home base of Rural Action, a southeastern Ohio nonprofit organization with the motto "weaving the fabric of community renewal." Rural Action's purpose is to organize, train, network, and support diverse groups of citizens for the revitalization of communities in eight counties in the southeastern corner of Ohio. Out of Rural Action's busy array of projects, the Monday Creek Restoration Project stands out as a model of the way restoration helps people rediscover their natural surroundings.

Even if you have lived in southeastern Ohio for 25 years, as one of us has, it is hard to fathom the social and environmental devastation stemming from more than a hundred years of coal mining. Social problems seem intractable — ranging from unemployment and illiteracy, high rates of teenage pregnancy and low rates of childhood immunization, to absentee landholding, tax delinquency, and a legal morass of surface and mineral rights ownership that ensnares even the federal government. Environmental problems, on and beneath the ground, are as profound. Surface water is so polluted by acid mine drainage that it's mostly lifeless. There are pock-marks of subsidence as former mine shafts and chambers collapse. And the landscape is littered with scarred and eroded former mine sites, decaying towns and illegal dumps. The official name of one township road in Athens County is "Trashpile Road."

This is Rural Action's perplexing daily reality, and it's nowhere better illustrated than in Monday Creek. One of Ohio's most polluted rivers, this stream was virtually killed four generations ago by acid mine drainage. "Nobody living remembers this stream as fishable," local resident Jim Dalton told us. But before coal became king, Monday Creek was a rich aquatic environment. Streams in the region were once habitat for diverse life with mayflies, stone flies, caddis flies and beetles at the base of the food chain, darters and daces next, and brook trout, spotted bass, small mouth bass, sauger, grass pike, sunfish, walleye and blue gills at the upper end of the chain — all under the shaded canopy of a mature bottomland forest.[9]

Fed by a poetry of intricately branched tributaries — Rock Run, Job's Run, Snow Fork, Snake Hollow, Long Run, Lost Run — Monday Creek ties together many small communities in Athens and Perry counties. Shawnee, Oreville, Carbon Hill, Pilgrims Rest — names with stories perhaps forgotten. This stream of 27 miles drains a small watershed of 116 square miles. In the dreams of some southeastern Ohio visionaries it need not be a regional sacrifice area. It could again become a thriving creek teeming with native life beneath a lush green canopy where people picnic and fish and swim. They ask: What if it were possible to fish for bass again?

Monday Creek's problem can be summed up in one word: coal. It was at the very core of the massive and highly prosperous coal industry of the Hocking Valley coal field. From the 1870s, when railroads punched into the region, to the 1930s, when the Depression hit, millions of tons of coal were taken from dozens of deep mines in this coal field — coal to power railroads and to fuel America's industrial machine in places like Pittsburgh, Wheeling and Youngstown. Among the most valuable Ohio coal seams was #6 Middle Kittaning, which underlies much of the watershed and crops out in hillsides adjacent to Monday Creek. Middle Kittaning provided a "walk through" vein (13-20 feet thick) of high quality, low-ash bituminous coal. It was thoroughly mined.[10]

Old mines, abandoned by the 1930s, underlie at least 20 per cent of Monday Creek's watershed. On the surface, about three thousand acres, 4 per cent of the watershed, were strip-mined in the 1940s to 1970s. Waste — in the form of household trash, mine refuse and tailings, gob piles, rotting structures, and surface water impoundments with pH values of 3.0 to 3.5 — is one legacy of the coal era.[11] Underground water pollution is another. Beneath the watershed is a honeycomb of mine shafts, tunnels and chambers, all of which store millions of gallons of water.[12] In the presence of oxygen and bacteria, this underground water interacts with iron sulphides around former coal seams forming acid mine drainage and a dissolved load of heavy metals. Finding its way to the surface through seeps, fractures, shafts and mine openings, acid mine drainage causes Monday Creek to look orange in some places, turquoise in others.

Monday Creek is one of dozens of Ohio watersheds despoiled by coal mining and left to pollute rivers downstream — the Hocking and Ohio in this case — with dilute sulphuric acid, iron precipitates and heavy metals. Neither federal nor state laws have resulted in significant restoration of water quality. And the coal companies, if they still exist, are not legally responsible. According to the U.S. Bureau of Mines, Monday Creek is part of a much bigger problem: more than 10,000 linear miles of streams in Appalachia are polluted by acid mine drainage.[13]

There had been some effort to clean up Monday Creek before this project. The Ohio Department of Natural Resources, Division of Mines and Reclamation, began working on reclamation projects in the watershed in 1977, but not specifically on water quality. Using federal Abandoned Mine Lands funds, the Division targeted "priority one" sites where "public health and/or safety were being adversely affected."[14] Some $760,000 were spent on plugging mine openings, rectifying subsidence and redirecting some of the most egregious examples of impounded waters.

In the early 1990s, a number of activists and projects focusing on Sunday and Monday creeks set the scene for the genuinely collaborative effort that emerged in 1994. John Winnenberg, editor of *Community Life News* in southern Perry County, wrote a two-part series on restoring life to local streams. In it he foresaw the importance of stream restoration in this impoverished land.

> Sunday and Monday Creeks won't be fixed overnight, perhaps not even in a decade or my lifetime. But this doesn't preclude our working hard at that change, or at least embarking on it. The streams in our presence here could be good indicators of our willingness to be responsible not only to ourselves and our immediate needs, but to the bigger picture — the tightly interwoven environment that includes our daily lives, how we sustain ourselves including how we make a living, how we interact with one another, raise and educate our children, spend our leisure time, care for the ill and those in need, raise our food as well as caring for the natural environment.[15]

Winnenberg was slightly ahead of his time.

Monday Creek really got its start as a citizens' project when, providentially, the paths of three hydrogeologists crossed in the watershed.

It happened this way.

In mid-1994, residents concerned about flooding along Snow Fork sought help from their county commissioners. Through another county agency, they approached Pam Stachler, an Ohio University hydrogeology graduate student, to look into flooding on Snow Fork. Stachler's advisor, Ohio University professor Mary Stoertz, the second hydrogeologist in this story, had long been seeking a way to tackle Monday Creek as part of her own research on Hocking River pollution. She encouraged Pam to do the project. That summer, Pam and five teen-aged boys spent many days on Snow Fork looking for things that may contribute to the flashy nature of the tributary.

By the end of the summer it became obvious to Stachler and Stoertz that Snow Fork had problems far worse than flooding: erosion, solid waste, septic pollution and, of course, acid mine drainage. In their report, they advocated creating a grassroots coalition and using a watershed approach to address the entire range of problems on Monday Creek. Although the grant proposal to launch such a coalition was never funded, the seed had been planted.

Meanwhile, Mary Ann Borch, the third hydrogeologist, came into the watershed as a staff member of Rural Action. With five years consulting experience in central Ohio, Mary Ann wanted to use her expertise to make a difference in southeastern Ohio. She brought new ideas. She was aware of a recent change in federal funding for the cleanup of acid mine drainage. This change, the Appalachian Clean Streams Initiative, enabled, for the first time, federal severance tax funds (raised under the Surface Mining Control and Reclamation Act of 1977) to be dedicated exclusively to cleanup of acid mine drainage. Borch also found a model that would show how Monday Creek could be restored.

Toby Creek, a watershed in western Pennsylvania similar to Monday Creek in size and setting, was the perfect analog. Like Monday Creek, Toby Creek watershed had been mined and was severely polluted with acidity. A 30-year effort to clean it provided a picture of what Monday Creek could be:

> We witnessed a fisherman enjoying native brown trout. We saw a variety of restoration techniques, and we saw a community that was prospering to the tune of a million dollars generated annually by tourism.... There are benefits to bridges because acid waters would no longer dissolve concrete structures. And I think there are intangible benefits for the environment and the people who live there. When our streams improve, so does our outlook.[16]

What was important about Toby Creek as a model, according to Stoertz, was "the agencies here did not believe we could clean up Monday Creek. I spent hours on the phone giving pep talks to guys who were highly doubtful. Toby Creek proved it was possible."

With Toby Creek in mind and the prospect of federal funding, in late 1994 Borch called a meeting of interested parties. Out of this has grown the Monday Creek Restoration Project, a partnership of 14 groups including residents, commissioners of three counties, the U.S. Forest Service (which owns 48 per cent of the land), Ohio University, Hocking College, and other federal, state and local resource agencies.

Among these, the partner that best symbolizes the third-wave spirit of this project is the National Environmental Training Co-operative (NETC), based at Hocking College in Nelsonville.[17] Itself an alliance of labor, coal industry, government, local businesses, community and education, NETC retrains displaced coal miners, then uses their skills in environmental restoration. So far, NETC is small. It's retrained a couple of dozen miners — all of whom have found jobs — but there is vast potential: there are 1,300 recently unemployed miners, thousands of others, and more than 200,000 acres to be restored in Ohio.[18] Jim Dalton, a retrained miner who is now an instructor at Hocking, told us "coal mining wrecked this area environmentally; now it's up to us to put it right again."

The Monday Creek Project began its work writing a plan and inventorying the watershed in various ways (including creation of a Geographic Information System). It then began to involve residents in stream sweeps and log-jam removals and to invite them to public meetings in various parts of the watershed. The project has also worked with schools in studying the science of acid mine drainage and leading field trips. In co-operation with the Forest Service and Ohio Department of Natural Resources, it has set up monitoring wells, planted trees, employed former miners in pilot reclamation projects, and submitted a raft of collaborative proposals. In 1996 the project was awarded a major grant from the U.S. Environmental Protection Agency.

Borch, Monday Creek Restoration Project co-ordinator, has in the short span of two years gathered the experts, promoted collaboration, energized residents and, in her person, provided a model for watershed work throughout Appalachia. She rightly concludes she did not "create" the project. She says "it was all converging to take place anyway." So far, the spirit of this project has infiltrated resource agencies in an unprecedented way. For example, the U.S. Forest Service has been taking bold steps to remedy mine problems on their land.[19] For forester Marcia Wikle, Monday Creek has become one of her most important responsibilities.

Of Rural Action's many efforts, Monday Creek comes closest to our vision of third-wave resource management — not because it was born in response to one of the nastiest kinds of water pollution known to humanity and not because the "Feds" changed the rules. Monday Creek is on the cusp of third-wave resource management because the vision of a swimmable and fishable Monday Creek is powered by innovative, pragmatic and flexible people — citizens and professionals — who are willing to collaborate and whose first concern is making the place they call home better.

Still, residents are not coming on board in numbers some may desire. Snow Fork may still flood as it did in the early 1990s. Monday Creek continues to flow with a pH as low as 3.0. Heavy metals and acidity stifle aquatic life. Mines still cave in. But change is clearly under way and people here are beginning to see the importance of restoration. Perhaps streams will soon be "good indicators of our willingness to be responsible not only to ourselves and our immediate needs, but to the bigger picture — the tightly interwoven environment."[20]

This strengthening partnership gives the dreamers in this watershed hope that Monday Creek will one day not only become a fisher's paradise but also a place whose future residents — the school kids of today — remember the good old days when they helped their watershed heal. Stoertz, one of the trio of hydrogeologists who helped get this thing going, is fond of saying "We will gather the people around the idea of life in their creeks." If this happens, the people and Monday Creek itself will have become part of the ecology of hope.

THE NORTH BRANCH PRAIRIE PROJECT

One day in the mid-1970s, naturalist Steve Packard was riding his bicycle in one of Cook County's forest preserves. Though Cook County is metropolitan Chicago, one of America's most heavily urbanized and industrialized regions, an area where eight million people live, it has the most extensive public forest system of any major city in North America — over 67,000 acres in all. North Branch, where Packard was riding, is a string of mostly forested preserves buffering the North Branch of the Chicago River, 15 or so miles directly north of downtown Chicago.

As he rode, Steve noted that the edges of the forest looked like they might once have been grassy and prairie-like. He began to doubt they were always forest. He got off his bike for a closer look and thought to himself:

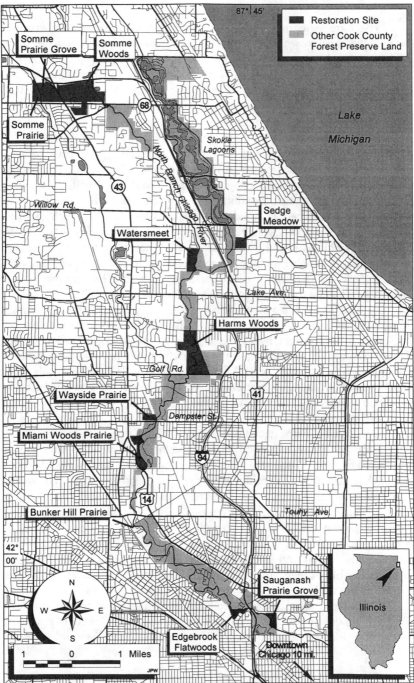

87° 45'

Restoration Site

Other Cook County
Forest Preserve Land

Somme
Prairie Grove

Somme
Woods

Lake

Michigan

68

Somme
Prairie

Skokie
Lagoons

43

Willow Rd.

Sedge
Meadow

Watersmeet

North Branch Chicago River

Lake Ave.

Harms Woods

Golf Rd.

41

Wayside Prairie

Dempster St.

Miami Woods Prairie

94

14

Bunker Hill Prairie

Touhy Ave.

42°
00'

Sauganash
Prairie Grove

Illinois

N

W   E

S

Edgebrook
Flatwoods

Downtown
Chicago 10 mi.

1   0   1 Miles

JPW

"These are remnant prairies. They're being massacred, mowed, wrecked by vehicles, overgrown with brush. But I could see that they were once prairies. At that moment, I remember becoming conscious of the commitment. I thought to myself: I could do something about this. But if I take this on, I could be stuck for a very long commitment. There is danger here. I'd hate to commit, involve lots of people, then have it crash. But then, can I just ride away from this?"

He decided he could not just ride away. He would work on saving the massacred prairies. He wrote letters, made phone calls, got in touch with a few key people. He was a '60s anti-war activist and he understood grassroots politics, the need to bring people together around a specific issue, the necessity of building an impassioned constituency. But what would be the issue around which people could rally? Packard recalled: "Though this was different, I understood how to organize people for a cause. I knew how to do this. The principles would be similar. That's when the idea of restoration came to me. I thought: we'll get people together to restore prairie in order to get people together, not really for restoration itself. The restoration idea was born of a need to build a constituency for these places."

But first Packard had to get the Cook County Forest Preserve District to agree to let ordinary people work on pulling brush and planting seeds on preserve lands. He kept badgering the supervisor of conservation of the Forest Preserve District, "badgering in a friendly sort of way — asking him the question in different ways," Packard recalled. "When he finally said, 'yes,' I yelled out loud, I was so happy. We were given the green light to do our little thing on five sites. I'm sure the guy thought: 'Oh, they'll get tired. This will go away.'"

Now, almost two decades later, it's clear that the conservation supervisor badly misjudged citizen involvement, as will many resource professionals steeped in first- and second-wave practice. He would later admit that there was some reluctance at having "outside forces" involved in the preserves for fear that their efforts could not be sustained.[21] Steve Packard, a man with unusual creative energy and passion for prairies and for engaging people in saving and enhancing biodiversity right in the midst of a major city, prevailed. Like Mary Ann Borch and Mary Stoertz, Packard provided the vision and inspired others. Then, everyday people, ready to touch something green and fascinated with restoring a native landscape, joined in the work.

With this in mind, we went to Chicago in mid-1994 to talk to Steve Packard and others who have now restored almost 20,000 acres of prairie in places just like the North Branch. Meanwhile, *New York Times* writer

William K. Stevens was at work on a book using the North Branch as its centerpiece. Stevens' book, published in 1995 as *Miracle Under the Oaks*,[22] engagingly relates the full story set in the context of what he interprets to be a national movement to revive nature. Here we highlight only a few of the accomplishments in this compelling story of environmental restoration in the midst of freeways and corporate parks.

ↄ

Once Steve Packard got permission for volunteers to try to restore prairies in the Forest District, he obviously needed some volunteers. At a local chapter meeting of the Sierra Club in 1977, he made a brief but apparently convincing presentation, got 13 people to sign up, and set off on a journey that has outlasted not only most of the county resource professionals on duty at the time but also the handful of people working on the first five sites. "The thirteen original people melted away," said Packard, "but I expected that." Seventeen years later, they had been replaced by 3,000 volunteers, members of a vast Volunteer Stewardship Network, restoring prairies at 150 sites around Chicago and its suburbs. Their ultimate goal is to restore 100,000 acres, including forest preserves, corporate campuses, greenways, and other as yet undeveloped tracts.

What was it like in the beginning? How did Packard and others create such an impressive volunteer system? He insists that building community was the key. With just a few volunteers, his strategy was to stay in touch with volunteers on and between work days. People would gather and work hard on Sunday mornings, have lunch together, decide what to do next. During the week, Steve would telephone them and ask "What did you think of last week? What should we be doing differently? Who do you know that might be interested? Do you talk to people about this? What do you tell them?" Early on, he says, the most important thing was making people feel part of an important effort — part of a community. "We didn't have meetings. We talked on a very personal level in the field. We made decisions, often by consensus, while we were having lunch. I would explain what we're doing: 'We're building a congregation for these sites; they're just like cathedrals over the centuries. They need a congregation that can last forever. Individual people will die but the congregation will go on forever.'" After a while, there was a kind of religious fervor about it."

In the formative years, Packard carefully built congregations and tenderly nurtured and protected "the creativity and good-heartedness" of communities of volunteers from conservation bureaucrats — people within the Nature Conservancy (his own employer), people in the scientific community who thought they knew more than the volunteers, and those working for state and county agencies. "I absorbed a lot of flak, took endless hits, threw my body in the path to protect this wonderful thing taking hold. I believed that the major threat to this effort was that creative, good-hearted, smart people would be driven off and the leadership would go to defensive, crabby, confrontational or passive, cynical people."

Packard wrote a grant to the Chicago Community Trust to stabilize the project, make it official, and to set up what would be called the "Volunteer Stewardship Network." The grant came through: a kingly sum of $15,000 spread over three years. Packard then had to spend the next three years convincing the Nature Conservancy that a volunteer network would work. It was a tough sale. The Conservancy felt their job was buying land and managing their own preserves, not engaging the community in the business of restoring biological diversity on public lands. "These are now accepted principles in the organization," says Packard. Laurel Ross, current co-ordinator of the Volunteer Stewardship Network, added "We've finally become known as the most mature volunteer program in the Nature Conservancy and we're getting serious attention at the national level."

"We've come a long way," Packard concludes. "In 1986, they wanted to close down the Volunteer Stewardship Network; they wanted to fire me."

As for the work itself, what began as "cutting a little brush and scattering a few seeds" in time expanded to a wide span of restorative activities such as cutting trees, collecting seeds from within a 50-mile radius of the site, growing plants in backyard nurseries all over the city, transplanting, and ultimately, controlled burning. No one had done exactly what the North Branchers were trying to do. No one had tried to rebuild a prairie with masses of volunteers starting from a forest. There were prairie restorationists at work who were starting from corn fields, plowing them and planting seed. But Packard intuitively sensed even though this prairie had been long covered with woodland, it would be possible to uncover a much richer prairie faster without disturbing the soil. He was reluctant at first to bring in too many scientists for fear of dampening volunteer enthusiasm. In Packard's opinion, "In the scientific community, there were some Eeyores out there who would say, 'No, this just won't succeed.'"

His intuition was on target, for the early projects were indeed successful, and not only at restoring prairie. As Steve Packard read more, studied maps and old photos, and worked in the emerging prairies, he became convinced that the remnant forested lands represented not only prairie edges but also a heretofore only partially described community. What he discovered, rediscovered really, was an oak/grassland community, historically influenced and maintained by regular burning by Indians over the centuries of occupation prior to contact.[23] As a picture of the tallgrass savanna took shape, the numbers of volunteer organizations and volunteers grew exponentially. The network now stretched beyond Cook County and Chicago into surrounding counties and suburbs.

Rediscovering a vegetation mosaic and ways to restore it are notable accomplishments in their own right. To us, however, the real story is how Packard and his colleagues invented a fresh and intoxicating way to draw neighborhood people into a huge citizens' workforce whose main purpose is none other than healing portions of their own city. People with little or no knowledge or experience in the restoration of native habitat, people for whom the concept of biodiversity is mostly unknown — at least at the onset — have taken up the work of prairie and savanna restoration in one of the world's biggest cities. They have become local experts in grasses, wildflowers, butterflies. They have sprouted seeds in their kitchens and turned their backyards into native nurseries. They have engaged themselves in "the particulars of the planet" as they experience them, to use the words of Mattole restorationist, Freeman House.[24]

Ultimately, thousands would join this network, they would raise funds and gather support from community organizations, businesses and schools, and they would restore not only North Branch but dozens of other sites around Chicago. Though on the surface this case looks nothing like the other places we've written about, in fact it is an exceptionally good illustration of third-wave resource management, for it is done by locally based citizen groups — each with its own structure and mission; it empowers ordinary people, who then have some of the same kinds of authority as the resource organizations with which they're in partnership. The key thing, according to Steve Packard, is that they are outside the guild structure of the resource professions, yet they have both the power and responsibility to make significant local resource decisions.

Their quest to understand the vegetation they were trying to restore is a consequence of tenaciously good research, curiosity about and deep knowledge of the plant world, reasonable hypotheses, and patience in the trial and error process of testing results in the field. Here in the most unlikely of places, the pathway to a more local form of resource management was the reconstruction of a phantom landscape. Like some powerful new religion, it attracted hundreds of converts — proselytes with pruning shears and disciples dedicated to restoring a patch of pre-contact biodiversity in their own neighborhoods. Their newly formed stewardship groups not only helped the Preserve District do work they could not afford, but also took on other projects, from river cleanups to community gardening.

The limited initial focus on restoration of prairies and savannas soon touched off a wildfire of new resource management proposals for Greater Chicago, including greenways and corridors, water quality improvements, naturally landscaped corporate parks, and attention to the Lake Michigan waterfront and surrounding rivers. The restored prairies and savannas would be the core of a vast biosphere reserve, not unlike that of the Eastern Shore of Virginia, but on a much grander scale. Ironic as it may sound, a diverse set of residents and representatives of many government agencies together with a number of private environmental organizations and foundations recently mapped out the "Chicago Wilderness Biosphere Reserve." They have received funding for the first steps. If they are successful, Chicago Wilderness would become one of the most dramatic and far-reaching attempts to plan, manage and restore natural functions in a complex urban area. It aims at nothing less than "rediscovering and saving native Chicago — its prairies, sloughs, river corridors, wetlands, savannas and forests."

This bunch of new Copernicans, empowered and energized by a virtually unlimited range of possibilities growing out of new values and new language, has inspired others to come on board. They now seem incapable of remembering the old way of doing business and they are willing to imagine an uncanny future. Will their dream of 100,000 acres of restored prairie and savanna come true? Who can say? Who would have predicted that Steve Packard's bike ride 20 years ago would have drawn thousands into his fold? Who would have ever imagined a Chicago Wilderness could exist again?

THE MORAL OF THE STORY

ც

———————— Part Three ————————

Envisioning the Goal
—— Chapter Eleven ——

In relation to the earth we have been autistic for centuries. Only now have we begun to listen with some attention and with a willingness to respond to the earth's demands that we cease our industrial assault, that we abandon our inner rage against the conditions of our earthly existence, that we renew our human participation in the grand liturgy of the universe.

— Thomas Berry[1]

We journeyed from Maine to California to determine whether there might be someone participating in the "grand liturgy of the universe" and beginning to fashion a more sustainable lifeway. We didn't find Eden. We found communities with myriad challenges and enormous, complex problems. None of them could be described as sustainable. Yet, all of them inspired optimism and had a hopeful story to share. Many of the people we encountered seemed to understand that radically different approaches will be required to solve the resource problems they have inherited and to ensure that they do not continue the legacy of exploitation into the next millennium. In their efforts to rebuild their communities, or save their communities, or define their communities, all of them seemed to have stumbled on a truth that was intimated thousands of years ago: "Without vision the people perish."[2]

If we are to move from this environmental Dark Age into an Age of Sustainability, we will need a new vision of the goal. Where are we going? What would success look like? What would a community need in order to practice sustainable resource management? To answer these questions, we coupled the hopeful visions of the people we met with the writings of Aldo Leopold and other teachers and our own observations and experiences. In doing so, we found a set of ideal characteristics. What follows are eight characteristics which, if practised, we believe would lead inexorably to a more sustainable relationship with the earth.

A GOOD WORKING KNOWLEDGE OF THE ECOSYSTEM

It's amazing. If I flipped to any bird in my bird book, most any person here could tell you what it was, whether it was here, and in which season you could find it.
— Steve Albert[3]

To practice sustainable resource management, a community must first understand the basic ecology of their home place. A good working knowledge of the ecosystem that sustains them would begin with an awareness of the smallest parts. It would continue through an attempt to understand the system as a whole to the greatest extent possible.

The decisions of this community would be based first on an understanding of the living framework that supports it. Members of this community would realize that they were a part of a community of interdependent parts and would strive to comprehend all they could about this vast, complex array of species and populations. They would look to see: What are the parts? How do they interact? Are some of them missing? Are some of them ailing? Soil microbes, burrowing animals, hurricanes — what natural processes are or should be at work? If lightning once resulted in regular fires, what was the natural frequency and intensity?

They would seek to understand the patterns: how animals move from place to place; how plants have sorted between different soils, altitudes or water regimes. They would have some understanding of how these inhabitants would change under different types of conditions. For as Paul Hawken notes, "In order to do anything about the planet where we live, we have to [first] know where we are."[4]

From soil processes to the dynamics of the atmosphere, from cycles that take days to those that take millennia, they would have as much understanding as possible about the place they wished to inhabit. And they would synthesize this knowledge in an overarching perspective on the system as a whole. They would recognize the truth of Kai Lee's observation that "the concept of ecosystem management...has a logical requirement: that one be able to see the ecosystem as a whole in some fashion." They would know that it takes "much less knowledge to exploit an ecosystem" than to try to live as a part of one.[5]

A COMMITMENT TO ECOSYSTEM HEALTH

How nature works should be a model for everything you do. Look to the river. Look to nature. You will find your answers there, no matter what the question.
— Dave Crockett[6]

When the visionaries of Chattanooga really looked at their river, they realized how profoundly out of balance they were. They also saw that by restoring the health of their river, they would find their way to a healthier community. In Plumas County, the community realized that the answer to what ailed them lay in healing their streams and forests. They would measure their success "not in board feet but in acres of forest and miles of stream restored."

To practice sustainable resource management, a community would have to possess a commitment to ecosystem health. They would know that the answers to any conflict lie not in balancing multiple demands but in seeking first to do no harm to the life-giving elements that sustain the future of the community. Armed with a workable understanding of the living infrastructure, the community would seek ecological balance as a guiding and underlying principle for all of their decisions.

This community would know that sustainability is not achieved by walking a tightrope between economic and environmental needs. This type of thinking leads to "habitats half protected,...economies weakened, and personal principles bargained away."[7] Like Virginia Eastern Shore residents, they would look, instead, for ways to create synergies: "ways that economic activity can promote a healthy environment and that healthy ecosystems can enrich their inhabitants, economically and otherwise."[8] When faced with the hard choices, however, a community seeking sustainability would have the wisdom and courage, like the Menominee, to make the decision to protect the health of the whole ecosystem of which humans are a part.

To be sustainable, a community would need to know something about how to read the vital signs of the health of their natural infrastructure. They would strive to understand and carefully monitor those aspects of the ecosystem that gave them a clear picture of the systemic overall health of the ecosystem. They would not be obsessed with monitoring only the "target" outputs from which they derived immediate economic returns.[9] Too often, communities are measuring only the amount of beef they can grow from the range or the oysters they can harvest in the bay. Using these outputs as the primary measures, grasslands turn to deserts and estuaries become salty, polluted lagoons before the community realizes that change is necessary if they are to appreciate those outputs over the long term. Sustainable resource management requires that the community track and protect the health of the "life-giving support systems. [Those ecological processes that] shape climate, cleanse air and water, regulate water flow, recycle essential elements, create and regenerate soil, and enable ecosystems to renew themselves. These are [what] keep the planet fit for life."[10]

Ultimately, the community would know that ecosystem health is still more than what science and scientific measures can ever tell them. In the words of David Ehrenfeld:

> Health is an idea that transcends scientific definition. It contains values, which are not amenable to scientific methods of exploration but are no less important or necessary because of that.... If used with care within ecology, the idea of health can enrich scientific thought with the values and judgements that make science a useful and durable human endeavor.[11]

A COMMITMENT TO LEARNING

Jim Enote, the leader of the Zuni Conservation Corps in New Mexico, described development of the tribe's resource management plan in this way: "It is really a hybrid of many ideas, lots of good work going on in different parts of the world, and very old traditional Zuni technologies." To develop their plan they reviewed reports and plans produced by the "Bureau of Indian Affairs, the Forest Service, the Soil Conservation Service, the Swiss Red Cross, the United Nations Environment Program and so on." They looked at seed banking in Bolivia, a forest program in a mountain village in Mexico, a cultural project in a Gandhian village in India. They networked with over 35 different projects all over the world. They consulted their elders and leaders. "All of these people have contributed something. So we have had this great cultural and intellectual diversity. We could have just opened up the resource management books and said 'Let's go.' But our path has opened up so much more. This enormous spectrum of knowledge has given us zest and has added layer upon layer of ideas."

The citizens of a sustainable community would be at least this curious.

They would possess a profound and unfailing commitment to learning. They would see themselves as perennial students. They would recognize that the knowledge necessary to make good decisions on behalf of the environment and future generations is always changing. Consequently, theirs would be a culture of learning, always open to new ideas and information. They would know that the task of living as if all life mattered required awesome awareness and profound understanding and that they would always have incomplete knowledge. This realization would inspire humility, as they constantly balanced the need to make decisions with less than complete data.

Far from discouraging, the realization that knowledge and understanding is a constantly evolving state would inspire a vitality and excitement in the community. The community would not be a closed, parochial one where different ideas or points of view were seen as threatening. A community seeking sustainability would be like Florence during the Renaissance. Genius would be attracted to it. The community would invest in the ideas and dreams of the most innovative thinkers of their times. Creativity would be prized and nurtured in its schools and institutions. As in Chattanooga, the people making the day-to-day decisions would welcome the input of those who dream of a different tomorrow.

The citizens of this community would be willing to look from many angles to gather knowledge of their place. They would see conventional science as one way of knowing and aboriginal wisdom as yet another. Ultimately, the goal would be to learn, in the words of Leopold, "to think like a mountain."[12] To do this the students would seek to "have the humility and wisdom to accept nature as [their] teacher."[13] They would "embrace the arrangements that have shaken down in the long evolutionary process and try to mimic them, ever mindful that human cleverness must remain subordinate to nature's wisdom."[14]

They would recognize that they must take action based on insufficient knowledge. This would prompt them to ensure that they had adequate feedback loops by setting up their actions as experiments with "testable hypotheses." This would be one way to learn from their actions.[15]

And they would surely value pristine wild areas. These would be the benchmarks from which they could evaluate the success of their efforts in the landscapes they were managing. For, as Leopold observed, "We literally do not know how good a performance to expect of healthy land, unless we have a wild area for comparison with sick ones."[16]

RESPECT FOR ALL PARTS

If the biota, in the course of eons, has built something we like but do not understand, then who but a fool would discard seemingly useless parts? To keep every cog and wheel is the first stage of intelligent tinkering.

— Aldo Leopold[17]

To achieve sustainability, a community must have a basic land ethic and a basic human ethic. Its members must know without question that the first law of ecology is inexorable. Everything is related to everything else. They would extend their respect to all parts of the community, whether grand or small, understood or enigmatic, commonly used or seldom seen.

The great diversity of the planet would be something to prize and celebrate as it adds texture, beauty, useful resources and wonder to life. Natural elements of the community would not be separated in walled preserves or reduced to name cards in tamed parks. The built and wild components of communities would be integrated, interacting without seams, woven into the daily patterns of life. In this way, there would be a living awareness of the essential interdependence and a constant opportunity to learn.

A community seeking sustainability would appreciate that "human intelligence could not have evolved in a lunar landscape, devoid of biological diversity."[18] They would know that "elemental things like flowing water, wind, trees, clouds, rain, mist, mountains, landscape, animals, changing seasons, the night sky, and the mysteries of the life cycle gave birth to thought and language."[19] Constant contact with this well-spring of knowledge would inspire the poet, instruct the farmer, challenge the engineer and guide the leaders.

Sustainability would require that the community understand and appreciate that the land "is not merely soil; it is a fountain of energy flowing through a circuit of soils, plants, and animals. Food chains are living channels which conduct energy upward; death and decay return it to the soil." They would see that this circuit, of which they are a part, "is a sustained circuit, like a slowly augmenting revolving fund of life."[20] They would respect this circuit and all its parts for they would know that it renews them and can teach them how to live as human beings connected to and respectful of the creative force that spawned them.

A SENSE OF PLACE

Sustainability will not come primarily from homogenized top-down approaches but from the careful adaptation of people to particular places.

— David Orr[21]

A sustainable community would be deeply attuned to its home place. Members would possess a sense of balance and, as Wendell Berry describes it, of "harmony with his or her surroundings."[22] They would be able to define what is singular about where they live. They would live somewhere, not just anywhere or worse yet, nowhere.

They would know their home place by its history, its geography and its natural cycles. They would take their home seriously, celebrating its triumphant stories, learning from the losses and struggles of the past, and sharing in the nurturing myths that provide wisdom and direction. They would take their cues for how to live from the "ecological realities"[23] of their lifescape.

Sense of place and citizenship rooted in place would not be static and ideological like nationalism. For they would be citizens of a place that was living and dynamic, defined not by political boundaries or outdated legal codes but by organic connections. What would constitute good citizenship would be rooted in one's ability to understand those connections and live as an integrated part.

Their commitment to a common place would be a common bond. Their home is worth caring about, sacrificing for, knowing and protecting. Decisions would be based on a shared desire that their children and their children's children will be able to live well in this place.

Sense of place would foster a community of people who understood they were connected deeply to each other by the inexorable workings of nature, the interconnectedness of life and the richness of their common history. Because they had this knowledge of their home and its history, they would understand that the Law of Thermodynamics ("For every action there is an equal and opposite reaction"), the Golden Rule, and the Law of Karma are one and the same thing. They would know that regardless of the rules they decree, these superordinate laws will be the final determinant of the health of the community.

Ultimately, to achieve sustainability members of a community must become "shaped" by their place. Being shaped by their country would not mean they all had the same thoughts, same ideas, beliefs, or angle of vision. Rather, inhabiting a place together would result in "shared values that give [them] the capacity to do difficult and important work together."[24]

ACCEPTANCE OF CHANGE

We're seeing so many changes on the land, in conservation, in the market, in the agencies. If we don't change, too, we aren't going to make it.
— Wendy Warner, Rancher, Douglas, Arizona[25]

A community in balance with its natural resource base understands that change is both inevitable and unpredictable. Knowing this, members would seek to foster natural and cultural systems that are capable of responding to change with the greatest resilience. As the Buddha stated, the only constant is change. In order to best adjust to this fundamental truth, a community practising sustainable resource management would not have such rigid and fixed expectations of its environmental resources that it would have no ability to be flexible in the face of change.

Ecologists C.S. Hollings and Kai Lee have the same advice for those who seek to manage environmental systems. They suggest that, given the inevitability of change and the unpredictable nature of the outcomes, it is always best not to aim for a rigid end product. It is better to aim for "resilience in the face of surprise."[26]

The management of ecological systems is thus a fundamental paradox. Before altering the environment, on whatever scale, sustainability requires that a community try to understand the behavior of the natural systems that sustain it, at the same time accepting that its knowledge will always be incomplete. The community would strive to make decisions that would be consistent with the natural direction of change in the ecosystem and attempt to identify, avoid and mitigate those changes that prove to be otherwise.

When a forest is made of different-aged trees it has many options. The older trees provide plenty of seed for reproduction. Their many branches, both living and dead, large and small, radiate in multiple directions and provide homes for many different animals. Their strength and stature inspires awe and gives good lumber for diverse uses. The middle-aged trees provide vigor to withstand the times of drought and are ready to occupy the canopy when an elder dies or is removed. Should there be a great storm that topples the larger trees, young trees will bend with the wind. Their resilience will ensure that there will be a forest over the long term.

To manage resources sustainably a community would have to think like this forest. They would understand that "to conserve well is to engineer within the rules of natural changes, patterns, and ambiguities; to engineer well is to conserve, to maintain the dynamics of the living systems."[27]

To embrace the inevitability of change is to realize that nature is replete with "discordant harmonies."[28] A sustainable community will be able to hear and play more than the simplest of melodies.

A Long-term Investment Horizon

Aldo Leopold spent his career working on the residual effects of over-grazing in the southwest, over-harvesting of wildlife and timber in the Midwest, and abusive farming in his home state of Wisconsin. He was constantly struck by the enormous impact that the settlers had in the brief time between their arrival and his. He recognized that these settlers came from a culture that was used to moving on when the land was depleted. He mused that "as long as six virgin continents awaited the plow, this was perhaps no tragic matter — eviction from one piece of soil could be recouped by despoiling another."[29] He also saw that on many of the projects he supervised, the cost of repairing damage generally outstripped the value of the land itself. Leopold noticed that often when the land became so despoiled as to be a threat to neighboring lands, it was the government that would be left with the burden of the cost of repair or acquisition. But as long as natural resources were thought of only as commodities to be traded in a market that had conceived of no way to truly value them, exploiting and moving on was the only thing that made sense.

Paul Hawken is talking about this same problem when he observes that "the single most damaging aspect of the present economic system is that the expense of destroying the earth is largely absent from the prices set in the marketplace."[30] This failing is not the domain of capitalism. The experiments of other economic systems have been no more effective at establishing the true worth of fundamental resources or the true cost of their loss.

A community prepared to make the right decisions on behalf of the natural infrastructure would have a means of valuing the natural capital and a commitment to preserving this capital long-term. Regardless of what economic "ism" they embraced they would ensure that it adequately incorporated ecological thinking and the ecological realities of living in their place.

They would think about "the seventh generation" and make decisions that would ensure that the natural resource returns, far into the future, would be as stable, diverse and secure as possible. In the face of absolute ignorance they would be conservative. Knowing that they would "never know more than a small part of what [they] need to know...[they] would keep the scale of their projects small, and...be ready to go back when things go sour."[31]

Just north of the Menominee reservation along the wild and scenic Wolf River, there is a proposal to mine a large deposit of copper. There is much concern in the surrounding communities about the proposed mining. Some of the Menominee have joined with other locals in urging that the copper mine be denied approval. We asked one of the tribe's leaders how the Menominee might react if a similar deposit were found on Menominee Land. He responded as follows:

> I don't believe the people would allow such major scarring of the land. The reason I say this is many times in the past these people were very poor. They could have liquidated their forest and been much better off but they chose not to. I don't think they would choose something that drastic today. They probably would say, 'If we destroyed our forest now to get the copper, we and our children wouldn't have the trees, the clean rivers, the fish and the deer. Maybe in time, someone will find a way to get copper out of the ground that would do less damage. Then it will be there for that generation and they will still have the forest and rivers, too. We can wait for that time.'[32]

As long as gold and stocks are seen as the necessary capital to sustain life, communities will be compelled to convert whole forests to cash and entire mountainsides to bonds. Sustainability requires that a community feel itself linked to the land and to those who will live there after its members. They must grasp the essential truth that the capital upon which their life and all life depends is the living infrastructure of the planet. If they do, they will fashion an economic system with the discipline and wisdom to invest for the long term.

ABILITY TO SET LIMITS

To be sustainable would be to act with the knowledge that ecosystems have tolerances and you cannot push them with abandon. To do so is reckless adolescent folly. To derive sustainable benefits from a resource, members of a community would have to have the maturity to tell themselves "no" when something is going to compromise the system's health. They would have to set limits.

Some of the lobstermen of Monhegan, Maine, had watched the demise of the halibut fishery in their lifetimes. They knew that to have a viable lobster fishery into the next generation they had to protect the reproductive capacity of the species and they had to limit the catch. They agreed amongst themselves to abide by the most restrictive conditions for their industry in all of Maine. As a result, 50 years later, they have a viable industry and a village that still maintains its relationship with the sea.

The Monhegan lobstermen's visionary act of setting limits to consumption and behavior was followed by the community's decision to restrict construction and uses in the recharge area of the island's freshwater aquifer and to place restrictions on development activities along the shoreline. Over 90 per cent of the residents of the island agree with these decisions. These people understand that they live together on a tiny island. They love the island and its way of life. They are setting limits on themselves in the interest of ensuring that their collective right to live safely together on a beautiful island is assured for the future.

In a sustainable community, decisions about how to use a resource would not be derived through an indifferent government process that focuses on procedure rather than common good. This type of "procedural politics" encourages individuals to ruthlessly pursue only those outcomes that are of importance to the one.[33] In this type of system, indifferent decision-makers will at best, strike a compromise. This approach, therefore, prompts each individual with a personal stake in the outcome to aggressively push for their singular interests. A community seeking sustainability would replace the whining harangues that represent procedural politics with what Steven Covey claims is the highest form of human functioning: highly self-actualized individuals collaborating towards a common good.[34]

The community would rely on its most informed understanding of the native ecosystem, its commitment and love of home place, and long-term economic interests to establish workable limits to resource use. This information would be considered and weighed through collaborative discussions. The many remaining unanswered questions would not be used to obfuscate and confuse a government bureaucrat whose main objective is to keep from getting sued. Threats and exposés would not be trumped up to neutralize a career politician with obvious ties to one or the other side. The decision would come from the participants themselves. They would understand that they directly bear the responsibility for the effects of their decision. The decision would be evaluated through disciplined monitoring programs designed to provide them with constant and honest feedback. Establishing limits and understanding the effectiveness of these limits would then become the true practice of resource management.

Caring parents do not allow their three-year-old to decide how many sweets to eat in a day. Nor will these parents give their teenager unlimited freedom, regardless of how loudly they cry "unfair." This type of parent understands that, over the long term, the effects of such indulgence will have negative consequences not just for them, but for the sanctity of the home and the health of the child. Similarly, a responsible community would not allow individuals with very limited knowledge or a short-term interest in the viability of the community to bludgeon them into making decisions that compromise the long-term health of the environment of their home place. The maturity to set and maintain limits will ultimately be the true measure of progress along the path towards sustainability.

IN SUMMARY

These eight characteristics (a good working knowledge of the ecosystem; a commitment to ecosystem health; a commitment to learning; respect for all parts; a sense of place; acceptance of change; a long-term investment horizon; ability to set limits) are facets of one central notion: all life does not revolve around the human species, any more than the sun revolves around the Earth. We human beings, though glorious in our complexity and endowed with a consciousness both profoundly inspiring and perplexing, are but one part of the global lifescape. Lacking this understanding, we have become deeply lost. When we begin to truly see that this new view of the cosmos is right, we will be inspired with new ideas and boundless new energy for the long journey home. And we will finally be able to navigate with grace and accuracy.

Finding the Path:
The Work We Must Do
———— Chaper Twelve ————

But each man and each woman of you I lead upon a knoll,
My left hand hooking you round the waist,
My right hand pointing to landscapes of continents and the public road,
Not I, not any one else can travel that road for you,
You must travel it for yourself.

— Walt Whitman[1]

The explorers we met are trying to chart a course toward a fresh definition of home and a new way of living there. Their course has taken them part way. As they told us their stories, we tried to stand on the "knoll." We tried to see if there was a discernible road that others might follow. As we listened and watched, a set of circumstances, practices, and personalities seemed to repeat themselves. We have come to think of these as mileposts along the path to sustainable resource management.

We can name these mileposts but we advise you to be wary of the comfortable linearity of the path; it is already well worn and it alone cannot bear truth. "In a sense everything...is off the path," writes poet Gary Snyder. "The relentless complexity of the world is off to the side of the trail.... We must wander through it to learn and memorize the field...holding the map in mind."[2]

What kind of map have we been holding?

The mileposts were not present in their entirety in every case. Yet communities who appeared to be making the most progress seemed to have moved past the greatest number of mileposts. The more we tried to draft a map, the more we realized how little we know. Our map will someday be viewed as a primitive first attempt. We invite you to mark up our map, to reconfigure it and to discover your own mileposts. We assume you'll find oversimplifications and misinterpretations. We present our map that it might inform your own journey and challenge you to chart your own course, away from the path we have found. For, after all, that is where the work must be done. That is where you will find your own ecology of hope.

VISIONARIES

Jeremy Seabrook, in a book about the Right Livelihood Award,[3] notes that all winners of this award have had a clear view of an alternative future, a future in which the consumptive, predatory culture is displaced by something gentler and saner. Being able to imagine a better future is a "necessary step," he says, "beyond the warnings and the analyses."[4] We concur. In every case we, too, have found a key person or persons who could envision a freshly conceived alternative future and who could put it into words the community understands.

What is essential about visionaries in these stories is that each possesses knowledge of vital connections between the natural ecosystem and the human community. All realize there is need for more ethical treatment of the living fabric that surrounds them. All can see a doorway between the old ways of their communities and a new future. They can point to the doorway so others can see it. Even if they cannot see beyond, they can see the value of going through. Dave Crockett knew that the river would bring Chattanooga back to life. The Menominee chiefs knew that if the forest remained whole the people would survive. Freeman House understood that if the people looked at the salmon, the whole valley would come into focus.

Aldo Leopold wrote that "the case for a land ethic would appear hopeless but for the minority which is in obvious revolt against these 'modern' trends."[5] The visionaries we encountered are part of this minority, not only revolting against destructive "modern" ways of managing the planet's resources but also possessed of wisdom and assurance, energy and new ideas, and the ability to inspire others. Ted Edison, deeply knowing Monhegan's beauty and its finely balanced political economy, returned with a plan to preserve for posterity Monhegan's wildlands. He knew that it would never be accomplished until put in the language of the people. Monhegan Associates was his particular stroke of genius. So also could it be said of the prophets of each place.

What drives these people? First, they seem to tap into a particular kind of wisdom; they not only have a picture of what the future might be but they also have words to describe it. "Gather the people around the idea of life in this creek," said Mary Stoertz of Monday Creek. "In ecosystem management, ecosystem is the capital and you live off the interest," Leah Wills teaches anyone in Plumas who will listen. "Start with the rising sun and work toward the setting sun" were the visionary words of the Menominee chiefs. "Enter the watershed through the life of the salmon," urge Mattole Salmon Group restorers.

The breakdown zone of clashing paradigms, the zone we now occupy, is a troubling time. Visionary personalities, few and often ignored, seem to understand the risks and obligations of this time. As futurist Richard Slaughter writes, for many reasons, ordinary people at first block out visionary thinking: "vested interests, dated attitudes, entrenched bureaucracies, and (initially at least) lack of public support" are all impediments.[6] But people with foresight know how to confront these obstacles, how to inspire the people.

"I know how to do this," said Packard, of restoring Chicago's faltering prairies, and indeed he did. What makes him a special person in our story is that his vision empowered thousands of others.

SMALL SUCCESSES

Any organizer of a volunteer effort will tell you that its future rests on building a track record, moving from small victory to small victory, building momentum, keeping people in the fold. Despite a bevy of setbacks in re-establishing prairie in the North Branch, Steve Packard kept his band of volunteers engaged from season to season by taking incremental steps that promised success. John Balaban, one of the most committed, told us that those early little successes seem in retrospect insignificant, but at the time they loomed large. "Little things — plants that would take hold, successful seed collecting missions, buckthorn successfully pulled from a site — these helped us get from one season to the next," he said.

Success tangibly demonstrates that a piece of the vision, however small, can be accomplished. This old axiom applies in case after case. For Plumas it was the early stream restoration projects that had immediate sensual and ecological impact: trout returned, the music of waterfowl reverberated across the meadows of Red Clover Creek. The stream projects also attracted a broad cross-section of local people who proved they could work together. As erosion co-ordinator Leah Wills whimsically remarked,

"After nine years of working together, the only thing that has sex appeal and lasts is success."

For the Mattole, it was an estuary project that pulled together citizen activists, government resource professionals, timber company people. At the end of the day there was a sense of accomplishment and a surge of new energy for the Watershed Alliance. Sanford Lowry told us, "We should do that again."

In Chattanooga, launching Vision 2000 required something small at first. After all, the river had been a sink for industrial wastes for 140 years; it could not be cleansed overnight. Nor would air quality be improved instantly, downtown be revitalized immediately, nor many of the dozens of other initiatives come to pass quickly. What worked was a highly visible and desperately needed women's shelter. Marty Bruell, the chair of Chattanooga Venture, called the project "a powerful beginning." It not only launched almost a billion dollars of new initiatives, it said to those members of the community who felt most alienated, "you are a critical part of this city's efforts to restore itself."

For Malpai, after a successful interagency burn, a grass bank plan, and agreement on a series of baseline studies, one rancher waxed lyrical, claiming "there isn't anything we can't do." It is precisely this sense of can-do optimism, grounded in small successes, that propels fragile experiments forward.

"Resist at all costs the temptation to do big fancy things. Go for success first."[7]

A PRECIPITATING CRISIS

If, as futurist Hazel Henderson believes, we are in a time of profound cultural change, a state of confusion "as our culture and those of most other industrial societies...shifts to the not-yet-defined 'post-industrial' phase,"[8] then it is not surprising that crises abound. Not only are institutions governing how resources are allocated and managed coming unstuck, but so also are the values underlying them. It is impossible, says Richard Slaughter, to think of the problems of our era "as if they were somehow separate from the systems of value and meaning which created them in the first place."[9] Diagnosing the meaning of crisis enables us to move beyond crisis. "Knowing what has gone wrong constitutes an important step in putting things right."[10]

A crisis has other advantages. When everyone's future is at stake, community pops into place; historic alliances and differences suddenly fade.

In traumas, such as accidents or earthquakes, psychologist Scott Peck says community almost automatically happens. A collective spirit and a consciousness of shared humanity well up and create strong bonds. Though genuine community may not survive the particular crisis and prolonged crisis can lead to retrenchment, far from being aberrant, crises are normal, just as natural ecological disturbances are normal. Community health may, in fact, be determined not by the absence of crisis but by the recognition of crisis and the way it is encountered.[11]

An activist in Virginia reminded us of the Chinese adage that the word for crisis in that language has two characters: one for "danger," the other for "hidden opportunity." She speculated that people in her community, the Eastern Shore, in dealing with the twin crises of an impoverished economy and runaway tourist development, seemed to have arrived at what Henderson calls "the politics of reconceptualization."[12] That is to say, crises shake people enough to let them break free of old conceptions.

Peck believes we achieve the greatest degree of psychological health when we can sense the drama of life, see the many "crises" that abound, and learn how to use them creatively.[13] In our communities, crises need not be contrived; they merely need to be recognized, met head-on, treated as hidden opportunities. Peck writes that the absence of community is itself a crisis:

> Indeed we must recognize that we live in a time in which our need for community has itself become critical. But we have a choice. We can keep on pretending that this is not so. We can continue refusing to face the crisis until the day when we individually and collectively destroy ourselves and our planet. We can avoid community until the end. Or we can wake up to the drama of our lives and begin to take the steps necessary to save them.[14]

Taking the steps necessary will require seizing opportunities perhaps now concealed by a misunderstanding of the role of crisis in our collective lives.

Crisis is surely one of the markers on our particular journey. In each place we stopped, a crisis opened doors, brought former adversaries to the table, cast new light on the dispiriting resource politics of "derision and division," and helped communities break through to hear the words of somebody with vision (and of each other). Whether loss of access to the shore for lobstermen on Monhegan or loss of wide open spaces for cattle farmers and ranchers in the Malpai, folks recognized things had gone awry, that their very way of life was at stake. And this became the first step to putting things right. In Plumas, Bill Coates recognized crisis as an opening for the Quincy Library Group when he lamented: "Our small towns were already endangered. This was going to wipe them out."[15]

By sensing the opportunity in crisis, Coates manifested an important quality of leadership. Good leaders know how to capitalize upon the sudden openness that a time of crisis creates. The reverse is true, too. Bad leaders will turn crises into fearful times by vilifying others and fanning the flames of prejudice.

Sensing hidden opportunities in a crisis may seem a transparently obvious marker. It's surprising that most communities haven't figured it out. Along the pathway, we encourage a search for the resource crises that mark special opportunities. This is when "the good news in the bad news becomes apparent."[16]

COLLABORATIVE ELEMENTS

When communities break through the barricades blocking sensible long-term management of local natural resources, they also seem to leap over the selfsame obstacles blocking good communication and decision-making. They appear to break into a new, more mature expression of democracy. The old conception of democracy, where the majority rules, leads to a system where every important decision is either a yes or no vote. This results in oversimplification of issues and to the formation of rancorous and unnecessarily polarized factions around every decision. Consequently, as David Chrislip notes, "the means to effect change in communities has pitted advocacy groups, elected leaders and influential citizens against one another." Thus, Chrislip continues, "leaders have focused on bringing together groups of people or interest coalitions to overpower others. When [this system] works, it leaves people divided. When it does not work, it leaves gridlock."[17]

The communities we visited have begun to see that the health of their environment cannot be left to the whimsy of such a process. When this realization begins to emerge, the black/white, either/or, them/us dichotomies that have stymied generations begin to be replaced by a spirit of complementarity. "The debate moves beyond the 'either competition or co-operation' argument, to the understanding that both these equally important principles are operating simultaneously and at every level in all human societies and in Nature."[18] Our case studies seem to substantiate this. Because people in these communities love the place they call home, they also seem to understand that neither rugged individualism nor government regulation will lead to resource management that fully respects the particularities of the place. Collaboration — working together in a joint effort in which self-interest becomes coterminous with community interest — is the answer.[19] Mary Walker counted collaboration as one of the most important qualities sustaining Chattanooga's momentum, and look where that led!

Collaboration itself is composed of several discernible elements:

Collaborative Leaders: People willing to work in collaborative ways are crucial to success. Collaborative leaders are respected long-time residents of the community; they can see the core idea clearly and communicate it effectively in language stakeholders and residents can understand. "Start where the people are in the language they are using," said Geri Spring, a truly collaborative leader in Chattanooga.

A collaborative leader is one who understands how to "bring the appropriate people together in constructive ways with good information [to] create authentic visions and strategies for addressing [the] shared concerns of the community."[20] The leaders we observed could bring the big idea to a cross-section of people in the community and allow others to develop connections and strategies themselves. Often these leaders are not very visible. They regularly prefer to put other people forward or to provide some tools or hints so that others will discover their own way.

Collaborative leaders are thus "servant leaders." In his book *Stewardship*, Peter Block describes a type of leadership that is dedicated to service rather than control. He recognizes that this type of leadership is necessary to move the culture of an organization from patriarchy to partnership.[21] In this type of organization individuals move toward becoming fully participatory and responsible adults concerned not only for themselves but also for the health and prosperity of the greater community.

Jane Cabarrus, NAACP President on Virginia's Eastern Shore, was effectively able to rise above historic divisions between the races, become an active participant in a wide range of partnerships, and assure her community that the current crisis on the Shore was unlike any other, that it represented new hope for African-Americans. Sherm Stanley on Monhegan, understanding full well what was at stake, took Edison's wildlands vision to the islanders and fishers, artists and summerfolk. Bill McDonald was able to bring other ranchers to an understanding of the need to come to the "radical center" if they were to find solutions to ecological and land subdivision threats to the lands of their ancestors. Sanford Lowry, the California rancher, took big risks with his own people when he opened up to ideas and information assembled by the Mattole Restoration Council. His request to have the council provide information to guide a proposed timber harvest on his own property legitimized the council to other long-standing residents of the region and helped launch the Mattole Watershed Alliance. All these leaders, and others we have not included, carefully used their own wisdom and authority to translate the new vision and to bring people into the emerging collaborative spirit.

And sometimes, "leadership isn't always leading," said Geri Spring of Chattanooga. "Leadership is sometimes standing back and letting things happen."

Collaborative Operators: If leaders are important in this new game of collaboration, so also are people who work hard to stitch together effective coalitions, task forces, work parties, and, above all, who understand group process. The "initiating group members," as Chrislip calls them, are absolutely essential to the collaborative effort. They are the ones who reflect diverse interests in the community. Collaborative operators are more than individuals who hold a place for one interest group or another. Collaborative operators are dedicated to insuring that any initiated process be fair and inclusive. These are people who have a natural talent for team work. They are good listeners, communitarians who see advantages in the emerging new coalitions, partnerships, and alliances. They are good information brokers. They are the ones who recruit other stakeholders into the process. They "assure the availability of sound information" and help to "locate resources — staff, facilitators, funding, etc — to carry out the collaborative process."[22] They are willing to be on the phone, to help set up meetings, smooth ruffled feathers, and, through their example and dedication, inspire others.

Susan Baremore, wife of logger Clay Baremore and Executive Director of Feather River Alliance for Resources and Environment, was a key collaborative member of the Quincy Library Group. Linda Blum, staunch environmentalist, a key person in the Friends of the Plumas Wilderness and local Audubon and Sierra Club chapters, was a driving force in the organized environmental movement in Plumas County. When these two women decided to talk directly to each other, to understand each other's points of view, and to search for a solution for their community that would work for both, they became an absolutely immutable force for positive change. The were highly effective collaborative operators. Theirs is the collaborative spirit that can break through winner/loser attitudes of the past.

Forum: In the stops along our journey, we often found that people had, of necessity, invented a new way of gathering divergent individuals and groups and enabling them to participate in a still-evolving vision. Such forums often bypassed established institutions. And it's no wonder. People are discouraged about the political and economic institutions of our day. A Kettering Foundation study a few years ago reported that people believe there has been "a hostile takeover" of the political process by special interests, lobbyists, and spin doctors. Yet Kettering also discovered that the concept of civic duty is not dead. People still want to participate; they just can't figure out how.[23]

More recently, Frances Moore Lappé and Paul Martin DuBois have uncovered a civic life, largely at the periphery of conventional politics and government, that is flourishing. If this "quickening democracy" is successful, they argue, the institutions taking shape will be unlike any we have known; they will take us to a different kind of government. Economist Robert Theobold thinks this implies the end of power as we know it. "People who say democracy is the end of the process...have completely missed the point. Democracy was a way of controlling power so it was not used as dangerously and as destructively as it used to be by dictators and kings. Now it is power itself that has to be abandoned."[24]

Nongovernment public interest groups often work collaboratively to offset "the other side." Government-appointed task forces with diverse interests such as corporations, government agencies, loggers, ranchers, bankers and real estate brokers are also a routine part of today's version of "open government." Public hearings that emerge from this process usually attract the same vocal people. "Other citizens, even when aware of the meeting," as Chrislip notes, usually "choose not to attend because they perceive no realistic possibility of making a difference."[25]

Forums that include all of these interests and provide for effective communication are still rare. Yet, as Daniel Kemmis rightly observes, it's difficult to imagine how communities can grow and once again become foundations of our civic culture without forums that include everyone. We agree. What is delightfully refreshing about the forums we've encountered — the councils, alliances, task forces, and visioning forums — is that they are much more inclusive than anything that preceded them. They are safe places for ideas to flow and for power, in the old sense, to be relinquished. And therefore they are paradoxically empowering.

Decision-making: Ideally, decisions in such forums are made by consensus. The group has to be willing to think like Quakers, to accept that everyone has a piece of the truth, to strive for solutions that break out of the tired legacies of compromise, Robert's Rules, winners and losers, and the politics of conflict where every issue is either right or wrong.

Intuitively, the Mattole Watershed Alliance understood this when they invited Quaker facilitator Caroline Estes to help them understand consensus and to train them. Out of that experience came the beginning of trust, though some still struggle with a process that is "clunky and slow." Freeman House's analogy describing the Mattole Watershed Alliance is typical of what we've seen — a 16-wheel cart with four wheels out of commission, a different four on different occasions.

Consensus isn't easy. People can be intoxicated by it in the early going. But when they get to the tough issues that have historically divided them, the honeymoon is over and many want to abandon the process. Few of the groups we came to know had really broken through to enduring consensus. Yet the "no blame" open nature of decision-making among partners in Co-ordinated Resource Management projects in Plumas has an impressive ten-year track record. "From day one all the CRM projects had to be voluntarily undertaken by the property owners and we agreed that the property owners would not be subject to blame for 100 years of resource history. All parties have to agree on the project design. We rarely vote."[26] Keeping the group together "through the long process of reaching implementable agreements" is a challenge for leaders and participants.

We asked Wendy Warner in the Malpai how they made decisions. She responded that they generally use consensus. The one time they failed to get consensus (one person didn't agree), they went ahead anyway and it turned out to be a bad decision. Everyone began to understand the benefits that come from laboring over consensus.

Our culture relishes individuality and competition, values that undercut consensus. "We live in a situation where people don't trust each other and the presumption is that everybody's out for themselves," Leah Wills observed. "But you still try to do something that's collaborative and involves many different participants." Keeping the ethic of consensus alive is important, for the process of seeking consensus is worthy in itself. When it works, it is inherently mystical and transformative.[27] And community is enriched beyond expectation.

For the more hard-nosed among us, those less enamored of mystery and transformation, the bottom line on consensus is that all parties, no matter their stature or power in the conventional sense, can be confident that their view of things, their piece of the truth, will be heard. The outcome is that virtually no one walks away the loser.

Inclusivity: It then follows that whoever is willing to contribute must be welcomed to the table. One of the roles of collaborative leaders is to assure that this will happen by using language that makes sense to a broad spectrum of viewpoints. The language, in other words, must speak of community, of common understandings of the place everyone calls home, whether a housing project in Chattanooga or an anciently occupied forest in northern Wisconsin. The Plumas proposal for "community stability" was drafted by environmentalists, loggers, timber executives, housewives and househusbands. Visioning in Chattanooga and the Eastern Shore of Virginia drew folk from the entire community, thousands of people in Chattanooga, hundreds in Virginia. MaiBelle Hurley, a city councilwoman of Chattanooga and a driving spirit of Vision 2000, encapsulates inclusivity in that city by saying "the only qualifications needed are that you must be hopeful and helpful."

Scott Peck writes that "the great enemy of community is exclusivity."[28] Exclusivity acts cliquishly to set up defensive bastions that make collaboration more difficult later. Since it is easier to exclude than to include, it takes leadership of the sort exercised by Coates at the Quincy Library or Weaver and Lowry in Mattole to open the door. The small society of Monhegan Island, with its New England town meeting, open to all, cannot easily be emulated on a larger scale. But the principle of allowing as much access as possible, that which Slaughter calls "a resurgent idea," is gaining ground across this continent. In light of the dark and divisive political landscape of our times it is an immensely positive sign, an idea whose time has come.[29] The advice one Chattanoogan gave us was, "Resist at all cost the thought that there are people who have nothing of significance to offer."

No matter how cumbersome collaboration may seem at first, over the long run it strengthens community. Collaboration helps people break through the unproductive resource battles that have divided us for a hundred years.

CELEBRATION OF PLACE

As the process of visioning and collaborative activities continue, trust and confidence build. The community begins to define a new sense of place, a sense which implies knowledge of ecological context. "Here" is distinctive. We realized how deeply important this could be when we read, with awe, the following on a sign near the Chattanooga River Plaza:

> Most of all this is Our Place. Chattanooga, Tennessee — Our Scale, Our History, Our Forms, Our ideas, Our river and mountains, Our festivals, Our ideals. Our energy.
>
> Ours is what will make a genuine place — belonging to, loved by, and cared for by the citizens of Chattanooga.

Chattanoogans have profoundly reinhabited their town not only as work but also as celebration.

We believe formal celebrations of place are vital benchmarks for sustainable community and ultimately for appreciation and good management of natural resources. They start to define home as unique. They encourage those who are already working and inspire others to join the caravan. They engender a sense of joy, pride and commonality of place. Chattanooga's river festival got Chattanoogans together, celebrating together, defining themselves as one community tied to the river. Celebrating those things that give life and context to a community can take a people to a new sense of place.

SHARED VISION

Wherever we went, when we asked community members what their place will be like in 20 years or 50 years, they responded in kind. They said they wish for stability and imagine a time of more quality, less consumption and waste, fewer "knock-down, drag-out battles." Or in the words of John Sheehan of Plumas: "I see a future in which we have retrieved the environmental integrity of this county, in which we are living off and managing the forests well, in which our children have both a prosperous economy and a high quality environment."[30] People may approach the future from different vantage points, but they share a similar vision and are letting go of their parochial interests. "I say when you've got a shared vision that something is possible, make it possible instead of hanging on to some parochial interest. Let that sucker go for the greater good."[31]

On Monhegan, decisions over the past two decades led to natural resource protection that over 90 per cent of the permanent residents passionately believed in. The historic village atmosphere, the beauty and biodiversity of the wildlands, fresh water from the aquifer, a stable fishing economy, no mass tourism, a year-round population: all are parts of an agreed-upon good life that will sustain generations to come. At the other end of the spectrum, a spectacular diversity of people in Chicago have divined a metro-biosphere reserve where red-tailed hawks forage along greenways, colorful and diverse prairie plants grace the edges of the forest preserves and highways, and wildlife and waterfowl inhabit corporate campuses.

"Sustainability," though not often mentioned per se, is somewhere near the heart of these dreams. Whether communities gradually mature into a more enduring relationship with the living resources of their neighborhoods or make the transition in great leaps, Lester Brown predicts it will be "extraordinarily satisfying." It will bring:

> a sense of excitement that our immediate forebears engaged in the building of fossil fuel-based societies did not have. In effect, we have embarked on a shared adventure, the building of a society that has the potential to be an enduring one. This awareness could begin to permeate almost everything we do, imbuing it with a sense of excitement — one that derives in part from the scale of the undertaking, which has no precedent, as well as from full knowledge of the risks and consequences of failure.[32]

This, in fact, is borne out by the hope that emerges from our stories.

Hope

If without vision the people perish, without hope, the vision withers. Hope, writes Bill McKibben, has sadly become a debased word, as overworked as "ecology" and "sustainability." Hope, McKibben argues, in environmental writing often means "wishing": wishing things were not as dire, wishing for scientific and technological fixes, wishing for fulfilment in the tinsel and trappings of our culture. But real hope, he says, "implies willingness to change."[33] We use all three words — ecology, sustainability and hope — unapologetically. Especially hope, for what distinguishes the people we've met and places we've visited is that they have vaulted beyond simply wishing. They are truly hopeful, for they are not only willing to change, they are changing. Even the Menominee, with thousands of years of forest life, like the forest itself, know they must be resilient. "I keep my mind open and clear," said Larry Waukau, "and I listen to the forest.... I have no fear...what I have is hope."

Wherever we travelled, we found this resiliency and optimism. "This can work." "An entirely new ball game...." "We can finally see some light." These are the words of our teachers, words which suggest that despair need not rule, even when all else seems gloomy. In spite of a grim short-term economy, the Quincy Library Group infuses the county with optimism. Bill Coates, the County Commissioner, put it this way: "I don't know anywhere in the United States an entire county has gotten environmentalists and people interested in jobs to agree on anything. All at once there are no sides. This is a brand new day." [34]

Tenacity

People draw strength from this optimism and extend it to another day. Tenacity, spirit, resolve are the very elements of endurance, elements required in the years ahead, years when the new paradigm of resource management will meet formidable resistance. There is no quick recipe for creating this kind of endurance. In Monhegan, when we asked a leader how he and others managed to abide with and constructively turn Maine's Land Use Regulatory Commission's complicated regulations into opportunities, he responded simply, "you just need resolve in dealing with the state. We stuck with it long enough to use it to our advantage."[35]

Against all odds, the Quincy Library Group keeps meeting, continues to push the Forest Service in new directions, continues to prove skeptics wrong. Environmental lawyer Michael Jackson says: "The power we have is the power of an idea we all agree on."[36] At this writing, after more than three years of struggle with the Forest Service, the Library Group continues to generate new initiatives, continues to gather the community around the vision of community stability.

Likewise, the Mattole Salmon Group, in their quest to bring back the salmon, encountered serious objections from bureaucrats in the resource agencies of California. Ultimately their competence and dedication yielded results. Not only did they get permission for the hatchbox program, but they also received state funding. Then, in the face of inflated community expectations, the group had to be honest: their program for salmon recovery would require the work of decades or even generations.

Most of the places we visited still need to learn the real meaning of tenacity, for their visions are fresh and their projects fledgling. They might note carefully Menominee resolve in staying with the instructions of their chiefs for six generations. Despite terrible poverty and the near collapse of their tribe, despite opportunities and temptations to liquidate their forest for quick profit, they kept their sights firmly locked on the long term: their forest productive and intact, in all senses, for many generations to come. That's the real meaning of tenacity.

Tenaciously staying with a resource program for the long haul, the

Menominee understand deeply, requires not only vision, collaboration and hope, it also requires a deep spiritual connection to the living community. This connection is alive and well in Menominee and sorely needed most everywhere else.

New Capital

No one can deny that money is needed to turn tentative volunteer-laden experiments into a lasting resource management framework. Capital is a powerful way of increasing resolve, extending energy, compounding good volunteer efforts, and attracting more visibility and support, monetary and otherwise. Capital in the thousands or hundreds of thousands of dollars seemed to be flowing into most project coffers. Chattanooga's initiatives have drawn almost a billion dollars of investment and the Eastern Shore of Virginia is pulling in tens of millions.

But money alone is not sufficient. Plumas Corporation Executive Director John Sheehan put it this way: "A good solution is the hardest thing to find. Good people to implement the solution...second hardest. And money the easiest." In Monday Creek's neighborhood, the Appalachian Regional Commission has thrown millions of dollars into environmental and community development projects over the past 30 years. Yet both degradation and poverty persist. By our reckoning, a home-grown partnership, rooted in a vernacular understanding of Monday Creek as a biophysical and cultural entity, implemented by people who live there, is likely to have a far better return on each dollar of investment. By the same token, in the absence of a community base, if just money had been thrown at the restoration of Red Clover Creek, Plumas residents might never have honed the skills necessary to craft a community stability proposal. Co-ordinated Resource Management projects in Plumas illustrate the importance of other ingredients: a shared vision of success, good working teams and leadership, a "no blame" rule, and a history of small successes. Money in the absence of changed values will usually just put a new face on a problem. When that wears off, the old face reappears, more battered than ever. Money without the shared vision embedded in an ecology of hope will never bring about systemic change of the order needed.

You Must Travel the Road Yourself

Leopold wrote that we must change our role from "conquerors" to "plain citizens." For at least three million years, humans have evolved with and impacted other life-forms, conquering the earth but never really divorcing themselves from it. We are all children of the Pleistocene, says David Orr, "...shaped by a wildness we can scarcely imagine."[37] If we and our natural companions are to survive and thrive, we must grasp this "wild" oneness and understand that the "conqueror role is eventually self-defeating."[38]

We believe this is beginning to happen.

Across the planet, there is a quiet revolution underway. It is called many things: sustainability, biophilia, collaborative planning, community-based conservation, ecological restoration, ecosystem management, bioregionalism, new resource management. It is taking people away from a view that the earth and its resources exist purely for humans to a belief that humans are part of the living earth. It is born of a new set of stories, a heightened ecological awareness, an understanding of limits, a new respect for all the "cogs and wheels." It is our best hope for a future on an earth in glowing good health, possessed of diversity, integrity, stability, and wild beauty.

We believe the revolution is happening at the bottom. It tiptoes into communities desperate for ways to escape legacies of bad resource management. What emerges — in the ways we list above and in much less time than we would have predicted — are partnerships among conventional adversaries, collaboration between government and nongovernment agencies, engagement of the private sector, deep involvement of ordinary people. Pride of place and confidence in a vision of a biologically and culturally restored region propel a new kind of activism, based not on resisting and finger pointing but on healing and working together, on collaborations as creative and diverse as the communities where they happen. It takes form in watershed restoration, saving species, forming land trusts, community forestry, clean-up campaigns, recycling, sustainable ways of using local resources like lobsters, rangelands, and forest preserves, and countless other imaginative ways. If you listen carefully to what people in these places are saying, if you observe what they are doing, you will see the stirrings of an ecology of hope. To experience it, you must travel the road yourself.

EPILOGUE

The questions which address themselves to each of us are: Will we recognize the mystery of this possibility? Will we be open to its opportunities: Are we willing to help it be pulled into the light of tomorrow? Will we turn away preoccupied or cynical, or will we step forward to assist?

These are not merely questions. They are the agenda of tomorrow, they are the exciting, irresistible invitation to each of us to abandon prejudgment and stubborn refusals to deeply hear one another. They are the program and means to make that leap of faith with each other which will move humanity and our earth into the new era of reconciliation and hope.

— Rabbi Herman Schaalman

ENDNOTES

Introduction

1. Thomas Berry, *The Dream of the Earth* (San Francisco: Sierra Club Books, 1988), 123.

2. Mary Pipher, *The Shelter of Each Other* (New York: G.P. Putnam Sons, 1996), 27.

3. William Stafford, as quoted in ibid., 271.

4. Pipher, *The Shelter of Each Other*, 25.

5. Aldo Leopold, "The Conservation Ethic," in *The River of the Mother of God and Other Essays by Aldo Leopold*, ed. Susan L. Flader and J. Baird Callicott (Madison: University of Wisconsin, 1933), 182.

6. Aldo Leopold, *A Sand County Almanac* (New York: Oxford Press, 1987), 224-225.

7. Ibid., 221.

8. Ibid., 223.

9. Wendell Berry, "Decolonizing Rural America," *Audubon* 3 (1993): 100-105.

10. David W. Orr, *Ecological Literacy* (Albany: State University of New York Press, 1992), 24.

11. James R. Hastings and Raymond M. Turner, *The Changing Mile: An Ecological Study of Vegetation Change With Time in the Lower Mile of an Arid and Semiarid Region* (Tucson: University of Arizona Press, 1965).

12. Daniel Kemmis, *Community and the Politics of Place* (Norman: University of Oklahoma Press, 1990), 114.

13. Pipher, *The Shelter of Each Other*, 271.

14. William Dietrich, *The Final Forest: The Battle for the Last Great Trees of the Pacific Northwest* (New York: Penguin Books, 1992).

15. Barry Lopez, as quoted in Pipher, *The Shelter of Each Other*, 266.

16. Pipher, *The Shelter of Each Other*, 271.

Chapter 1

1. Colin A. Ronan, *Changing Views of the Universe* (New York: Macmillan, 1961), 88-91.

2. A. Pannekoek, A *History of Astronomy* (London: George Allen and Unwin, 1961), 188.

3. Thomas S. Kuhn, *The Copernican Revolution: Planetary Astronomy in the Development of Western Thought* (Cambridge: Harvard University Press, 1957), 134.

4. Thomas S. Kuhn, *The Structure of Scientific Revolutions* (Chicago: University of Chicago, 1970), 92-110.

5. Marilyn Ferguson, *The Aquarian Conspiracy: Personal and Social Transformation in Our Time* (Los Angeles: J.P. Tarcher, 1980), 26.

6. Thomas Berry, *The Dream of the Earth* (San Francisco: Sierra Club Books, 1988), 203.

7. E.O. Wilson, *The Diversity of Life* (New York: W.W. Norton, 1992), 277.

8. World Resources Institute, *World Resources 1994-95, A Report by the World Resources Institute* (New York: Oxford University Press, 1994), 38.

9. Lester R. Brown et al., Vital Signs 1993: *The Trends That are Shaping Our Future* (New York: Norton, 1993), 32-33.

10. Paul Schneider, "When a Whistle Blows in the Forest," *Audubon* (January/February 1992), 42-49.

11. Kirkpatrick Sale, *The Green Revolution: The American Environmental Movement 1962-1992* (New York: Hill and Wang, 1993), 72-94.

12. Michael Frome, "Heal the Earth, Heal the Soul," *Crossroads: Environmental Priorities for the Future*, ed. Peter Borelli (Covelo, CA: Island Press, 1989), 249.

13. Matthew Fox, *Original Blessing* (Salt Lake City: Bear and Company, 1983).

14. Berry, *The Dream of the Earth*, p. 35.

Chapter 2

1. Roderick Frazier Nash, *American Environmentalism*, 3rd ed. (New York: McGraw-Hill, 1990), 6.

2. Roderick Frazier Nash, "The Potential of Environmental History," in *American Environmentalism: Readings in Conservation History*, 3rd ed. (New York: McGraw-Hill, 1990), 1-8.

3. Robert Gottlieb, *Forcing the Spring: The Transformation of the American Environmental Movement* (Covelo, CA: Island Press, 1993).

4. Edward Goldsmith, *The Way: An Ecological World-View* (Boston: Shambhala, 1993).

5. Aldo Leopold, A *Sand County Almanac* (New York: Oxford University Press, 1987), 188.

6. David Lilienthal, *Democracy on the March* (New York: Harper and Row, 1944), 50.

7. Conrad Richter, *The Awakening Land* (New York: Alfred A. Knopf, 1989), 8.

8. Freeman House, "Forgetting and Remembering the Instructions of the Land: The Survival of Places, Peoples, and the More-than-human" (Rufus Putnam Lecture, Ohio University, Athens, Ohio, April 1996).

9. Michael W. Robbins, "Environmentalists Defined," *Audubon* (September/October 1995), 4.

10. Quoted in Roderick F. Nash, *American Environmentalism*, 85.

11. Philip Shabecoff, *A Fierce Green Fire: The American Environmental Movement* (New York: Hill and Wang, 1993), 67.

12. Gifford Pinchot, *Breaking New Ground* (New York: Harcourt, Brace, 1947), 285.

13. Pinchot, *Breaking New Ground*, 505.

14. Pinchot, *Breaking New Ground*, 31.

15. Quoted in Stephen Fox, *John Muir and His Legacy: The American Conservation Movement* (Boston: Little, Brown), 289.

16. David Brower, *Let the Mountains Talk, Let the Rivers Run* (New York: Harper Collins West, 1995), 41.

17. Quoted in Fox, *Muir and His Legacy*, 290.

18. John Muir, *Our National Parks* (Boston: Houghton Mifflin, 1901), 1.

19. Oliver S. Owen and Daniel D. Chiras, *Natural Resource Conservation: Management for a Sustainable Future*, 6th ed. (Englewood Cliffs, NJ: Prentice Hall), 314.

20. Roderick F. Nash, *Wilderness and the American Mind*, 3rd ed. (New Haven: Yale, 1982), 326.

21. William Cronon, "The Trouble With Wilderness," *New York Times Magazine*, 27 August 1995, 42.

22. Donald C. Swain, *Federal Conservation Policy, 1921-1933*, University of California Publications in History, LXXVI (Berkeley: University of California Press), 169-170.

23. Stuart L. Udall, *The Quiet Crisis* (New York: Holt, Rhinehart and Winston), 137-138.

24. Les Line, "A System Under Siege," *Wilderness* 59, 210 (Fall 1995): 10-27; Ted Williams, "Seeking Refuge," *Audubon* 98, 3 (May-June, 1996): 34-45, 90-94.

25. Ron MacIsaac and Anne Champagne, eds., *Clayoquot Mass Trials: Defending the Rainforest* (Gabriola Island: New Society Publishers, 1994).

26. Garrett Hardin, "The Tragedy of the Commons," *Science* 162 (1968): 1243-1248.

27. H. Patricia Hynes, *The Recurring Silent Spring* (New York: Pergamon Press, 1989), 163.

28. Samuel P. Hays, *Beauty, Health and Permanence: Environmental Politics in the United States, 1955-1985* (Cambridge: Cambridge University Press, 1987), 14-15.

29. Public Law 91-190, 42, U.S.C 4221-4347, January 1, 1970, as amended by Public Law 94-83, August 9, 1975.

30. Gottlieb, *Forcing the Spring*, 124-125.

31. Kirkpatrick Sale, *The Green Revolution: The American Environmental Movement 1962-1992* (New York: Hill and Wang, 1993).

32. Wes Jackson, *Becoming Native to This Place* (Lexington: The University Press, 1994), 25.

33. Bill Devall and George Sessions, *Deep Ecology: Living as if Nature Mattered* (Salt Lake City: Gibbs Smith, 1985), 43.

34. Timothy O'Riordan, *Environmentalism* (London: Pion, 1981), 11-19.

35. H. Patricia Hynes, *The Recurring Silent Spring* (New York: Pergamon Press, 1989), 162-163.

36. Hynes, *The Recurring Silent Spring*, 163.

37. Jeff DeBonis, "Natural Resource Agencies: Questioning the Paradigm," in *A New Century for Natural Resources Management*, ed. Richard L. Knight and Sarah E. Bates (Covelo, CA: Island Press, 1995), 159-170.

38. Thomas Berry, *The Dream of the Earth* (San Francisco: Sierra Club Books, 1988), 5.

39. Leopold, *A Sand County Almanac*, 203-204.

40. Daniel B. Botkin, *Discordant Harmonies: A New Ecology for the Twenty-first Century* (New York: Oxford University Press, 1990), 188.

41. Edward Goldsmith, *The Way: An Ecological World-View* (Boston: Shambhala, 1993), 381.

42. Curt D. Meine, "The Oldest Task in Human History," in *A New Century for Natural Resources Management*, 25-26.

43. Meine, "The Oldest Task," 26.

44. Kirkpatrick Sale, *The Green Revolution: The American Environmental Movement 1962-1992* (New York: Hill and Wang, 1993), 63-64.

45. For example, Steve Chase, ed., *Defending the Earth: A Dialogue Between Murray Bookchin and Dave Foreman* (Boston: South End Press, 1991), 19-21.

46. Planet Drum Foundation, P.O. Box 31251, San Francisco, CA 94131; New Society Publishers, P.O. Box 189, Gabriola Island, B.C. V0R 1X0, which publishes The New Catalyst Bioregional Series; Kirkpatrick Sale, *Dwellers in the Land: The Bioregional Vision* (Gabriola Island: New Society Publishers, 1991).

47. Van Andruss, Christopher Plant, Judith Plant, and Eleanor Wright, *Home: A Bioregional Reader* (Gabriola Island: New Society Publishers, 1990).

48. Jim Dodge, "Living by Life: Some Bioregional Theory and Practice," in *Home: A Bioregional Reader*, 10.

49. "Bioregional Directory and Map," *Raise the Stakes: The Planet Drum Review* 24 (Winter 1994/Spring 1995).

50. Scott Peck, *The Different Drum: Community Making and Peace* (New York: Simon and Schuster, 1987), 25.

51. Quoted in Edward Dumbold, ed., *The Political Writings of Thomas Jefferson* (Indianapolis: Bobbs Merrill, 1955), 97.

52. Jeffrey Friedman, *Planning in the Public Domain* (Princeton: Princeton University Press, 1987); Daniel Kemmis, *Community and the Politics of Place* (Norman: University of Oklahoma Press, 1990); Herman E. Daly and John B. Cobb Jr., *For the Common Good: Redirecting the Economy Toward Community, the Environment, and a Sustainable Future* (Boston: Beacon Press, 1989); Frances Moore Lappé and Paul Martin DuBois, *The Quickening of America: Rebuilding Our Nation, Remaking Our Lives* (San Francisco: Jossey-Bass, 1994).

53. Daly and Cobb, *For the Common Good*, 360.

54. Peter F. Drucker, *Post-Capitalist Society* (New York: HarperBusiness, 1993), 174.

55. Kemmis, *Community and the Politics of Place*, 11.

56. John Leo, "Community and Personal Duty," in *Changing Community*, ed. Scott Walker (Saint Paul: Graywolf Press, 1993), 30.

57. Peck, *The Different Drum*, 59.

58. S.T.A. Pickett and Richard S. Ostfeld, "The Shifting Paradigm in Ecology," in *A New Century for Natural Resources Management*, 261-278; Daniel S. Botkin, *Discordant Harmonies: A New Ecology for the Twenty-First Century* (New York: Oxford University Press, 1990).

59. Pickett and Ostfeld, "The Shifting Paradigm," 263.

60. Botkin, *Discordant Harmonies*, 189.

61. Pickett and Ostfeld, "The Shifting Paradigm," 266-267.

62. Kai N. Lee, *Compass and Gyroscope: Integrating Science and Politics for the Environment* (Covelo, CA: Island Press, 1993).

63. Jackson, *Becoming Native to This Place*.

64. Pickett and Ostfeld, "The Shifting Paradigm," 273.

65. Goldsmith, *The Way*, 222.

66. Bill McKibben, "Buzzless Buzzword," *New York Times*, 10 April 1996, A 16.

67. The World Commission on Environment and Development (Brundtland Commission), *Our Common Future* (New York: Oxford University Press, 1987), 8.

68. Paul Hawken, *The Ecology of Commerce: A Declaration of Sustainability* (New York: Harper Business, 1993).

69. David W. Orr, *Ecological Literacy: Education and the Transition to a Postmodern World* (Albany: State University of New York Press, 1992), 23-40.

70. Hazel Henderson, "A Guide to Riding the Tiger of Change: The Three Zones of Transition," in *Gaia, A Way of Knowing: Political Implications of the New Biology*, ed. William Irwin Thompson (Great Barrington, MA: Lindisfarne Press, 1987), 144-166.

71. Henderson, "Riding the Tiger," 156.

72. André Clewell, "Downshifting," *Restoration and Management Notes* 13, 2 (Winter 1995): 171.

73. Ehrenfeld, *Beginning Again*, 193.

74. Jackson, *Becoming Native*, 57.

75. See the *Greenpeace Guide to Anti-Environmental Organizations*, Berkeley: Odonian Press, 1993.

Chapter 3

1. Monhegan Associates, Certificate of Organization, State of Maine, Chapter 50 of the Revised Statutes and Amendments, 2 (a).

2. Aldo Leopold, *A Sand County Almanac* (New York: Oxford University Press, 1987), 223.

3. Philip W. Conkling, "Toward an Island Ethic," *The New Monhegan Press*, III, 3 (May 1991), 3.

4. According to *Monhegan Island Plantation: An Inventory and Analysis*, in 1991 Monhegan had zero unemployment, and in the decade of the 1980s had enjoyed an 83.7 per cent growth in per capita income and a 61.3 per cent decrease in property taxes. The latter, however, has begun to increase in the 1990s.

5. Maine Land Use Regulatory Commission, *Monhegan Island Plantation: An Inventory and Analysis* (Augusta: LURC, 1991), 3-2.

6. Ibid.

7. Larry Cooper, "Where Have All the Flowers Gone?" *The New Monhegan Press*, II, 4 (July 1990), 1.

8. Raquel D. Boehmer, "Annual Town Meeting," *The New Monhegan Press*, IV, 1 (April 1994), 3.

9. LURC, *An Inventory and Analysis of Monhegan Plantation*, 1-1.

10. Charles B. McLane, *Islands of the Mid-Maine Coast*, Vol. III (Rockland, ME: The Island Institute, 1982), 226.

11. Shea Wheelwright, *Along the Maine Coast* (Barre, MA: Barre Publishers, 1967), 90.

12. James M. Acheson, *The Lobster Gangs of Maine* (Hanover, N.H.: University Press of New England, 1988), 158-59.

13. William P.E. Graves, "Monhegan: Maine's Lobster Island," *National Geographic Magazine* (Feb. 1959), 285-298.

14. Sherman Stanley, retired lobsterman, interview, 6 May 1994.

15. Peter Boehmer, Editor of *The New Monhegan Press*, interview, 5 May 1994.

16. LURC, *An Inventory and Analysis of Monhegan Plantation*, 3-9.

17. Trail and fire road maintenance and cutting deadfall near homes are so far the only management practices approved by the Associates.

18. Boehmer, interview, 5 May 1994.

19. *Lighthouses of Maine*, 129.

20. Bill Boynton, Monhegan resident and business owner, interview, 8 May 1994.

21. Land Use Regulatory Commission Memorandum, 17 November 1989, from David E. Boulter, Director of LURC, to Paul Dutram, State Groundwater Management Strategy (Augusta: LURC files).

22. Barry S. Timson, *Monhegan "Meadow" Aquifer: Preliminary Hydrogeology and Management Considerations* (Franklin, ME: James Haskell and Associates, 1989).

23. James S. Haskell Jr. and Barry S. Timson, *Final Recommendations to the Monhegan Advisory Committee* (Franklin, ME: James S. Haskell Associates, 1989).

24. *An Inventory and Analysis for Monhegan Plantation*, 3-9.

25. James S. Haskell Jr., "Revisions to the Commission's Land Use Districts and Standards Requested on Behalf of Assessors of Monhegan Plantation" (Augusta: LURC files, 1989).

26. Richard Farrell, Monhegan resident and business owner, interview, 6 May 1994.

27. Bill Baker and Amy Melenbacker, Monhegan residents and business owners, interview, 6 May 1994.

28. Letter from Willard J. Boynton, Charles L. MacDonald, and Gretel N. Stanley, Plantation Assessors, to David E. Boulter, Director of LURC, 19 February 1992 (Augusta: LURC Files).

29. Barry S. Timson, letter to the editor, *The New Monhegan Press*, III, 6 (August 1991): 5.

30. Boynton interview, 8 May 1994.

31. *Monhegan Island Plantation: An Inventory and Analysis*, 4.

32. Katy Bogel, Monhegan resident, business owner, and First Assessor of Plantation, interview, 8 May 1994.

33. Peter Boehmer, personal communication, 23 January 1996.

Chapter 4

1. Mary Beth Sutton, Director of the Chattanooga Nature Center, interview, 14 December 1994.

2. Dave Crockett, Chattanooga City Councilman, interview, 14 December 1994.

3. Bruz Clark, Lyndhurst Foundation Officer, interview, 15 December 1994.

4. Mary W. Walker, "Cradle to Cradle Industries," *Envirolink* (February 1995), 1-3.

5. Vernon Summerlin, "Chattanooga: Becoming 'The Environmental City,'" *The Tennessee Conservationist* (September/October 1992), 14-17.

6. Gene Roberts, "Mayor Gene Roberts on Sustainable Development in Chattanooga," World Wide Web, America OnLine, Chattanooga Development Online, Chattanooga Community Link, December 1995.

7. Steve Lerner, "Brave New City?" *The Amicus Journal* (Spring 1995), 22-28.

8. Monty Bruell, Former Chair of Chattanooga Venture, interview, 15 December 1994.

9. Mary Walker, Editor, *Envirolink*, interview, 14 December 1994.

10. Geri Spring, Chattanooga Neighborhood Network Co-ordinator, interview, 14 December 1994.

11. Chattanooga Venture, *Revision 2000: Take Charge Again*, informational brochure, 1993, 25.

12. Ibid., 6.

13. James Catanzaro, President, Chattanooga State Technical Community College, interview, 13 December 1994.

14. Lerner, "Brave New City," 26.

15. Chattanooga Venture, 8.

16. Lerner, "Brave New City," 25.

Chapter 5

1. From Robinson Jeffers' poem "To the Rock That Will be a Cornerstone," as quoted in *The Shorter Bartlett's Familiar Quotations*, ed. Christopher Morley (New York: Permabooks, 1953), 190.

2. Curtis J. Badger, "Getting Back to the Roots," *Nature Conservancy* (January/February, 1995), 20.

3. John E. Bright and Marc Sagan, *Beaches, Islands, Marshes, and Woodlands: Outdoor Recreation Plan on Virginia's Eastern Shore* (Washington: National Park Service, 1987), 18.

4. Curtis J. Badger, *Salt Tide: Cycles and Currents of Life Along the Coast* (Harrisburg, PA: Stackpole Books, 1993), 53.

5. Badger, Salt Tide, 3.

6. Curtis J. Badger, "Eastern Shore Gold," *The Nature Conservancy Magazine* (July/August, 1990), 10-11.

7. Badger, "Eastern Shore Gold," 8.

8. Sustainable Development Task Force, *The Sustainable Development Action Strategy for Northampton County, Virginia* (Eastville, VA: Northampton County Board of Supervisors, 1994), 3-6.

9. Ibid.

10. *Sustainable Development Action Strategy*, 4-3; Community Resource Development, *Northampton County Statistical Profile* (Blacksburg, VA: Virginia Tech, 1994), 16, 35.

11. Jane G. Cabarrus, President, Northampton County Branch, NAACP, personal communication, 15 June 1994.

12. T. Charles Renner, Assistant Vice-President, Crestar Bank, Cheriton, Virginia, personal communication, 16 June 1994.

13. Ian L. McHarg, *Design With Nature* (Garden City, N.Y.: Doubleday, 1969), 79.

14. Quoted in *Beaches, Islands, Marshes, and Woodlands*, 6.

15. Badger, "Eastern Shore Gold," 13.

16. Badger, "Eastern Shore Gold," 9.

17. Karen Jolly Davis, "Creating Jobs From Conservation," *The Virginian Pilot and the Ledger-Star*, 13 June 1994, B4.

18. James Kirkly, Virginia Institute of Marine Science, personal communication, 5 June 1996.

19. *Sustainable Development Action Strategy*, 5-3.

20. Ibid.

21. Steve Parker, Director of Economic Programs, the Nature Conservancy, Virginia Coast Reserve, Brownsville, Virginia, 16 June 1994.

22. John Nottingham, Sustainable Development Task Force Co-chair, quoted in Karen Jolly Davis, "Creating Jobs From Conservation," *The Virginian Pilot and the Ledger-Star*, 13 June 1994, B1.

23. Badger, "Eastern Shore Gold," 10.

24. World Resources Institute, *World Resources 1994-95* (New York: Oxford University Press, 1994), 318.

25. Michel Batisse, "The Bioreserve: A Tool for Environmental Conservation and Management," *Environmental Conservation* 9, no. 2 (1982): 101-103 and Stephen R. Kellert, "Public Understanding and Appreciation of the Biosphere Reserve Concept," *Environmental Conservation* 10, no. 3 (1986): 101-102.

26. Tim Hayes, Northampton County Director of Sustainable Development, personal communication, 22 May 1996.

27. Quoted in Badger, "Eastern Shore Gold," 12-13.

28. *Beaches, Islands, Marshes, and Woodlands*, 7.

29. *Beaches, Islands, Marshes, and Woodlands*, 12.

30. *Beaches, Islands, Marshes, and Woodlands*, 14.

31. The Northampton Economic Forum, *A Blueprint for Economic Growth* (Eastville, VA: The Northampton Economic Forum, 1992), 3.

32. Editorial: "Leadership for the future," *Eastern Shore News*, 24 July 1993, 4.

33. Tom Harris, Northampton County Administrator and Tim Hayes, Northampton County Director of Sustainable Development, personal communication, 11 July, 1996.

34. The plan did get a healthy jump-start from a four-year National Oceanic and Atmospheric Administration grant partly based on ensuring good water quality in bayside creeks and lagoons to protect shellfish and finfish nursery areas.

35. Davis, "Creating Jobs," B1.

36. *Sustainable Development Action Strategy*, frontispiece.

37. Harris and Hayes, personal communication, 11 July 1996.

Chapter 6

1. Steve Wall, *Wisdom's Daughters: Conversations With Women Elders of Native America* (NY: Harper Perennial, 1993), 138.

2. John Kotar, J.A. Kovach, and Craig T. Locey, *Field Guide to Forest Habitat Types of Northern Wisconsin* (Madison: Department of Forestry, University of Wisconsin and Wisconsin Department of Natural Resources, 1988).

3. The history of the Menominee people was taken from the following sources: Felix M. Keesing, *The Menomini Indians of Wisconsin: A Study of Three Centuries of Cultural Contact and Change* (Philadelphia: American Philosophical Society, 1939); Patricia K. Ourada, *The Menominee* (New York: Chelsea House Publishers, 1990); Patricia K. Ourada, *The Menominee Indians* (Norman: University of Oklahoma Press, 1979); Nicholas C. Peroff, *Menominee Drums: Tribal Termination and Restoration, 1954-1974* (Norman: University of Oklahoma Press, 1982); George D. Spindler, *Sociocultural and Psychological Processes in Menomini Acculturation* (Berkeley and Los Angeles: University of California Press, 1955).

4. Neopit, His Mark, in *Shawano County Advocate*, 16 March 1882.

5. Keesing, *The Menominee*, 185.

6. U.S. Senate Hearings, 1965-66, 228.

Chapter 7

1. Daniel Kemmis, *Community and the Politics of Place* (Norman: University of Oklahoma, 1990), 135.

2. Robert R. Humphrey, *The Desert Grassland: A History of Vegetational Change and an Analysis of Causes* (Tucson: University of Arizona Press, 1958), 16-17.

3. Will C. Barnes, "Herds in San Simon Valley," *American Forests* (October 1936), 456, 457, 480, 481.

4. J.J. Wagoner, "Development of the Cattle Industry in Southern Arizona, 1870s and '80s," *New Mexico Historical Review*, 26 (1951), 204-24.

5. James S. Findley, *Natural History of New Mexican Mammals* (Albuquerque, NM: University of New Mexico Press, 1987), 3.

6. R.J. Morrisey, "The Early Range Cattle Industry in Arizona," *Agricultural History* 24 (1950): 151-56.

7. Barnes, "Herds," 456-481.

8. Morrisey, "The Early Range," 151-56.

9. Ronald Bemis, "Range Manuscript for the Douglas Tombstone Soil Survey Area 671," 1991.

10. Conrad Joseph Bahre, *A Legacy of Change: Historic Human Impact on Vegetation*

in the Arizona Borderlands (Tucson: University of Arizona Press, 1991), 117.

11. Barnes, "Herds," 456-481.

12. Hooker, from Bahre, *A Legacy*, 117.

13. Aldo Leopold, "The Conservation Ethic," in *The River of the Mother of God and Other Essays by Aldo Leopold*, ed. Susan L. Flader and J. Baird Callicott (Madison: University of Wisconsin, 1933), 184.

14. Tony Povilitis, "The Gila River-Sky Island Bioregion: A Call for Bold Conservation Action," *Natural Areas Journal* 16, no. 1 (1996), 62-66.

15. Frederick R. Gehlbach, *Mountain Islands and Desert Seas: A Natural History of the U.S.-Mexican Borderlands* (College Station: Texas A&M Press, 1981), 158.

16. Brian Power, Forester, Douglas, Arizona, interview, October 1994.

17. Daniel Kemmis, "The Last Best Place: How Hardship and Limits Build Community, in *Changing Community*, ed. Scott Walker (Saint Paul: Graywolf Press, 1993), 277-78.

Chapter 8

1. Peter Berg and Raymond Dasmann, "Reinhabiting California," in *Home! A Bioregional Reader*, ed. Van Andruss, Christopher Plant, Judith Plant and Eleanor Wright (Gabriola Island: New Society Publishers, 1990), 35.

2. David Simpson, *Meat* (Petrolia, CA: Privately Published, n.d.), 8.

3. The Mattole Restoration Council, *Elements of Recovery: An Inventory of Upslope Sources of Sedimentation in the Mattole River Watershed* (Petrolia, CA, December 1989), 11.

4. *Elements of Recovery*, 10-11.

5. *Elements of Recovery*, 12.

6. Freeman House, "To Learn the Things We Need to Know: Engaging the Particulars of the Planet's Recovery," in *Home! A Bioregional Reader*, 112.

7. Freeman House, "Dreaming Indigenous: One Hundred Years from Now in a Northern California Valley," *Restoration and Management Notes*, 10, no. 1 (Winter 1992), 60.

8. Mattole Restoration Council, "Distribution of Old-Growth Coniferous Forests in the Mattole River Watershed," Map (Petrolia: MRC, 1988).

9. *Elements of Recovery*, 6.

10. David Simpson, "A Report From the Mattole Watershed Salmon Support Group," *Mattole Restoration Newsletter*, 9 (Winter 1994-95), 6.

11. House, "Dreaming Indigenous," 61.

12. House, "To Learn the Things," 111.

13. Sanford E. Lowry, personal communication, 1 May 1996.

14. House, "Dreaming Indigenous," 61.

15. William Poole, "For the Sake of the Salmon," *This World Magazine*, San Francisco *Chronicle*, 28 June 1987, 9.

16. Gary Peterson, "Mattole Salmon Runs Show Improvement, *The Mattole Spawning News* (Winter 1996): 4.

17. House, "To Learn the Things," 111.

18. House, "To Learn the Things," 112.

19. David Simpson, "A Report From the Mattole Watershed Salmon Support Group," *Mattole Restoration Newsletter* (Winter 1994-95): 6.

20. Simpson, "Report from MSG," 6.

21. House, "To Learn the Things," 112.

22. House, "To Learn the Things," 117.

23. Howard T. Odum, *Environment, Power, and Society* (New York: Wiley, 1971).

24. Simpson, "Report from MSG," 6.

25. Freeman House, "Salmon and Settler: Toward a Culture of Reinhabitation," in *Turtle Talk: Voices for a Sustainable Future*, ed. Christopher Plant and Judith Plant (Gabriola Island: New Society Publishers, 1990), 110.

26. David Simpson, telephone interview, 12 February 1996.

27. Simpson, "Report from MSG," 6.

28. Peterson, "Mattole Salmon Runs," 4.

29. House, "Salmon and Settler," 108.

30. Freeman House, "Watersheds as Unclaimed Territories," in *Boundaries of Home: Mapping for Local Empowerment*, ed. Doug Aberley (Gabriola Island: New Society Publishers, 1993), 36.; Mattole Restoration Council, *Mattole Restoration Newsletter*, 10 (Winter 1995-96): 3.

31. House, "To Learn the Things," 116.

32. MRC, *Mattole Restoration Newsletter* (Winter 1995-96): 2.

33. Thomas Dunklin, "The Road to Nowhere Disappears," *Mattole Restoration Newsletter*, 10 (Winter 1995-96): 1.

34. Sanford E. Lowry, personal communication, 1 May 1996.

35. Caroline Estes, "Consensus and Community," in *Turtle Talk: Voices for a Sustainable Future* (Gabriola Island: New Society Publishers, 1990), 99.

36. Sanford E. Lowry, written communication, 1 May 1996.

37. Freeman House, "There Must Be a Better Way," *Natural Resources News*, University of California Extension Service (June 1993): 7.

38. House, "Better Way," 7.

39. Sanford E. Lowry, 1 May 1996.

40. Sanford E. Lowry, personal communication, 1 May 1996.

41. David Simpson, "The Mattole Mouth Opens to a New Age," *The Mattole Spawning News* (1996): 4.

42. House, "Salmon and Settler," 112.

Chapter 9

1. Paul Hawken, *The Ecology of Commerce* (New York: HarperCollins Publishers, Inc., 1993), 5.

2. Collins Pine Co., "All Quiet in the Forest," in *Crow's Forestry Industry Journal* 7, no. 3 (June 1992).

3. L.W. Potts, Vice-President and General Manager of Collins Pine Company, interview by authors, April 1994.

4. Plumas National Forest, *Forest Statistics: 1991-1994* (Quincy, CA: Plumas National Forest Supervisor, 1994).

5. Susan Baremore, Executive Director of Feather River Alliance for Resources and the Environment, interview, April 1994.

6. John Sheehan, "A Grassroots Perspective, Feather River Co-ordinated Resource Management," unpublished report, Plumas Corporation, November 1993.

7. Ibid.

8. J.B. Little, "The Quincy Library Group," *American Forests*, 101 (1995): 22-24, 56.

9. Wayne Thornton, Plumas National Forest Supervisor, interview, April 1994.

10. Little, "The Quincy Library Group," 23.

11. Quincy Library Group, "Community Stability Proposal" (Quincy, CA: 1993).

12. Ibid.

13. Brad Knickerbocker, "Forest Managers Learn How to Grow 'Green' Lumber," *The Christian Science Monitor*, (November 29, 1993), 11.

14. Thornton, interview.

15. John Sheehan, "Overview of the Community Stability Proposal of the Quincy Library Group," unpublished report, December 1994.

16. Little, "Quincy Library Group," 25.

17. Hawken, *The Ecology of Commerce*, 12.

18. John Schramel, interview, April 1994.

19. Hawken, *The Ecology of Commerce*, 11, 12.

20. Michael Jackson, Attorney, Quincy, CA, interview, April 1994.

Chapter 10

1. Stephanie Mills, *In Service of the Wild: Restoring and Reinhabiting Damaged Lands* (Boston: Beacon Press, 1995), 19-20.

2. Aldo Leopold, *A Sand County Almanac* (New York: Oxford, 1987), 196.

3. William R. Jordan III, "Restoration and the Re-entry of Nature," in *Finding Home*, ed. Peter Sauer (Boston: Beacon Press, 1992), 98.

4. David R. Brower, *Let the Mountains Talk, Let the Rivers Run* (New York: Harper Collins West, 1995), 91-98.

5. Richard Nilsen, *Helping Nature Heal* (Berkeley, CA: Ten Speed Press, 1991); William K. Stevens, *Miracle Under the Oaks* (New York: Pocket Books, 1995); Stephanie Mills, *In Service of the Wild: Restoring and Reinhabiting Damaged Land* (Boston: Beacon Press, 1991); John J. Berger, *Restoring the Earth: How Americans Are Working to Renew Our Damaged Environment* (New York: Anchor Doubleday, 1987).

6. Jordan, "Restoration and the Re-entry of Nature," 105-12.

7. John Winnenberg, "Restoring Life to Local Streams," *Community Life News* 6, no. 1 (Winter 1995): 1.

8. Mary Ann Borch, "Monday Creek Cleanup Seeks Planning Expertise," *Monday Creek News* 1, no. 1 (January 1995): 1.

9. Quoted in John Winnenberg, "Restoring Life to Local Streams," *Community Life News* 6, no. 2 (March 1993): 2.

10. Mitch Farley, "A Historical Coal Mining Perspective," *Monday Creek News* 2, no. 1 (April 1996): 3.

11. The pH scale measures acidity/alkalinity, with 1 being highly acid and 14 highly basic. an increase or decrease from one whole number to the next represents a tenfold change, so that pH 3 is 10 times more acid than pH 4.

12. Mitch Farley, Ohio Department of Natural Resources, Division of Mines and Reclamation, "Monday Creek Mining and Reclamation," presentation given at Reclaiming Watersheds in Appalachia Workshop, 3 May 1996.

13. Michael D. Morgan, Joseph M. Moran, and James H. Wiersma, *Environmental Science: Managing Biological and Physical Resources* (Dubuque, IA: Wm. C. Brown Publishers, 1993), 375.

14. Ohio Department of Natural Resources, Division of Mines and Reclamation, *Acid Mine Drainage Abatement Program* (Columbus: ODNR, December 1995), 3.

15. John Winnenberg, "The Big Picture for the Long Haul," *Community Life News* (January 1993): 2.

16. Mary Ann Borch, "Toby Creek: A Testimony to the Future," *Monday Creek News* 2, no. 1 (April 1996): 3.

17. Jennifer Rice, "Miners Rebuild the Earth: College Program Reclaims Land and Jobs," *Southeast Ohio* (Summer/Fall 1995), 8-11.

18. "Partner Profile: Nation Environmental Training Co-operative," *Monday Creek News* 1, no. 2 (February 1995): 2.

19. Mary Ann Borch, personal communication, 18 May 1996.

20. Winnenberg, "The Big Picture," 2.

21. William K. Stevens, *Miracle Under the Oaks: The Revival of Nature in America* (New York: Pocket Books, 1995).

22. Stevens, *Miracle Under the Oaks*, 51.

23. Steve Packard, "Just a Few Oddball Species: Restoration and Rediscovery of the

Tallgrass Savanna," in *Helping Nature Heal: An Introduction to Environmental Restoration*, ed. Richard Nilsen (Berkeley: Ten Speed Press, 1991), 28-38.

24. Freeman House, "To Learn the Things We Need to Know: Engaging the Particulars of the Planet's Recovery," in *Helping Nature Heal*, 46-61.

Chapter 11

1. Thomas Berry, *The Dream of the Earth* (San Francisco: Sierra Club Books, 1988), 215.

2. Proverbs 29:18. This passage is taken from the King James Version of the Bible.

3. Steve Albert, Zoologist, Zuni Conservation Corps, interview, October 1994.

4. Paul Hawken, "The Ecology of Commerce," *Inc.* (April 1992): 94.

5. Kai N. Lee, *Compass and Gyroscope: Integrating Science and Politics for the Environment* (Washington, D.C.: Island Press, 1993), 58, 59.

6. Dave Crockett, Chattanooga City Councilman, interview, December 1994.

7. Kirk Johnson, "Reconciling Rural Communities and Resource Conservation," *Environment* 35 (September 1993): 18.

8. Ibid.

9. Lance H. Gunderson, C.S. Holling, and Stephen S. Light, eds., *Barriers and Bridges to the Renewal of Ecosystems and Institutions* (New York: Columbia University Press, 1995), 7, 8.

10. The World Conservation Union (IUCN), UN Environment Program (UNEP), and World Wide Fund for Nature (WWF), *Caring for the Earth: A Strategy for Sustainable Living* (Gland, Switzerland: IUCN, UNEP, and WWF, 1991), 9.

11. David Ehrenfeld, *Beginning Again: People and Nature in the New Millennium* (New York: Ballantine Books, 1970), 137.

12. Aldo Leopold, *A Sand County Almanac with Essays on Conservation from Round River* (New York: Ballantine Books, 1970), 137.

13. Wendell Berry, "Decolonizing Rural America," *Audubon* 3 (May/June 1993): 100-105.

14. Wes Jackson, "Listen to the Land," *The Amicus Journal* (Spring 1993): 32-34.

15. Lee, *Compass and Gyroscope*, 53.

16. Leopold, *Sand County Almanac*, 221.

17. Aldo Leopold, "The Round River," *A Sand County Almanac* (New York: Oxford University Press, 1953), 190.

18. David Orr, *Earth in Mind: On Education, Environment and the Human Prospect* (Washington, D.C.: Island Press, 1994), 140.

19. Ibid., 141.

20. Leopold, *A Sand County Almanac*, 216.

21. David W. Orr, *Ecological Literacy: Education and the Transition to a Post Modern World* (Albany: State University of New York Press, 1992), 33.

22. Wendell Berry, "Living with the Land," *Journal of Soil and Water Conservation* 46: 391.

23. Wes Jackson, *Becoming Native to This Place* (Lexington, Kentucky: University Press of Kentucky, 1994), 3.

24. David Kemmis, "The Last Best Place: How Hardship and Limits Build Community," in *The Graywolf Annual Ten: Changing Community*, ed. Scott Walker (St. Paul, Minnesota: Graywolf Press, 1993), 284.

25. Wendy Warner, *Rancher*, interview, 1 Nov. 1994

26. Lee, *Compass and Gyroscope*, 63.

27. Daniel B. Botkin, *Discordant Harmonies: A New Ecology for the Twenty-First Century* (New York: Oxford University Press, 1990), 190.

28. Ibid.

29. Aldo Leopold, "The Conservation Ethic," in *The River of the Mother of God and Other Essays by Aldo Leopold*, ed. Susan L. Flader and J. Baird Callicott (Madison: University of Wisconsin, 1933), 183.

30. Hawken, *The Ecology of Commerce*, 13.

31. Jackson, *Becoming Native to This Place*, 24.

32. Marshall Pecore, Chief Forester, Menominee, interview, May 1994.

33. Daniel Kemmis, "The Art of the Possible in the Home of Hope," in *Community and the Politics of Place* (Norman: University of Oklahoma Press, 1990), 109-142.

34. Stephen R. Covey, *The 7 Habits of Highly Effective People: Restoring the Character Ethic* (New York: Simon & Schuster, 1990).

Chapter 12

1. Walt Whitman, "Song of Myself," in *Leaves of Grass*, ed. Emory Holloway (Garden City: Doubleday, 1926).

2. Gary Snyder, "On the Path, Off the Trail," *The Practice of the Wild* (New York: Farrar, Straus and Giroux, 1990), 145.

3. The Right Livelihood Foundation was established by Swedish philanthropist Jacob von Uexkull. It gives annual Right Livelihood Awards, much in the style of the Nobel Prize, to practitioners of peace, sustainable development, environmental integrity, social justice and human rights.

4. Jeremy Seabrook, *Pioneers of Change: Experiments in Creating a Humane Society* (Gabriola Island: New Society Publishers, 1993), 216.

5. Aldo Leopold, "The Land Ethic," in *A Sand County Almanac* (New York: Oxford University Press, 1987), 224.

6. Richard Slaughter, *The Foresight Principle: Cultural Recovery in the 21st Century* (Westport, CN: Praeger, 1995), 53.

7. John Sheehan, Executive Director of the Plumas Corporation, personal communication, 12 April 1994.

8. Hazel Henderson, "A Guide to Riding the Tiger of Change: The Three Zones of Transition," in Gaia: *A Way of Knowing*, ed. William Irwin Thompson (Great Barrington, MA: Lindisfarne Press, 1987), 146.

9. Slaughter, *The Foresight Principle*, 15.

10. Ibid.

11. Scott Peck, *The Different Drum: Community Making and Peace* (New York: Simon and Schuster, 1987), 77-81.

12. Henderson, "Riding the Tiger," 159.

13. Peck, *The Different Drum*, 77-85.

14. Peck, *The Different Drum*, 80-81.

15. Jane Braxton Little, "The Quincy Library Group," *American Forests* 101 (February 1995): 23.

16. Henderson, "Riding the Tiger," 156-157.

17. David Chrislip, "Pulling Together: Creating a Constituency for Change," *National Civic Review* (Winter 1995): 21-29.

18. Slaughter, *The Foresight Principle*, 63.

19. Henderson, "Riding the Tiger," 166.

20. Chrislip, "Pulling Together," 23.

21. Peter Block, *Stewardship* (San Francisco: Barrett Koehler, 1993), pp. 15-17.

22. Chrislip, "Pulling Together," 26.

23. The Kettering Foundation, *Citizens and Politics: A View from Main Street America* (Dayton, 1991).

24. Alan Atkisson, "Portrait of a Political Instigator: An Interview with Robert Theobold," *In Context* 30 (Fall/Winter 1991), 26-31.

25. Chrislip, "Pulling Together," p. 27.

26. John Sheehan, Executive Director, The Plumas Corporation, personal communication, April 1994.

27. Peck, *The Different Drum*, 63-64.

28. Peck, *The Different Drum*, 61.

29. Slaughter, *The Foresight Principle*, 60-63.

30. John Sheehan, Executive Director, The Plumas Corporation, personal communication, April 1994.

31. John Schermel, personal communication, April 1994.

32. Lester Brown, *Building a Sustainable Society* (New York: Norton, 1981), 369.

33. Bill McKibben, *Hope, Human and Wild: True Stories of Living Lightly on the Earth* (Boston: Little, Brown and Company, 1995), 3.

34. Little, "The Quincy Library Group," 23-24.

35. Willard Boynton, Monhegan Island resident and business owner, personal communication, May 1994.

36. Little, "The Quincy Library Group," 55.

37. David Orr, "Love It or Lose It: The Coming Biophylia Revolution," *Orion* 13 (Winter 1994): 15.

38. Leopold, *Sand County Almanac*, 204.